NATURAL LANGUAGE PROCESSING (NLP)

The Complete Guide

By

Dr. Hesham Mohamed Elsherif

ABOUT THE AUTHOR

 Dr. Hesham Mohamed Elsherif stands at the forefront of library management and research, boasting an impressive 22-year tenure in the field. Holding dual doctoral degrees, one in Management and Organizational Leadership and the other in Information Systems and Technology, Dr. Elsherif brings a unique blend of knowledge to any intellectual endeavor.

An expert in Empirical research methodology, Dr. Elsherif specializes particularly in the Qualitative approach and Action research. This specialization has not only strengthened his research endeavors but has also allowed him to contribute invaluable insights and advancements in these areas.

Over the years, Dr. Elsherif has made significant contributions to the academic world not only as a professional researcher but also as an Adjunct Professor. This multifaceted role in the educational landscape has further solidified his reputation as a thought leader and pioneer.

Furthermore, Dr. Elsherif's expertise isn't confined to one region. He has served as a consultant to numerous educational institutions on an international scale, sharing best practices, innovative strategies, and his deep insights into the ever-evolving realms of management and technology.

Combining a passion for education with an unparalleled depth of knowledge, Dr. Elsherif continues to inspire, educate, and lead in both the library and academic communities.

PREFACE

Welcome to "Natural Language Processing (NLP): The Complete Guide." In today's digital age, where vast amounts of textual data are generated every second, the ability to understand, analyze, and generate human language is more crucial than ever. Natural Language Processing (NLP) serves as the bridge between human communication and machine understanding, empowering us to extract valuable insights, automate tasks, and enhance user experiences across diverse domains.

This book is crafted to be your comprehensive companion on the journey through the multifaceted world of NLP. Whether you're a seasoned practitioner seeking to deepen your expertise or a newcomer eager to explore this dynamic field, our goal is to equip you with the knowledge, skills, and practical insights needed to succeed in the realm of NLP.

The "Natural Language Processing (NLP): The Complete Guide" is designed with a learner-centric approach, guiding you from foundational concepts to advanced techniques in a structured and accessible manner. We begin by laying a solid groundwork with an overview of NLP, its applications, and its significance in various fields. From there, we delve into the essentials of text processing, feature extraction, and representation, providing you with a strong foundation to build upon.

As you progress through the chapters, you'll explore a wide range of NLP tasks and techniques, including text classification, sentiment analysis, named entity recognition, machine translation, and more. Each topic is presented with clarity and depth, supported by practical examples, code snippets, and hands-on exercises to reinforce your understanding.

Moreover, this guide goes beyond mere theory, offering practical insights and best practices gleaned from real-world experience. We showcase industry-standard tools, libraries, and frameworks commonly used in NLP projects, empowering you to apply your newfound knowledge to solve real-world problems and create impactful applications.

In addition to covering core concepts and techniques, this book also explores emerging trends and cutting-edge developments in NLP. From deep learning architectures to ethical considerations and bias mitigation strategies, we aim to provide you with a comprehensive understanding of the current landscape of NLP and prepare you for the challenges and opportunities that lie ahead.

We understand that learning NLP can be a daunting endeavor, given the complexity and rapid pace of innovation in the field. However, we believe that with dedication, curiosity, and the right guidance, anyone can master NLP and harness its transformative power. With this guide as your companion, we invite you to embark on a journey of exploration, discovery, and mastery in the fascinating world of Natural Language Processing.

Thank you for choosing "Natural Language Processing (NLP): The Complete Guide." We hope that it serves as a valuable resource on your journey to mastering NLP and inspires you to push the boundaries of what's possible with language and technology. Let's embark on this adventure together and shape the future of human-computer interaction with the power of NLP.

Dr. Hesham Mohamed Elsherif

WHO SHOULD READ THIS BOOK?

This book, "Natural Language Processing (NLP): The Complete Guide," is intended for a wide range of readers who are interested in mastering the principles, techniques, and applications of NLP. Here's a comprehensive overview of who should read this book:

1. **Students and Researchers**: Whether you're pursuing a degree in computer science, linguistics, data science, or a related field, this book provides a solid foundation in NLP concepts and techniques. Students and researchers seeking to understand the fundamentals of NLP and explore advanced topics will find this book invaluable.

2. **Professionals in AI and Data Science**: Professionals working in artificial intelligence, machine learning, and data science industries will benefit from this book's practical insights and hands-on approach. Whether you're a data scientist, AI engineer, or software developer, mastering NLP opens up new opportunities for building intelligent systems and extracting valuable insights from text data.

3. **Language Enthusiasts and Linguists**: Language enthusiasts and linguists interested in exploring the intersection of language and technology will find this book fascinating. From understanding the inner workings of language processing algorithms to analyzing linguistic patterns, this book offers a comprehensive overview of NLP from a linguistic perspective.

4. **Software Engineers and Developers**: Software engineers and developers looking to integrate NLP

capabilities into their applications will find practical guidance and code examples in this book. Whether you're building chatbots, recommendation systems, or sentiment analysis tools, this book provides the necessary knowledge and tools to implement NLP solutions effectively.

5. **Business Professionals and Decision Makers**: Business professionals and decision-makers seeking to leverage NLP for competitive advantage will gain valuable insights from this book. Understanding the capabilities and limitations of NLP enables business leaders to make informed decisions about implementing NLP technologies and leveraging text data for strategic purposes.

6. **Educators and Trainers**: Educators and trainers teaching courses or workshops on NLP will find this book to be a valuable resource for structuring their curriculum and providing comprehensive coverage of NLP concepts and techniques. With its clear explanations and practical examples, this book is suitable for both classroom instruction and self-paced learning.

7. **Anyone Curious About NLP**: Finally, anyone with a curiosity about how machines understand and process human language will find this book engaging and informative. Whether you're a hobbyist, a lifelong learner, or simply intrigued by the possibilities of NLP, this book provides a comprehensive guide to understanding and exploring the fascinating world of natural language processing.

In summary, "Natural Language Processing (NLP): The Complete Guide" is designed to cater to a diverse audience, including students, professionals, language enthusiasts, educators, and anyone curious about NLP. Whether you're looking to build intelligent systems, analyze text data, or simply deepen your understanding of human language, this book offers the knowledge, insights, and practical guidance you need to succeed in the field of NLP.

Happy Reading!

Dr. Hesham Mohamed Elsherif

WHY THIS BOOK IS ESSENTIAL READING?

"Natural Language Processing (NLP): The Complete Guide" is an indispensable resource for anyone seeking to understand, master, and leverage the power of natural language processing. Here's why this book is essential reading:

1. **Comprehensive Coverage**: This book offers a comprehensive exploration of NLP, covering fundamental concepts, advanced techniques, and practical applications. From basic text processing tasks to complex machine learning algorithms, readers gain a thorough understanding of NLP principles and methodologies.

2. **Practical Approach**: With its hands-on approach and practical examples, this book bridges the gap between theory and practice. Readers not only learn NLP concepts but also gain practical experience through coding exercises and real-world projects, enabling them to apply their knowledge effectively.

3. **Clear Explanations**: Complex NLP concepts are presented in a clear and accessible manner, making them easy to understand for readers of all backgrounds. Whether you're a beginner or an experienced practitioner, the explanations provided in this book ensure that you grasp key concepts with clarity and confidence.

4. **Real-World Relevance**: This book emphasizes real-world applications of NLP, demonstrating how NLP techniques are used to solve practical problems in various domains. From sentiment analysis and text

classification to language translation and chatbots, readers gain insights into how NLP is applied in industry and research.

5. **Up-to-Date Content**: NLP is a rapidly evolving field, with new techniques, algorithms, and applications emerging regularly. This book provides up-to-date content, covering the latest advancements in NLP, including deep learning architectures, state-of-the-art models, and ethical considerations.

6. **Learning Path**: The book offers a structured learning path, guiding readers from foundational concepts to advanced topics in a logical progression. Each chapter builds upon the previous one, ensuring a gradual and comprehensive understanding of NLP principles and techniques.

7. **Resource for Practitioners**: For practitioners working in AI, data science, linguistics, and related fields, this book serves as a valuable reference and guide. Whether you're building NLP models, conducting research, or developing applications, the insights and techniques provided in this book enhance your skills and expertise.

8. **Educational Resource**: This book is an essential educational resource for students, educators, and researchers interested in NLP. It serves as a textbook for courses on NLP, providing a structured curriculum and supplementary materials for classroom instruction and self-paced learning.

9. **Insight into Language Processing**: Even for readers with a general interest in language and technology, this book offers valuable insights into how machines understand and process human language. It sheds light

on the inner workings of language processing algorithms, revealing the complexities and intricacies of language understanding.

In summary, "Natural Language Processing (NLP): The Complete Guide" is essential reading for anyone interested in understanding, mastering, and applying NLP. With its comprehensive coverage, practical approach, and real-world relevance, this book equips readers with the knowledge, skills, and insights needed to succeed in the dynamic field of natural language processing.

Enjoy Reading!

Dr. Hesham Mohamed Elsherif

Table of Contents

Introduction

In the evolving landscape of artificial intelligence, Natural Language Processing (NLP) stands as a transformative technology that bridges the gap between human communication and machine understanding. "Natural Language Processing (NLP): The Complete Guide" is designed to be an authoritative text on the subject, offering readers a comprehensive exploration into the vast world of NLP. This book serves as both an introduction for those new to the field and a detailed guide for advanced practitioners looking to deepen their understanding of specific techniques and applications.

NLP, at its core, involves the development of algorithms and systems that allow computers to process, understand, and generate human language. This technology underpins a variety of applications that we use daily, from search engines and chatbots to translation services and voice-activated assistants. As we delve into the book, we embark on a journey through the history of NLP, its foundational theories, the latest advancements in the field, and a look toward the future where NLP technology may lead us.

The book is structured to provide a clear and logical progression through the complexities of NLP. It begins with an overview of the fundamentals, including linguistic principles and the evolution of NLP technologies. This foundation is crucial for understanding how machines interpret the nuances of human language, such as syntax, semantics, and pragmatics.

Following the basics, we explore the various methodologies and algorithms that form the backbone of NLP, including both traditional rule-based approaches and modern machine learning techniques. Special attention is given to deep learning models that have significantly advanced NLP capabilities in recent years.

Practical application is a core focus of this guide. Each chapter includes real-world examples, case studies, and detailed explanations of how NLP techniques are applied in various industries. From automating customer service to analyzing social media sentiment, we illustrate the transformative impact of NLP across different sectors.

The book also addresses the challenges and ethical considerations in NLP, such as bias in language models and privacy concerns. We engage with ongoing debates and discussions in the field, offering readers insights into the complexities of developing fair and responsible NLP systems.

"Natural Language Processing (NLP): The Complete Guide" is more than just a textbook; it's a gateway to one of the most exciting areas of artificial intelligence. Whether you're a student, a professional, or simply curious about the capabilities of NLP, this book offers a wealth of knowledge, insights, and inspirations to explore the endless possibilities that NLP brings to our world.

Definition and significance of NLP:

Natural Language Processing (NLP) is a pivotal area within artificial intelligence (AI) that focuses on the interaction between computers and humans through natural language. At its core, NLP strives to enable machines to understand, interpret, and respond to human languages in a way that is both meaningful and useful. This ambitious goal involves a myriad of computational linguistics techniques, including parsing, semantics, syntax, and machine learning algorithms, to bridge the gap between human communication and computer understanding.

The significance of NLP cannot be overstated. In an era where data is omnipresent, much of the world's information is stored in the form of unstructured text. NLP is the key that unlocks this vast repository, allowing for the automated analysis and interpretation of massive volumes of natural language data. This capability is revolutionary, paving the way for advancements across numerous fields such as healthcare, finance, customer service, and education.

NLP technologies facilitate a wide array of applications that influence our daily lives. Search engines leverage NLP to understand and process user queries, providing relevant results. Digital assistants like Siri, Alexa, and Google Assistant rely on NLP to interpret voice commands and offer helpful responses. In the customer service sector, chatbots and virtual assistants use NLP to provide automated support to users, improving efficiency and user satisfaction. Furthermore, NLP plays a crucial role in sentiment analysis, language translation, and content summarization, enhancing our ability to communicate, access information, and make informed decisions.

Beyond practical applications, the significance of NLP also lies in its contribution to bridging cultural and linguistic barriers. By advancing language translation and multilingual models, NLP technologies foster better understanding and communication among people of diverse linguistic backgrounds. This democratization of information and knowledge has profound implications for global collaboration, education, and accessibility.

The challenges in NLP are as vast as its potential. Languages are inherently complex, with nuances, idioms, slang, and evolving usage patterns that present ongoing challenges for computational models. Moreover, the ethical considerations surrounding NLP, such as bias in language models and privacy concerns, require careful attention and ongoing research. These challenges underscore the importance of NLP as a field that not only pushes the boundaries of what is technologically possible but also navigates the moral and ethical implications of AI in society.

In summary, NLP stands as a cornerstone technology of the AI revolution, with its significance rooted in its ability to transform how we interact with machines, access information, and connect with one another across the globe. "Natural Language Processing (NLP): The Complete Guide" aims to unravel the complexities of NLP, offering readers an in-depth understanding of both its transformative potential and the challenges it faces. As we embark on this exploration, we invite readers to appreciate the profound impact NLP has on our world and envision the future it helps to shape.

NLP stands not just as a bridge between human languages and machine processing but as a transformative force that redefines the boundaries of interaction, accessibility, and data analysis.

Enabling Complex Interactions

One of the most compelling aspects of NLP is its role in enabling complex interactions between humans and machines. Through the development of sophisticated models that understand context, sarcasm, and even humor, NLP technologies have made significant strides in making computer interactions feel more natural and human-like. This progression has not only improved user experience but also expanded the possibilities for AI applications in education, therapy, and entertainment, where nuanced language understanding is crucial.

Advancements in Machine Translation

The advancements in machine translation are a testament to the profound impact of NLP. Early machine translation systems struggled with accuracy and fluency, often producing literal translations that missed the nuances of language. However, with the advent of neural machine translation and context-aware algorithms, we have seen remarkable improvements in the quality of translated text. This leap forward has been instrumental in breaking down language barriers, promoting cross-cultural exchanges, and making information universally accessible, regardless of the reader's native language.

Facilitating Access to Information

NLP's significance extends to the realm of information accessibility. By enabling machines to summarize texts, extract relevant information, and generate answers to questions, NLP technologies have transformed how we access and consume information. These capabilities are crucial for fields like legal research, medical diagnostics, and academic study, where the ability to quickly analyze vast amounts of text can save time, resources, and even lives.

Addressing Ethical and Social Challenges

As we delve deeper into the potential of NLP, it's imperative to address the ethical and social challenges that accompany its advancement. The issue of bias in language models, where AI systems may perpetuate or amplify societal biases present in training data, is a significant concern. NLP research is increasingly focusing on developing more equitable and fair models that represent the diversity of human language and experience. Furthermore, privacy and consent in language data processing are critical considerations, as the use of personal information raises concerns about surveillance and data protection. These challenges are not insurmountable but require concerted effort from researchers, practitioners, and policymakers to ensure that NLP technologies benefit society equitably.

The Future of NLP

Looking toward the future, the potential of NLP seems boundless. From enhancing human-AI collaboration to unlocking the secrets of historical texts and driving global connectivity, NLP stands at the forefront of the next wave of technological and societal advancements. As computational power increases and our understanding of language deepens, we can anticipate NLP technologies that are more sophisticated, inclusive, and capable of handling the complex subtleties of human communication.

In conclusion, "Natural Language Processing (NLP): The Complete Guide" aims to not only chart the technical landscape of NLP but also to illuminate its profound implications for the future. As we explore the intricate dance between language and computation, we uncover the vast potential of NLP to transform our world, making it more connected, accessible, and understanding. Through this comprehensive exploration, readers are invited to join in shaping the future of NLP, a field at the heart of the human experience and technological innovation.

Importance Of NLP In Various Fields:

Natural Language Processing (NLP) occupies a unique position at the crossroads of artificial intelligence (AI), linguistics, and data science, offering transformative insights and capabilities that are reshaping these disciplines.

AI and NLP: Pioneering Intelligent Systems

In the realm of artificial intelligence, NLP is a critical component that enables machines to perform tasks that require understanding of natural language. This capability is fundamental to creating AI systems that can interact with humans in a natural and intuitive manner. NLP allows for the development of intelligent agents that can comprehend instructions, respond to queries, and engage in dialogue, thereby making AI technologies more accessible and useful in everyday life. By equipping machines with the ability to process and understand human language, NLP is pushing the boundaries of AI, enabling more sophisticated and human-like AI applications.

The synergy between Artificial Intelligence (AI) and Natural Language Processing (NLP) forms the cornerstone of creating pioneering intelligent systems. This collaboration is reshaping the landscape of AI, pushing the frontier of what machines can understand and how they interact with humans.

Enabling Human-like Interaction

One of the paramount achievements of integrating NLP with AI is the ability to facilitate human-like interactions between machines and people. NLP serves as the bridge that allows AI systems to not only parse and understand human language but also to generate responses that are coherent, contextually relevant, and indistinguishable from human communication. This capability is vital for the development of chatbots, virtual assistants, and interactive AI applications that require a high degree of linguistic intelligence to function effectively. By incorporating NLP, AI systems can achieve a deeper understanding of user intent, enabling them to provide more accurate and helpful responses, thereby enhancing user experience and satisfaction.

Understanding Context and Nuance

At the heart of NLP's contribution to AI is its ability to grasp the subtleties of human language, including context, tone, idioms, and even humor. These aspects of language present significant challenges for AI systems, as they require not only a surface-level understanding of words and phrases but also an appreciation of the deeper meanings and implications. NLP methodologies and models, especially those leveraging advancements in deep learning, are instrumental in tackling these challenges. They enable AI systems to analyze the context in which language is used, understand nuances, and respond in a manner that is both appropriate and contextually aware.

This level of understanding is critical for applications ranging from sentiment analysis in social media monitoring to natural language understanding in voice-activated systems.

Advancing Machine Learning Models

NLP is also at the forefront of advancing machine learning models within AI. The development of models such as transformers and recurrent neural networks (RNNs) has been driven by the need to improve NLP tasks, including language translation, text generation, and speech recognition. These models have significantly enhanced the ability of AI systems to process sequential data, understand the structure of language, and generate text that is coherent and contextually relevant. Furthermore, the success of these models in NLP tasks has led to their application in other areas of AI, demonstrating the cross-disciplinary impact of NLP research.

Pioneering Research and Applications

The importance of NLP in AI extends to pioneering research and the exploration of new applications. NLP-driven AI research is continually pushing the boundaries of what is possible, from developing models that can write original prose and poetry to creating systems that can interpret and summarize complex legal documents. These advancements not only showcase the potential of combining AI with NLP but also open up new avenues for application in fields such as education, law, and creative writing. The ongoing research and development in NLP and AI promise to deliver even more sophisticated and capable systems, further bridging the gap between human intelligence and machine understanding.

The integration of NLP with AI is not merely an enhancement of AI capabilities but a fundamental shift towards creating intelligent systems that can truly understand and engage with human language. As we continue to explore the depths of NLP and AI, we pave the way for a future where machines can communicate and understand with the complexity and subtlety of human language.

Linguistics and NLP: A Synergistic Relationship

The relationship between linguistics and NLP is deeply synergistic. Linguistics provides the theoretical framework and insights into the structure, use, and meaning of language that are essential for developing effective NLP systems. Understanding linguistic principles such as syntax (sentence structure), semantics (meaning), and pragmatics (contextual use of language) is crucial for tackling the nuances of natural language processing. Conversely, NLP offers linguistics a powerful set of tools for analyzing vast amounts of language data, enabling linguists to uncover patterns and insights that were previously inaccessible. This interplay between linguistics and NLP not only advances our understanding of human language but also improves the capabilities of NLP systems.

The relationship between linguistics, the scientific study of language, and Natural Language Processing (NLP), the AI field that applies algorithms to understand and manipulate human language, is inherently synergistic. This collaboration enriches both domains, leveraging the insights of human language understanding to advance computational models, and vice versa. We explore the profound importance of this relationship, detailing how it drives progress in NLP, enhances linguistic research, and ultimately contributes to our understanding of human cognition and communication.

Linguistic Theories Informing NLP Models

Linguistics provides the theoretical underpinnings necessary for the development of effective NLP systems. Fundamental linguistic concepts such as phonology (the study of speech sounds), morphology (the study of word formation), syntax (the study of sentence structure), semantics (the study of meaning), and pragmatics (the study of language use in context) are crucial for designing algorithms that can process and generate natural language. By applying these principles, NLP researchers can create more nuanced and sophisticated models that better capture the complexities of human language. For instance, understanding syntax is essential for parsing sentences, while semantics aids in interpreting the meaning of words and phrases within different contexts.

NLP Advancing Linguistic Analysis

Conversely, NLP technologies offer linguists powerful tools for analyzing language on a scale previously unimaginable. Corpus linguistics, which involves the study of language as expressed in corpora (samples) of "real world" text, has been revolutionized by NLP methods. These technologies enable the processing and analysis of large volumes of textual data, allowing linguists to identify patterns, trends, and anomalies in language use. NLP tools facilitate the automatic tagging of grammatical features, parsing of sentence structures, and extraction of semantic relationships, significantly accelerating linguistic research and expanding its potential scope.

Bridging Computational and Theoretical Linguistics

The interplay between NLP and linguistics is also evident in the bridging of computational linguistics—a discipline that applies computer science to the analysis and synthesis of language—and theoretical linguistics, which seeks to understand the underlying principles of language structure and function. This convergence has led to a richer, more comprehensive approach to studying language, combining the precision and scalability of computational methods with the depth and nuance of theoretical insights. Through this synergy, researchers can test linguistic theories on extensive datasets, refine computational models with linguistic insights, and explore new hypotheses about language learning, variation, and evolution.

Enhancing Language Understanding and Processing

The collaborative efforts between linguistics and NLP are pushing the boundaries of how machines understand and interact with human language. By incorporating linguistic theories into NLP models, developers can create systems that are more adept at interpreting the subtleties and variations of language, including slang, idioms, and dialectal differences. This enhanced understanding is critical for a wide range of applications, from machine translation and speech recognition to sentiment analysis and conversational agents, ensuring that they can operate effectively across diverse linguistic and cultural contexts.

Contributing to Cognitive Science

Finally, the relationship between linguistics and NLP contributes to broader scientific understanding, particularly in cognitive science. By exploring how machines can be taught to understand and produce language, researchers gain insights into human cognition, language acquisition, and the neural mechanisms underlying language processing. This cross-pollination not only advances our understanding of human intelligence but also informs the development of AI systems that more closely mimic human cognitive processes.

In conclusion, the symbiotic relationship between linguistics and NLP is a cornerstone of both fields' evolution, fostering advancements that have a profound impact on technology, science, and society. As explored in "Natural Language Processing (NLP): The Complete Guide," this synergy is essential for developing more sophisticated and human-like NLP systems, advancing linguistic research, and deepening our understanding of the fundamental nature of language and cognition.

Data Science and NLP: Extracting Value from Text Data

In the field of data science, NLP is a vital tool for extracting valuable insights from text data. With the explosion of digital content, from social media posts and online articles to customer reviews and open-ended survey responses, there is an unprecedented amount of unstructured text data available. NLP techniques are essential for analyzing this data, enabling data scientists to perform sentiment analysis, topic modeling, trend analysis, and more. Through NLP, data scientists can transform raw text into structured data that can be analyzed statistically, uncovering trends, patterns, and insights that inform decision-making across various domains, including marketing, finance, healthcare, and public policy.

In the digital era, where data is the new oil, Natural Language Processing (NLP) stands out as a crucial tool in the data scientist's toolkit, especially when it comes to unlocking the value hidden within text data.

Transforming Text into Data

The first step in understanding the value of NLP within data science involves recognizing the sheer volume and variety of text data generated daily, from social media posts and customer reviews to emails and news articles. Unlike structured data, text data is unstructured and requires specialized methods for processing and analysis. NLP bridges this gap by providing the tools and techniques necessary to convert text into a structured form that can be analyzed using statistical and machine learning methods. This transformation allows data scientists to extract meaningful patterns, trends, and insights from text data, which would otherwise remain inaccessible.

Sentiment Analysis and Opinion Mining

One of the most prominent applications of NLP in data science is sentiment analysis, also known as opinion mining. This process involves analyzing text data to determine the sentiment expressed within it, whether positive, negative, or neutral. Businesses extensively use sentiment analysis to gauge customer satisfaction, monitor brand reputation, and understand consumer preferences by analyzing customer reviews, social media conversations, and feedback surveys. The ability to automatically analyze and interpret sentiment at scale offers companies invaluable insights into their customers' perceptions and experiences, enabling them to tailor products, services, and marketing strategies more effectively.

Topic Modeling and Trend Analysis

NLP also plays a critical role in topic modeling and trend analysis, techniques that identify prevalent themes or topics within large datasets of text. By uncovering the underlying topics in documents, news articles, or social media feeds, data scientists can track trends over time, understand the discourse in various communities, and identify emerging issues or interests. These insights are particularly valuable for market research, content strategy development, and competitive analysis, allowing organizations to stay ahead of industry trends and align their offerings with consumer needs.

Information Extraction and Knowledge Discovery

Information extraction is another area where NLP significantly impacts data science. This process involves automatically extracting structured information from unstructured text, such as entities (names, places, organizations), relationships between entities, and specific facts or events. By transforming text into a structured database, information extraction enables the creation of knowledge bases that support decision-making, research, and automated reasoning. Applications include automating data entry, enhancing search and recommendation systems, and supporting natural language interfaces that allow users to query data in conversational language.

Enhancing Machine Learning Models

Finally, NLP enriches data science by enhancing machine learning models with the ability to understand and generate human language. Text data can be used to train models for a variety of tasks, including classification, prediction, and recommendation systems. Moreover, NLP techniques like word embedding, which represents words in high-dimensional space based on their context, have proven to be invaluable for improving the accuracy and effectiveness of machine learning models across not only text-related tasks but also broader applications in data science.

In conclusion, the intersection of data science and NLP represents a powerful alliance that enables the extraction of valuable insights from text data, a resource that is abundantly available but underutilized. As outlined in "Natural Language Processing (NLP): The Complete Guide," NLP's contribution to data science extends from transforming unstructured text into actionable data to enabling advanced analyses such as sentiment analysis, topic modeling, information extraction, and the enhancement of machine learning models. Through these applications, NLP not only enriches the field of data science but also empowers organizations to make more informed, data-driven decisions.

Bridging Fields and Facilitating Innovations

The importance of NLP extends beyond its direct applications, acting as a bridge that facilitates collaboration and innovation across fields. By bringing together AI, linguistics, and data science, NLP fosters a multidisciplinary approach to solving complex problems related to human language. This convergence is driving the development of new methodologies, technologies, and applications, from enhancing human-computer interaction to improving the accuracy of information retrieval and enabling more effective communication across language barriers.

The intersection of Natural Language Processing (NLP) with fields such as artificial intelligence (AI), linguistics, and data science is not merely a convergence of disciplines but a fertile ground for innovation. This synergy, as detailed in "Natural Language Processing (NLP): The Complete Guide," highlights NLP's pivotal role in bridging diverse fields, fostering cross-disciplinary collaboration, and driving forward groundbreaking advancements. Here, we explore how NLP acts as a catalyst for innovation, facilitating the development of technologies and methodologies that transcend traditional boundaries.

Facilitating Cross-disciplinary Research

NLP stands at the confluence of AI, linguistics, and data science, drawing upon the methodologies and insights of each to advance our understanding and processing of natural language. This intersection encourages a cross-pollination of ideas, where computational models inspired by linguistic theory enhance AI algorithms, and data-driven approaches inform linguistic research. Such collaboration is essential for tackling the complex challenges of language processing, from understanding the nuances of human speech to interpreting the vast, unstructured datasets that define the digital age. By bridging these disciplines, NLP fosters an environment where interdisciplinary teams can work together to solve problems that were once considered beyond reach.

Enhancing Human-Computer Interaction

One of the most tangible impacts of NLP's interdisciplinary nature is its contribution to human-computer interaction (HCI). By integrating linguistic insights with AI technologies, NLP has significantly advanced the development of natural language interfaces, voice-activated assistants, and conversational agents. These innovations have transformed the way users interact with technology, making it more intuitive, accessible, and efficient. The ability to communicate with machines in natural language breaks down barriers between humans and computers, opening up new possibilities for user engagement and accessibility.

Revolutionizing Information Access and Knowledge Discovery

NLP has also revolutionized the fields of information retrieval and knowledge discovery, making it easier to navigate and extract value from the vast expanses of digital information. Search engines, recommendation systems, and automatic summarization tools rely on NLP techniques to understand and organize content in ways that are meaningful to users. By improving the accuracy and relevance of information retrieval, NLP enhances our ability to access knowledge, fostering informed decision-making and driving innovation across industries, from healthcare and education to finance and entertainment.

Accelerating Scientific Research

The capabilities of NLP extend into the realm of scientific research, where it accelerates discovery by enabling the automated analysis of scientific literature and data. Text mining and natural language understanding tools can sift through thousands of research papers, extracting relevant findings, identifying trends, and even generating hypotheses. This automation not only speeds up the research process but also allows scientists to uncover connections and insights that might otherwise go unnoticed, promoting a more integrated and holistic approach to science.

Driving Social and Ethical Innovation

Finally, NLP plays a critical role in driving social and ethical innovation. As NLP technologies become increasingly integrated into our lives, they raise important questions about privacy, bias, and ethical use. The interdisciplinary nature of NLP, involving experts from computer science, linguistics, ethics, and law, facilitates a comprehensive approach to addressing these issues. By considering the societal impacts of NLP applications, researchers and developers can work towards creating technologies that are not only effective but also responsible and inclusive, ensuring that the benefits of NLP are accessible to all.

The importance of NLP in bridging fields and facilitating innovations is a recurring theme in "Natural Language Processing (NLP): The Complete Guide." Through its unique position at the intersection of AI, linguistics, and data science, NLP not only advances our ability to process and understand natural language but also encourages a collaborative and interdisciplinary approach to research and development. This cross-disciplinary synergy is essential for driving technological advancements, enhancing our interaction with digital systems, and addressing the complex challenges of the modern world.

In conclusion, the significance of NLP in AI, linguistics, and data science is profound and multifaceted. As a cornerstone of artificial intelligence, a valuable tool in linguistics research, and a critical asset in data science,

NLP is not only advancing our capabilities in processing and understanding human language but also facilitating interdisciplinary research and innovation. "Natural Language Processing (NLP): The Complete Guide" seeks to illuminate these contributions, exploring how NLP is reshaping these fields and highlighting the endless possibilities it offers for the future.

Objectives And Scope of The Book:

"Natural Language Processing (NLP): The Complete Guide" is crafted with the dual purpose of demystifying the field of NLP and serving as a comprehensive resource for learners, practitioners, and enthusiasts alike. This book aims to bridge the gap between theoretical knowledge and practical application, providing a detailed exploration of NLP's principles, technologies, and their implications across various domains. Here, we outline the primary objectives and the scope of the book, detailing what readers can expect to gain from this extensive guide.

Objectives

1. **Foundational Understanding**: To offer a solid foundation in NLP principles, covering linguistic theories, computational methods, and machine learning techniques that underpin the field. This includes an exploration of syntax, semantics, pragmatics, and the evolution of NLP technologies from rule-based systems to advanced neural networks.

2. **Technical Proficiency**: To equip readers with the technical skills required to implement NLP solutions, including hands-on tutorials on processing and

analyzing text data, building NLP models, and leveraging existing NLP libraries and frameworks. Practical exercises and examples will be provided to reinforce learning and application.

3. **Real-world Applications**: To showcase the wide-ranging applications of NLP across industries such as healthcare, finance, customer service, and more. This will involve case studies and discussions on how NLP technologies are being used to solve real-world problems, automate processes, and enhance decision-making.

4. **Ethical and Societal Implications**: To address the ethical considerations and societal impacts of NLP technologies, including discussions on data privacy, algorithmic bias, and the responsible use of NLP. This objective underscores the importance of developing and deploying NLP solutions that are fair, transparent, and inclusive.

5. **Research and Future Directions**: To provide insights into the cutting-edge research and emerging trends in NLP, fostering an understanding of where the field is headed. This includes an examination of ongoing challenges, potential breakthroughs, and the future possibilities of NLP technologies.

Scope

The scope of "Natural Language Processing (NLP): The Complete Guide" encompasses a broad spectrum of topics and themes within NLP, ensuring a comprehensive coverage that caters to a diverse audience.

1. **Theoretical Frameworks and Linguistic Principles**: An in-depth look at the linguistic and computational theories that form the basis of NLP, offering readers a theoretical understanding necessary for mastering the field.

2. **Machine Learning and Deep Learning in NLP**: An exploration of how machine learning and deep learning techniques are applied in NLP, including discussions on neural networks, transformers, and state-of-the-art models.

3. **Toolkits and Libraries**: Guidance on using popular NLP libraries and frameworks such as NLTK, spaCy, and TensorFlow, providing readers with the practical skills to build and deploy NLP applications.

4. **Ethics and Governance**: A critical examination of the ethical challenges and governance issues surrounding NLP, aiming to promote a responsible approach to the development and application of NLP technologies.

5. **Interdisciplinary Perspectives**: Insights into how NLP intersects with other fields, such as AI, data science, and linguistics, highlighting the multidisciplinary nature of NLP and its impact across various sectors.

By achieving these objectives and covering this scope, "Natural Language Processing (NLP): The Complete Guide" aspires to be an indispensable resource for anyone looking to deepen their understanding of NLP, from beginners seeking an introduction to the field, to advanced practitioners aiming to expand their knowledge and explore new horizons in NLP research and applications.

Chapter 1: Foundations of the NLP

The section on the Foundations of NLP serves as the cornerstone of the reader's journey into understanding and mastering NLP. This foundational segment is meticulously designed to equip readers with the essential concepts, theories, and methodologies that form the basis of natural language processing. Here, we delve into the linguistic and computational underpinnings of NLP, setting the stage for more advanced topics and applications covered later in the book.

Linguistic Principles

The exploration begins with an overview of key linguistic principles that are crucial for NLP. This includes an introduction to the components of language such as phonetics (the sounds of speech), morphology (the structure of words), syntax (the arrangement of words to form sentences), semantics (the meaning of words and sentences), and pragmatics (the use of language in context). Understanding these linguistic aspects is vital for developing NLP systems that can accurately interpret and generate human language.

Introduction to Linguistics and Language Structure

The journey into linguistic principles begins with a broad overview of linguistics — the scientific study of language. It outlines the major components of linguistic analysis: phonetics and phonology, morphology, syntax, semantics, and pragmatics. Each of these components plays a crucial role in how information is encoded and interpreted in human language, thus representing critical areas of study for NLP.

Phonetics and Phonology: These areas study the sounds of human language (phonetics) and the rules governing how those sounds are combined in languages (phonology). Though more relevant for speech recognition and synthesis in NLP, understanding phonetics and phonology is crucial for developing systems that interact with spoken language.

Morphology: This is the study of the structure of words. Understanding morphology helps in developing NLP applications that deal with word formation, inflection, and the creation of new words. Morphological analysis is vital for tasks such as stemming and lemmatization, which reduce words to their base or root form, aiding in the normalization of text data.

Syntax: The study of sentence structure and the rules that govern the construction of sentences in a language. Syntax analysis is foundational for parsing techniques, where sentences are broken down and analyzed to understand their grammatical structure. This understanding is crucial for tasks requiring sentence-level analysis, such as machine translation and grammatical error correction.

Semantics: Semantics involves the study of meaning in language, encompassing the interpretation of words, phrases, and sentences. In NLP, semantic analysis helps in understanding the intended meaning behind a text, which is essential for applications like question answering systems, text summarization, and semantic search.

Pragmatics: This area examines how context influences the interpretation of meaning. Pragmatics is key in understanding how the same phrase can have different meanings in different situations. Incorporating pragmatic analysis into NLP systems allows for a more nuanced understanding of language use, improving the performance of dialogue systems and conversational agents.

The Role of Linguistic Theories in NLP

The book delves into how linguistic theories have influenced NLP methodologies and technologies. It explores the transition from rule-based approaches, which heavily relied on linguistic insights to encode grammar and syntax rules, to statistical and machine learning models that learn from the linguistic characteristics of large datasets. The discussion underscores the importance of linguistic principles in training more advanced NLP models, such as neural networks and transformers, which require an understanding of language structure and use to accurately process and generate text.

Linguistics Applied to NLP Tasks

Practical applications of linguistic principles in NLP are highlighted through examples and case studies. These include the application of phonetics in speech recognition systems, morphology in text normalization, syntax in syntactic parsing, semantics in natural language understanding (NLU), and pragmatics in dialogue systems. By applying these principles, NLP systems can achieve a deeper and more accurate understanding of human language, leading to more effective and human-like interactions between computers and humans.

In summary, the section provides a comprehensive overview of how the structure and function of human language are analyzed and applied in NLP. This foundation is not only crucial for those entering the field but also enriches the knowledge of seasoned practitioners, offering insights into the linguistic complexities that NLP seeks to model and interpret. Through this exploration, readers gain a deeper appreciation for the interdisciplinary nature of NLP, poised at the intersection of computer science, artificial intelligence, and linguistics.

Computational Models of Language

Following the linguistic principles, the book delves into the computational models used to process and understand language. The evolution of machine learning in NLP is discussed, highlighting how models have become increasingly sophisticated, moving from simple bag-of-words approaches to complex deep learning architectures like recurrent neural networks (RNNs) and transformers. Each model's workings, advantages, and limitations are examined to provide readers with a comprehensive understanding of NLP's computational landscape.

Evolution of Computational Models

The narrative begins with a historical overview of computational models in NLP, tracing their evolution from early rule-based systems to the current state-of-the-art deep learning models. This historical context sets the stage for understanding the advancements in the field and the motivations behind the development of newer models.

Rule-Based Models: Early NLP systems relied heavily on rule-based models, which utilized sets of linguistic rules crafted by experts to parse and understand text. These models, while effective for specific tasks with limited scope, struggled with the complexity and variability of natural language, leading to rigid systems that were difficult to scale or adapt to new languages or domains.

Statistical Models: With the advent of larger text corpora and increased computational power, statistical models began to gain prominence. These models, including hidden Markov models (HMMs) and n-gram models, leverage the probability distributions of words and sequences to make predictions about language. They marked a significant shift towards data-driven approaches in NLP, offering more flexibility and robustness than rule-based systems.

Machine Learning Models: The incorporation of machine learning techniques further advanced NLP, introducing models such as decision trees, support vector machines (SVMs), and later, ensemble methods like random forests. These models are trained on annotated datasets to learn the patterns of language, enabling more accurate classification, tagging, and parsing tasks.

Deep Learning Revolution in NLP

The section then delves into the deep learning revolution that has transformed NLP in recent years. It covers the fundamentals of neural networks, including feedforward networks, recurrent neural networks (RNNs), and long short-term memory networks (LSTMs), explaining how these architectures model language data.

Transformers and Attention Mechanisms: A significant focus is placed on the transformer architecture and its underlying mechanism of attention. Introduced with the seminal paper "Attention is All You Need," transformers have set new benchmarks in a wide range of NLP tasks. The book explains how transformers work, their advantages over previous models, and their role in the development of large-scale language models like BERT, GPT, and others.

Challenges and Considerations

Challenges including the handling of ambiguity, context-dependence, and the diversity of linguistic structures across languages. It discusses the importance of training data quality, the risk of bias in models, and the computational resources required for training state-of-the-art models.

Practical Applications and Future Directions

Lastly, the exploration of computational models concludes with discussions on the practical applications of these models in NLP tasks such as machine translation, sentiment analysis, question-answering, and automated content generation. Future directions in computational modeling of language are contemplated, considering potential advancements in model architecture, efficiency, and the ongoing quest for models that better capture the nuances of human language.

Text Processing and Analysis

A critical aspect of NLP is the ability to process and analyze text data. These techniques form the building blocks for many NLP applications and are essential skills for practitioners.

Preprocessing Techniques

The journey into text processing begins with an examination of preprocessing techniques. These initial steps are crucial for cleaning and standardizing text data, making it more amenable to analysis and modeling. Key preprocessing tasks discussed include:

Tokenization: The process of breaking down text into smaller units, such as words or phrases. This step is foundational for most NLP tasks, as it transforms raw text into a format that algorithms can work with more effectively.

Normalization: Techniques such as lowercasing, removing punctuation, and correcting misspellings are covered under normalization. These methods help in reducing the complexity of the text data and improve the performance of NLP models by ensuring consistency.

Stemming and Lemmatization: These processes reduce words to their base or root form, aiding in the consolidation of variations of a word into a single representation. The distinction between the crude heuristic approach of stemming and the more sophisticated morphological analysis performed by lemmatization is explained.

Stop Word Removal: The elimination of common words that carry little semantic value (such as "the", "is", "and") is discussed. Removing these words can help focus on the more meaningful parts of the text for analysis.

Text Analysis Techniques

Following preprocessing, the book delves into text analysis techniques that allow for the extraction of insights and features from text:

Part-of-Speech Tagging: Identifying the grammatical parts of speech (e.g., nouns, verbs, adjectives) in a text. This technique is crucial for understanding the structure of sentences and for tasks that require knowledge of grammatical roles.

Named Entity Recognition (NER): The process of identifying and classifying key elements in text into predefined categories, such as person names, organizations, locations, dates, and quantities. NER is essential for extracting structured information from unstructured text data.

Syntax Parsing: Discussing the methods for analyzing the syntactic structure of sentences to understand their grammatical constituents. Syntax parsing is fundamental for applications that require a deep understanding of sentence structure, such as machine translation and natural language understanding.

Sentiment Analysis: The technique of determining the sentiment expressed in a piece of text, whether positive, negative, or neutral. This analysis is particularly valuable for monitoring public opinion, customer feedback, and social media analysis.

Topic Modeling: Exploring methods such as Latent Dirichlet Allocation (LDA) for identifying the underlying themes or topics in a large collection of documents. Topic modeling is useful for summarizing and discovering the main ideas within extensive text datasets.

Challenges and Considerations

Also addresses the challenges encountered in text processing and analysis, including dealing with ambiguity, the complexity of human language, and the scalability of processing large datasets. It underscores the importance of careful preprocessing and the selection of appropriate analysis techniques based on the specific requirements of the NLP task at hand.

Practical Applications

Each technique is accompanied by practical examples and applications, demonstrating how text processing and analysis form the foundation for tasks such as information retrieval, content categorization, question answering, and many more. This approach not only solidifies the theoretical understanding but also illustrates the real-world utility of these foundational NLP techniques.

Machine Learning and NLP

The foundations of NLP are deeply intertwined with machine learning, and explores how machine learning algorithms are applied to NLP tasks. It covers the basics of supervised, unsupervised, and semi-supervised learning, as well as specific algorithms commonly used in NLP, such as decision trees, support vector machines, and neural networks. The discussion includes how these algorithms are trained on text data, the challenge of handling high-dimensional data, and strategies for feature extraction and selection. It explores the transformative impact machine learning has had on NLP, offering a deep dive into the methods, algorithms, and practices that have propelled NLP into new frontiers. It's designed to equip readers with both a conceptual understanding and practical knowledge of applying machine learning to solve complex language processing tasks.

Introduction to Machine Learning in NLP

The section begins with an introduction to machine learning, setting the stage for its application in NLP. It outlines the distinctions between supervised, unsupervised, and semi-supervised learning, alongside reinforcement learning, and their relevance to NLP tasks. Key concepts such as feature extraction, model training, validation, and testing are discussed, providing a solid foundation for understanding how machine learning models learn from linguistic data.

Supervised Learning for NLP

A significant focus is placed on supervised learning, the most common paradigm in NLP applications. This part explains how labeled datasets are used to train models to perform a variety of NLP tasks, such as classification (e.g., spam detection, sentiment analysis), and sequence labeling (e.g., part-of-speech tagging, named entity recognition). The discussion includes an overview of traditional algorithms like Naive Bayes, decision trees, and support vector machines, as well as the rationale behind choosing specific models based on the nature of the NLP task and the characteristics of the data.

Unsupervised Learning and NLP

Unsupervised learning's role in NLP is explored next, highlighting how algorithms discover hidden patterns in unlabeled data. Techniques such as clustering (for grouping similar text documents) and dimensionality reduction (for reducing the complexity of text data) are covered. The section on topic modeling, particularly Latent Dirichlet Allocation (LDA), exemplifies unsupervised learning's power in uncovering latent topics within large collections of texts, showcasing its utility in organizing, summarizing, and navigating text corpora.

Deep Learning in NLP

The advent of deep learning has ushered in a new era for NLP, marked by significant advancements in model performance and capabilities. The evolution from simple feedforward networks to more complex architectures like Recurrent Neural Networks (RNNs), Long Short-Term Memory networks (LSTMs), and Convolutional Neural

Networks (CNNs) is discussed, with an emphasis on their applications in processing sequential text data.

A considerable part of the narrative is dedicated to the revolutionary impact of transformer models, such as BERT (Bidirectional Encoder Representations from Transformers), GPT (Generative Pre-trained Transformer), and their variants. The guide explains the concepts of self-attention mechanisms and pre-training, detailing how these models achieve state-of-the-art results across a wide range of NLP tasks by capturing deep contextual meanings of words.

Challenges and Ethical Considerations

The section does not shy away from addressing the challenges associated with applying machine learning to NLP, including issues related to data bias, model interpretability, and the computational resources required for training large models. Ethical considerations, such as privacy concerns and the potential for misuse of powerful NLP technologies, are also discussed, urging practitioners to adopt responsible AI practices.

Practical Applications and Future Directions

Practical examples and case studies are woven throughout the section to demonstrate how machine learning models are applied in real-world NLP tasks, from automated customer service chatbots to sophisticated language translation services. The discussion concludes by speculating on future directions in the intersection of machine learning and NLP, pondering advancements in unsupervised learning, the quest for generalizable AI, and the ongoing efforts to make NLP models more efficient, interpretable, and ethically sound.

Ethics and Challenges in NLP

An understanding of the foundations of NLP would be incomplete without addressing the ethical considerations and challenges inherent in the field.

Ethical Considerations in NLP

The section begins by addressing the fundamental ethical considerations inherent in NLP technologies. It explores the implications of algorithmic bias, where models may inadvertently perpetuate or amplify societal biases present in their training data. Examples such as gender or racial bias in word embeddings and language models are discussed to illustrate how biases can manifest in NLP applications, affecting everything from job search algorithms to sentiment analysis tools.

Privacy concerns are also highlighted, especially in relation to the collection and use of personal data for training NLP models. The guide discusses the importance of data anonymization, consent, and the ethical use of data in accordance with privacy regulations and standards.

Another significant ethical consideration covered is the impact of NLP on misinformation and the spread of harmful content. The section examines the role of NLP in detecting and mitigating fake news, hate speech, and online harassment, balancing the benefits of content moderation with the risks of censorship and the suppression of free speech.

Challenges in NLP

The scalability of NLP solutions is discussed, highlighting the difficulties in processing and analyzing large volumes of text data in real-time, especially for languages with limited resources or complex grammatical structures.

Interoperability poses another challenge, as the section examines the need for NLP systems to integrate with existing software ecosystems and standards, ensuring that NLP technologies can be effectively deployed and utilized across different platforms and applications.

Addressing Ethical Challenges

The guide emphasizes the importance of adopting a proactive approach to ethical challenges in NLP. It advocates for the development of ethical guidelines and standards for NLP research and applications, including the need for transparency, accountability, and fairness in algorithmic decision-making.

Strategies for mitigating bias in NLP models are explored, such as diversifying training data, implementing fairness-aware algorithms, and conducting rigorous bias audits. The section also discusses the role of interdisciplinary collaboration, involving ethicists, sociologists, and domain experts, in identifying and addressing ethical issues in NLP projects.

Introduction To NLP and its Applications:

This introductory chapter is crafted to provide a comprehensive overview of NLP, demystifying what it is, its significance, and the myriad ways it intersects with our daily lives through various applications. It sets the tone for the entire book, establishing a solid foundation of understanding and appreciation for the field's depth and breadth.

What is Natural Language Processing?

The introduction begins by defining Natural Language Processing as a subfield of artificial intelligence (AI) focused on enabling computers to understand, interpret, and generate human language in a meaningful way. It outlines the historical development of NLP, from its early days rooted in computational linguistics to its modern incarnation powered by advanced machine learning and deep learning technologies. This historical context helps readers grasp the evolutionary trajectory of NLP and its growing impact on technology and society.

This foundational chapter demystifies NLP, presenting it not merely as a technological field but as an interdisciplinary endeavor that sits at the confluence of computer science, artificial intelligence, linguistics, and data science. It aims to provide a clear, comprehensive understanding of NLP, its scope, and its transformative potential in bridging human communication and computational processes.

Defining Natural Language Processing

The section begins by defining NLP as the scientific and engineering discipline dedicated to enabling computers to understand, interpret, and generate human languages (natural languages) in a way that is both meaningful and useful. It emphasizes the dual focus of NLP on understanding (comprehension) and generation (production) of natural language by machines, highlighting the complexity and challenges inherent in these tasks due to the nuanced and dynamic nature of human language.

Historical Overview and Evolution

An overview of the historical development of NLP is provided to give readers a sense of the field's evolution. From early rule-based systems and the advent of machine learning approaches to the current era dominated by deep learning and neural networks, this narrative outlines the major milestones and technological breakthroughs that have shaped NLP. This historical context helps readers appreciate the progress made in the field and the accelerating pace of innovation driven by advances in algorithms, computational power, and data availability.

The Interdisciplinary Nature of NLP

This segment highlights the interdisciplinary nature of NLP, underscoring how it draws upon principles and methodologies from linguistics (the study of language), computer science (the study of computation and information processing), artificial intelligence (the pursuit of creating intelligent agents), and data science (the extraction of knowledge and insights from data). This convergence of disciplines is presented as a strength of NLP, enabling it to tackle the complexity of human language by leveraging diverse perspectives and techniques.

Core Challenges in NLP

The discussion then shifts to the core challenges that define NLP, including ambiguity (lexical, syntactic, and semantic), context-dependence, and the vast diversity of linguistic expressions and structures across different languages and dialects. These challenges underscore the sophistication required in NLP models and algorithms to accurately process and generate natural language, reflecting the ongoing research efforts and innovations aimed at overcoming these obstacles.

Applications and Impact of NLP

Finally, the section introduces a broad spectrum of NLP applications to illustrate the field's impact and practical relevance. From machine translation and speech recognition to sentiment analysis, chatbots, and automated summarization, these examples demonstrate how NLP technologies are integrated into various aspects of daily life, business operations, and societal functions. This exploration of applications sets the stage for subsequent chapters, which delve deeper into specific NLP technologies, techniques, and use cases.

By providing a clear, engaging introduction to Natural Language Processing, "What is Natural Language Processing?" lays the groundwork for readers to navigate the complex, rapidly evolving landscape of NLP. It offers a solid foundation from which to explore the detailed methodologies, challenges, and innovations discussed throughout "Natural Language Processing (NLP): The Complete Guide," equipping readers with the knowledge and context needed to understand the profound impact of NLP on technology and society.

The Significance of NLP

The importance of NLP in breaking down language barriers and making information more accessible is also emphasized, showcasing its potential to drive global communication and knowledge sharing.

Bridging Human and Machine Communication

The discourse begins by framing NLP as a crucial bridge between human language and machine comprehension. It underscores how NLP technologies enable computers to perform tasks that require an understanding of natural language, such as translating texts, answering questions, and recognizing speech. This bridging function of NLP is presented not merely as a technological achievement but as a paradigm shift in how humans interact with machines, making technology more accessible, intuitive, and responsive to our natural modes of communication.

Democratizing Information Access

A significant portion of the discussion on the significance of NLP is devoted to its role in democratizing access to information. NLP technologies, particularly in machine translation and information retrieval, have broken down language barriers, making vast amounts of knowledge and information accessible to people regardless of their linguistic backgrounds. This aspect of NLP is celebrated for fostering global communication, enabling cross-cultural exchanges, and facilitating equal access to educational and informational resources.

Enhancing Business and Social Enterprises

The section further explores how NLP applications are revolutionizing business practices and social enterprises. From automating customer service interactions through chatbots to analyzing consumer sentiments on social media, NLP is at the forefront of enhancing business intelligence, operational efficiency, and customer engagement. Moreover, the text highlights NLP's impact on social good initiatives, such as monitoring public health through sentiment analysis of social media posts and enhancing accessibility for individuals with disabilities through speech recognition and generation technologies.

Advancing Artificial Intelligence

The significance of NLP extends into the broader field of artificial intelligence, where it serves as a key area of research and development. This segment of the discussion delves into how NLP challenges and advances in machine learning models, such as deep learning, are pushing the boundaries of what AI can achieve. By tackling the intricacies of natural language understanding and generation, NLP is not only advancing the capabilities of AI systems but also providing insights into human cognition and language processing.

Addressing Ethical and Societal Implications

The exploration of NLP's significance concludes with a thoughtful examination of the ethical and societal implications of NLP technologies. This includes a discussion on the responsibility of developers and researchers to address issues of bias, privacy, and security inherent in NLP applications. The guide posits that the significance of NLP also lies in its potential to reflect and influence societal norms and values, underscoring the importance of ethical considerations in the development and deployment of NLP technologies.

Through this comprehensive analysis, illuminates the profound significance of NLP in modern society. By detailing the ways in which NLP bridges the gap between human and machine, democratizes information, revolutionizes business and social initiatives, advances AI, and raises important ethical considerations, the section invites readers to appreciate the vast potential and critical importance of NLP in shaping the future of technology and human interaction.

Core Components and Techniques

An overview of the core components and techniques of NLP is provided to familiarize readers with the fundamental aspects of the field. This includes discussions on syntax, semantics, pragmatics, and discourse, explaining how these linguistic principles are applied in computational models. The introduction also touches on essential NLP techniques such as tokenization, part-of-speech tagging, named entity recognition, and sentiment analysis, setting the stage for deeper exploration in subsequent chapters.

Core Components of NLP

The exploration begins by delineating the core components that constitute the framework of NLP:

Syntax: The study of the rules that govern the structure of sentences. Understanding syntax is crucial for parsing sentences and extracting structural information, which is foundational for many NLP tasks. Techniques like tokenization (breaking text into tokens, such as words and phrases) and syntactic parsing (analyzing the grammatical structure of sentences) are vital tools in this domain.

Semantics: Concerned with the meaning of words, phrases, sentences, and texts. Semantic analysis enables NLP systems to comprehend the meanings conveyed in texts, going beyond mere word recognition to grasp the nuances of language. Techniques such as Named Entity Recognition (NER), which identifies and categorizes key information in text, and Word Sense Disambiguation (WSD), which determines the meaning of words based on context, are central to semantic processing.

Pragmatics: The aspect of linguistics that deals with language use in context and how context influences the interpretation of meaning. Pragmatics in NLP involves understanding the intended message, tone, and conversational dynamics within communication. It's key for tasks requiring a deeper level of understanding, such as sentiment analysis and dialogue systems.

Discourse: The examination of how sequences of sentences (discourses) convey meaning and how they are interconnected. Discourse analysis in NLP helps in understanding the coherence and cohesiveness of longer texts, essential for summarization, topic segmentation, and cohesive text generation.

Fundamental Techniques in NLP

Following the introduction to core components, the book delves into the fundamental techniques that are applied across various NLP tasks:

Text Preprocessing: Techniques such as cleaning text, removing stopwords, stemming, and lemmatization prepare data for further processing. These initial steps are crucial for standardizing text input and enhancing the performance of NLP models.

Feature Extraction and Representation: Methods to convert text into a format that machine learning algorithms can process. This includes bag-of-words, TF-IDF (Term

Frequency-Inverse Document Frequency), and word embeddings (such as Word2Vec and GloVe). These techniques transform raw text into numerical representations, capturing the semantic properties of words.

Machine Learning Algorithms: The application of machine learning in NLP, including both traditional algorithms (like Naive Bayes, Decision Trees, and Support Vector Machines) and neural network-based models.

Deep Learning and Neural Networks: An introduction to the use of deep learning models, particularly RNNs (Recurrent Neural Networks), LSTMs (Long Short-Term Memory networks), CNNs (Convolutional Neural Networks), and Transformers in NLP. These advanced models are capable of capturing complex language patterns and have significantly improved the performance of various NLP tasks, including machine translation, text generation, and sentiment analysis.

Evaluation Metrics: Understanding how to assess the performance of NLP models is critical.

Applications of NLP

The heart of the introduction is its exploration of the diverse applications of NLP, illustrating the technology's versatility and utility across various domains. Key applications covered include:

Machine Translation: Transforming text or speech from one language to another, enabling cross-linguistic communication and content accessibility.

Speech Recognition and Generation: Powering voice-activated assistants, dictation software, and other tools that interpret spoken language and convert it into text or generate spoken responses.

Chatbots and Virtual Assistants: Enhancing customer service and user interaction through automated, natural language-based communication systems.

Sentiment Analysis: Analyzing opinions, emotions, and sentiments in text data, widely used in marketing, product development, and social media monitoring.

Information Retrieval: Improving search engines and recommendation systems by enabling them to understand and process natural language queries.

Basic Linguistic Concepts for NLP:

The exploration of basic linguistic concepts forms a critical foundation for understanding how NLP systems are designed to interpret, process, and generate human language.

Syntax: The Structure of Language

Syntax refers to the set of rules, principles, and processes that govern the structure of sentences in a language. It involves the arrangement of words and phrases to create well-formed sentences, encompassing the grammatical structure that dictates how words combine to convey meaning. In NLP, understanding syntax is crucial for parsing sentences, which involves breaking down a sentence into its constituent parts and analyzing its grammatical structure.

Parsing and Syntactic Analysis: NLP utilizes parsing algorithms to analyze the syntactic structure of sentences, helping to identify the relationships between words and phrases. Techniques such as constituency parsing (which identifies the syntactic structure based on the constitution of sentences) and dependency parsing (which focuses on the dependencies and relationships between words) are fundamental.

Applications in NLP: Syntactic analysis is essential for numerous NLP tasks, including grammatical error correction, machine translation, and question answering. By understanding the syntax of a sentence, NLP systems can accurately interpret queries, translate between languages while maintaining grammatical integrity, and generate text that adheres to the rules of syntax.

Semantics: The Meaning of Language

Semantics is the branch of linguistics concerned with the meaning of words, phrases, sentences, and texts. It deals with how linguistic signs convey meaning, how meaning is constructed, and how it varies across different linguistic contexts. In NLP, semantic analysis enables systems to comprehend the intended meaning behind the text, a crucial step for tasks that require a deep understanding of language.

Semantic Analysis Techniques: This includes Named Entity Recognition (NER) for identifying and classifying entities within text, Word Sense Disambiguation (WSD) for determining the correct meaning of a word based on context, and Semantic Role Labeling (SRL) for identifying the underlying relationships and roles in a sentence.

Applications in NLP: Semantics powers applications such as information extraction, where the goal is to retrieve structured information from unstructured text, and natural language understanding (NLU) systems, which aim to comprehend user queries in a manner akin to human understanding.

Pragmatics: The Use of Language in Context

Pragmatics focuses on the use of language in context and how context influences the interpretation of meaning. It examines how the same expression can convey different meanings in different situations and how understanding is negotiated between speakers and listeners (or readers and writers). Pragmatics in NLP is about interpreting the intended meaning, inferring the speakers' intentions, and understanding the implications of the language used.

Pragmatic Modeling in NLP: Techniques for modeling pragmatics include discourse analysis, which looks at how sequences of sentences convey information cohesively, and context modeling, which involves using external knowledge and situational context to interpret text accurately.

Applications in NLP: Pragmatics is crucial for developing effective dialogue systems and chatbots, which must understand and generate responses that are appropriate to the context of the conversation. It also plays a role in sentiment analysis, where the sentiment conveyed by a text can depend heavily on contextual clues.

Overview Of the NLP Pipeline:

Tokenization: The First Step in Text Processing

Tokenization is the process of dividing text into smaller units, known as tokens, which can be words, phrases, or symbols. It's the foundational step in the NLP pipeline, setting the stage for more complex analyses by breaking down the text into manageable pieces.

Importance of Tokenization: Understanding the significance of tokenization involves recognizing its role in standardizing text input and facilitating subsequent processing steps. Accurate tokenization is essential for parsing, part-of-speech tagging, and other NLP tasks that rely on the discrete analysis of text components.

Techniques and Challenges: The guide discusses various tokenization techniques, including whitespace tokenization, punctuation-based tokenization, and advanced methods that account for complex linguistic phenomena such as contractions and multi-word expressions. Challenges such as tokenizing languages without clear word boundaries are also addressed.

Parsing: Analyzing Syntactic Structure

Parsing in NLP involves analyzing the grammatical structure of sentences to identify their constituent parts and relationships. This process is crucial for understanding the syntactic organization of text, which informs both meaning and function.

Constituency and Dependency Parsing: The section explores the differences between constituency parsing, which breaks down sentences into sub-phrases, and dependency parsing, which focuses on the relationships between words. Examples and applications of both parsing types are provided to illustrate their utility in NLP.

Applications in NLP: Parsing is fundamental to applications requiring a deep understanding of sentence structure, such as machine translation, natural language understanding (NLU), and automated text summarization.

Named Entity Recognition (NER): Identifying and Classifying Entities

Named Entity Recognition is the process of locating and classifying named entities within text into predefined categories such as persons, organizations, locations, dates, and quantities. NER is a critical step in extracting structured information from unstructured text.

Techniques for NER: The book outlines various approaches to NER, including rule-based methods, statistical models, and recent advancements leveraging deep learning. The challenges of ambiguity and context in entity recognition are also discussed.

Role in Information Extraction: NER's significance in information extraction is highlighted, demonstrating its application in creating knowledge bases, enhancing search and recommendation systems, and supporting question-answering applications.

Beyond Basic Processing: Advanced NLP Techniques

Following the foundational steps of the NLP pipeline, the section introduces more advanced techniques essential for fully realizing the potential of NLP:

Part-of-Speech Tagging: The process of assigning parts of speech to each token in a sentence, vital for understanding grammatical structure and meaning.

Coreference Resolution: Identifying when different words refer to the same entity in a text, crucial for maintaining coherence and understanding discourse.

Sentiment Analysis: Analyzing the sentiment expressed in text, useful for monitoring opinions and attitudes in customer feedback, social media, and more.

Word Embeddings and Language Models: Discussing the development and use of word embeddings and language models (such as BERT and GPT) for capturing semantic relationships and context in text.

Key Challenges in NLP:

The exploration of key challenges in NLP is critical for understanding the complexities and intricacies of human language that NLP systems strive to decode.

Ambiguity in Language

Language ambiguity presents a significant challenge for NLP systems. Ambiguity occurs when a word, phrase, or sentence can be interpreted in multiple ways, making it difficult for machines to determine the intended meaning without human-like levels of inference and reasoning.

Lexical Ambiguity: This type of ambiguity arises when a single word has multiple meanings. For example, the word "bank" can refer to a financial institution, the side of a river, or the act of tilting an airplane. NLP systems must use context to resolve which meaning is relevant in a given situation.

Syntactic Ambiguity: Syntactic or structural ambiguity occurs when a sentence can be parsed in multiple ways, leading to different interpretations. For instance, "I saw the man with the telescope" can mean either that the speaker used a telescope to see the man or that the man had a telescope. Parsing algorithms and understanding sentence structure context are crucial for addressing this challenge.

Semantic Ambiguity: Semantic ambiguity happens when the meaning of a sentence as a whole can be interpreted in multiple ways, often due to complex relationships between the words and phrases. This requires deep semantic analysis and real-world knowledge to resolve.

Context: The Key to Meaning

The challenge of context involves understanding the situation, background, or conditions surrounding a piece of text. Context can significantly affect the interpretation of language, and NLP systems must be adept at using contextual clues to correctly understand and generate language.

Pragmatic Understanding: This involves interpreting language based on the social context, the speaker's intent, and unstated assumptions. Pragmatic understanding is vital for tasks like sarcasm detection, humor recognition, and effective dialogue management in conversational agents.

Cohesion and Coherence: Achieving text cohesion and coherence requires understanding how different parts of a text relate to each other and to the larger discourse. NLP systems need to track entities, themes, and narrative structures across sentences and paragraphs to maintain continuity and relevance.

Understanding Nuances: Capturing the Subtleties of Language

The subtleties and nuances of language pose another layer of complexity for NLP. This encompasses aspects like emotion, tone, style, and the connotative meanings of words and phrases, which are often challenging for machines to capture and interpret.

Sentiment and Tone Analysis: Accurately gauging the sentiment or emotional tone of text requires a nuanced understanding of language, including idioms, euphemisms, and intensity modifiers. NLP models must be trained on diverse datasets to recognize these subtleties across different contexts and cultures.

Figurative Language: Metaphors, similes, and idiomatic expressions are common in natural language but can be particularly challenging for NLP systems to interpret correctly. Addressing this requires advanced semantic analysis and, often, knowledge beyond the text itself.

Cultural and Linguistic Diversity: Language use varies significantly across cultures and communities, affecting vocabulary, grammar, and communication styles. NLP systems must be adaptable and sensitive to this diversity to function effectively in a global context.

Chapter 2: Text Processing and Tokenization

The segment on Text Processing and Tokenization provides an in-depth exploration of the foundational steps required to prepare text data for further NLP tasks. This chapter is critical as it lays the groundwork for understanding how raw text is transformed into a structured format that NLP models can efficiently process and analyze. It underscores the significance of meticulous text processing and the pivotal role of tokenization in the broader context of NLP pipelines.

Understanding Text Processing

Text processing involves a series of preprocessing steps aimed at converting raw text into a cleaner, more uniform format suitable for analysis.

Key preprocessing tasks discussed include:

Normalization: This involves standardizing the text by converting it to a uniform case (usually lowercase), removing punctuation, special characters, and extraneous whitespace. Normalization helps in reducing the variability of the text, making it easier for algorithms to detect patterns.

Removing Stop Words: Stop words are common words that carry minimal semantic weight (such as "the", "is", "at") and are often removed from the text to focus on more meaningful words. This step is crucial for tasks where the semantic content of the text is important, such as in topic modeling or keyword extraction.

Dealing with Spelling Errors: Techniques for correcting spelling errors or standardizing spelling variations are discussed, emphasizing their role in ensuring consistency and accuracy in text representation.

Tokenization: The First Step in Text Analysis

Tokenization is presented as the foundational step in the analysis of text, where the raw text is divided into meaningful elements called tokens. These tokens can be words, phrases, or sentences, depending on the level of granularity required for the NLP task at hand.

Word Tokenization: The process of splitting the text into individual words or terms. The section details various approaches to word tokenization, including the use of whitespace, punctuation, and advanced linguistic rules to accurately identify word boundaries.

Sentence Tokenization: Breaking down text into individual sentences. This involves identifying sentence boundaries, which can be challenging due to the use of punctuation for purposes other than sentence demarcation. Techniques for accurately detecting sentence endings are explored.

Subword Tokenization: For certain languages or specialized applications (such as dealing with unknown words or names in machine translation), tokenizing text into subword units (like syllables or morphemes) can be beneficial.

Text Preprocessing Techniques:

This comprehensive portion emphasizes the critical role of cleaning, normalization, and encoding in the text preprocessing pipeline, illustrating how these steps enhance the quality and utility of text data, laying the groundwork for effective tokenization and subsequent analysis.

Cleaning: The Initial Step in Text Preprocessing

Definition and Importance:

Cleaning refers to the process of removing irrelevant or extraneous information from the text data. This initial step is crucial for eliminating noise that could detract from the performance of NLP models.

Text processing and tokenization form the bedrock of Natural Language Processing (NLP), enabling computers to understand, interpret, and generate human language. This chapter delves into the fundamental techniques of text preprocessing: cleaning, normalization, and encoding, which are pivotal for preparing raw text for further NLP tasks such as parsing, sentiment analysis, and machine translation. Understanding these techniques is crucial for anyone venturing into the field of NLP, as they significantly influence the performance and effectiveness of algorithms applied later in the processing pipeline.

Text Preprocessing: Definition and Importance

Text preprocessing is the initial phase in the NLP pipeline, involving a series of steps designed to transform raw text into a more manageable and uniform format for algorithms to process. Given the vast diversity in human language, including variations in syntax, semantics, and grammar, preprocessing is vital for reducing complexity and enhancing computational efficiency. The primary goal is to strip text of noise and inconsistencies, making it more amenable to analysis and pattern recognition by algorithms.

Cleaning

Text cleaning is the process of removing irrelevant characters, symbols, and formatting from the text. This step is crucial because raw data often comes laden with HTML tags, URLs, social media entities (like hashtags and mentions), as well as punctuation and special characters, which may not be useful for specific NLP tasks. Cleaning ensures that the text is stripped down to its essential content, reducing the computational load and focusing the analysis on meaningful data only.

Normalization

Normalization involves converting text into a more uniform format to ensure consistency across the dataset. It includes tasks such as converting all characters to lower case, removing accents, and expanding contractions (e.g., transforming "don't" to "do not"). Normalization also encompasses stemming and lemmatization, which reduce words to their base or root form. This step is vital for reducing the complexity of the text and for treating different forms of the same word as equivalent, thus facilitating better comparison and analysis.

Encoding

Encoding is the process of converting text into a format that can be understood by machine learning models. Since algorithms typically operate on numerical data, encoding transforms text into numerical values or vectors. Common encoding techniques include one-hot encoding, Bag of Words (BoW), and Term Frequency-Inverse Document Frequency (TF-IDF). More advanced methods, such as word embeddings (Word2Vec, GloVe), provide a dense representation of words based on their context, capturing semantic relationships between them. Encoding is a critical step as it directly impacts the model's ability to learn from the text data.

The initial stages of text preprocessing—cleaning, normalization, and encoding—are foundational for effective NLP. By preparing the raw text through these techniques, we significantly enhance the efficiency and accuracy of subsequent NLP tasks. Proper preprocessing not only streamlines the analysis but also unveils the nuanced patterns and insights within the text, making it indispensable for anyone looking to master Natural Language Processing. As NLP continues to evolve, the methods and technologies for text preprocessing also advance, offering more sophisticated tools for tackling the complexities of human language.

Common Cleaning Tasks:

The guide outlines typical cleaning tasks, including the removal of HTML tags, URLs, email addresses, and special characters, which often do not contribute to the understanding of text. Additionally, it discusses the importance of removing or handling duplicated entries, which can skew analysis and model training.

Text preprocessing is an indispensable stage that prepares raw text for subsequent analytical tasks. Cleaning text is essential for removing noise and irrelevant information, thereby simplifying the data and making it more amenable to processing and analysis. Here, we explore the common tasks involved in cleaning text data, shedding light on their importance and implementation.

Removing HTML Tags and URLs

Raw text, especially when extracted from web pages or social media, often contains HTML tags, URLs, and other web-specific noise. These elements can disrupt text analysis by introducing irrelevant characters and structures. Removing HTML tags and URLs is thus a fundamental cleaning task, ensuring that the text reflects pure content without markup or web artifacts.

Dealing with Special Characters and Punctuation

Special characters and punctuation marks can either be noise or carry semantic weight depending on the context of the NLP task. For instance, punctuation is critical in sentiment analysis but may be irrelevant in topic modeling. Cleaning involves either removing these characters or transforming them in a way that serves the analytical goals, such as converting currency symbols to standard text expressions or handling apostrophes in contractions.

Case Normalization

Case normalization is a simple yet impactful cleaning task that involves converting all text to a uniform case, typically lowercase. This process is crucial for consistency and ensures that algorithms do not treat words differently based on case variation alone, such as "Apple" and "apple" being recognized as the same word.

Removing Stop Words

Stop words are common words that carry minimal semantic weight in a given language, such as "the", "is", and "and" in English. These words can significantly clutter and dilute the focus of text analysis. Removing stop words is a common cleaning task that helps highlight more meaningful words, thereby improving the efficiency and accuracy of NLP models.

Handling Numbers and Dates

Numbers and dates can introduce a level of variability in text that may not be useful for certain NLP tasks. Depending on the context, it may be beneficial to remove them or convert them into a standardized format. In some cases, numbers and dates carry critical information and must be preserved in a way that aligns with the analytical objectives, such as transforming dates into a uniform format for temporal analysis.

Text Tokenization

Tokenization is the process of breaking down text into smaller units, such as words or phrases. While not strictly a cleaning task, tokenization is a preparatory step that often follows initial cleaning efforts. It transforms the cleaned text into tokens that can be further processed, analyzed, or encoded for machine learning models. Tokenization is fundamental to NLP, as it delineates the basic units of text for subsequent tasks like parsing, stemming, and lemmatization.

Common cleaning tasks in text preprocessing set the stage for effective NLP by reducing noise and standardizing the text. These tasks—ranging from removing HTML tags to tokenizing text—facilitate a cleaner, more focused dataset that is primed for analysis. Mastering these cleaning techniques is essential for anyone looking to delve into the complexities of Natural Language Processing, as they directly impact the performance and accuracy of downstream NLP tasks. As we continue to explore the vast domain of NLP, the role of diligent text cleaning remains paramount, ensuring that the foundation upon which we build our analyses is solid and reliable.

Normalization: Standardizing Text Data

Purpose of Normalization:

Normalization involves converting text into a more uniform format to reduce data redundancy and improve the consistency of input for NLP tasks. This step is vital for ensuring that variations in the text do not affect the analysis or the outcomes of NLP models.

Normalization in the context of NLP involves a series of processes aimed at converting varying forms of text data into a uniform format. This standardization is essential for several reasons:

Consistency Across Text Data: Natural language is inherently diverse and fluid, with numerous ways to express the same idea. Variations in spelling, capitalization, and usage of synonyms can introduce discrepancies in text data. Normalization minimizes these variations, ensuring that similar ideas are represented in a consistent manner, thereby reducing the complexity for NLP models to understand and process the text.

Improving Computational Efficiency: By standardizing the text data, normalization reduces the variability within the data, which in turn decreases the computational complexity involved in processing the text. This efficiency is crucial for large-scale NLP projects where the volume of text data can be substantial.

Enhancing Model Performance: Machine learning models, including those used in NLP, often perform better with standardized input data. Normalization helps in reducing the dimensionality of the feature space (the number of unique tokens) by consolidating different variants of a word into a single representative form. This reduction in feature space can lead to improvements in model accuracy and performance.

Facilitating Better Comparison and Analysis: For tasks that involve comparing text documents or analyzing text patterns, normalization ensures that the comparisons are not skewed by superficial differences in text representation. This is particularly important in tasks like sentiment analysis, topic modeling, and document clustering, where the inherent meaning and context of the text are more significant than its form.

Key Processes in Normalization

Normalization encompasses several key processes, each aimed at standardizing different aspects of the text:

- **Case Conversion:** Converting all characters in the text to a uniform case (usually lowercase) to avoid distinguishing between words simply based on case.

- **Removing Accents and Diacritics:** Standardizing characters by removing accents and diacritics, especially in languages where these can significantly alter the appearance of words without affecting their meaning.

- **Lemmatization and Stemming:** Reducing words to their base or root form. Lemmatization involves using vocabulary and morphological analysis, while stemming is a cruder approach that chops off word endings based on common rules.

- **Standardizing Spelling and Abbreviations:**
  Correcting misspellings and standardizing abbreviations
  and contractions (e.g., transforming "isn't" to "is not")
  to ensure that they are represented uniformly across the
  text.

- **Handling Synonyms and Near-Synonyms:** In some
  advanced applications, normalizing synonyms or near-
  synonyms to a common representative term can further
  reduce complexity and enhance the model's ability to
  learn from the data.

Normalization is a fundamental aspect of text
preprocessing in NLP, serving the critical purpose of
standardizing text data to improve consistency,
computational efficiency, and model performance. By
addressing the inherent variability and complexity of
natural language, normalization lays the groundwork for
more accurate and effective analysis, comparison, and
processing of text data. As NLP technologies advance, the
methods and approaches to normalization continue to
evolve, further refining the ability to standardize and
understand the vast and varied landscape of human
language.

Encoding: Transforming Text into Machine-Readable
Format

Significance of Encoding:

Encoding is the process of converting text into a
format that can be easily processed by machine learning
algorithms. This step is fundamental for translating the
natural language into numerical or symbolic representations
that capture linguistic properties.

Encoding is a transformative step that converts text into a format that machines can interpret and analyze. Encoding not only facilitates the bridge between human language and machine processing but also plays a pivotal role in the performance of NLP models.

Encoding: The Purpose

The primary purpose of encoding is to translate the textual data into a numerical or symbolic form that computer algorithms can work with. Since machines do not understand text in the way humans do, encoding helps in representing the text in a way that encapsulates its semantic and syntactic essence, allowing for effective machine learning and analysis.

Encoding Strategies

Several encoding strategies have been developed to address different aspects of text representation, each with its advantages and specific use cases:

One-hot Encoding: This is the simplest form of text encoding where each word in the vocabulary is represented by a vector. In this vector, only one element is "hot" (set to 1) while all other elements are "cold" (set to 0), corresponding to the presence of a specific word. While straightforward, one-hot encoding suffers from high dimensionality and sparsity, especially in large vocabularies, and does not capture word relationships.

Bag of Words (BoW): The BoW model extends one-hot encoding by considering the frequency of words within a document. It represents text data as a bag of its words, disregarding syntax and word order but keeping multiplicity. BoW is effective for document classification but still fails to capture the semantic relationships between words.

Term Frequency-Inverse Document Frequency (TF-IDF): This strategy enhances the BoW model by adjusting the word frequencies based on how common they are across all documents. Words that are frequent in a document but rare in other documents are given more weight, helping to highlight unique terms that might be more relevant for analysis. TF-IDF is useful for search and information retrieval systems.

Word Embeddings: Word embeddings such as Word2Vec, GloVe, and FastText offer a dense representation of words in a continuous vector space where semantically similar words are mapped to proximate points. These models capture deeper linguistic patterns and word associations based on the context of their use, enabling a nuanced understanding of language beyond mere word presence or frequency.

Contextual Embeddings: With the advent of models like BERT (Bidirectional Encoder Representations from Transformers), encoding has taken a leap forward by generating context-sensitive embeddings. Unlike static word embeddings, contextual embeddings reflect the meaning of a word in relation to its surrounding words, allowing for a dynamic representation of language that accounts for polysemy and nuanced usage.

Encoding is a foundational step in text preprocessing, pivotal for transforming textual data into a machine-readable format that retains the richness and subtleties of human language. Through various encoding strategies, from basic one-hot encoding to advanced contextual embeddings, NLP practitioners can choose the appropriate method to suit their specific task requirements. The evolution of encoding techniques continues to enhance the ability of machines to understand and process natural language, marking a critical advancement in the field of NLP. As these strategies evolve, they promise to unlock even deeper insights into the complexities of human communication, paving the way for more sophisticated and intuitive NLP applications.

Implications for Tokenization and NLP Tasks

The segment on text preprocessing techniques—cleaning, normalization, and encoding—sets the stage for a crucial subsequent process: tokenization. Tokenization, the act of breaking down text into its constituent elements (tokens), is foundational for almost all NLP tasks.

Implications for Tokenization

The efficacy of tokenization - and the subsequent success of NLP models - relies heavily on how well the text has been cleaned, normalized, and encoded. Each of these preprocessing steps shapes the input for tokenization, influencing the quality and nature of the tokens generated.

Cleaning: By removing irrelevant characters, symbols, and formatting, cleaning ensures that tokenization focuses only on meaningful elements of the text. For instance, stripping HTML tags and handling special characters like punctuation can prevent the generation of spurious tokens that could dilute the semantic signal in the data.

Normalization: This step directly impacts tokenization by creating a uniform representation of text. Case conversion, for instance, ensures that 'Apple', 'apple', and 'APPLE' are recognized as the same token, rather than being treated as distinct. Lemmatization and stemming reduce words to their base or root form, significantly reducing the variety of tokens and aiding in the consolidation of semantic meaning across different morphological variants of a word.

Encoding: While not directly influencing the tokenization process, the choice of encoding method has downstream implications for how tokenized data is represented and used in NLP models. Encoding strategies determine the vector space in which tokens are represented, affecting the model's ability to discern and utilize the relationships between tokens.

Impact on NLP Tasks

The combined effect of text preprocessing and tokenization is profound across a wide range of NLP tasks:

Text Classification: For tasks like sentiment analysis or spam detection, clean and well-normalized tokens improve model accuracy by focusing on the essential elements of the text. Encoding methods like TF-IDF can highlight significant tokens, making models more sensitive to the features that differentiate classes.

Machine Translation: Tokenization is critical in identifying the units of translation. Effective preprocessing ensures that tokens accurately represent words or phrases, which is essential for translation models to capture and translate the semantic essence of the source text accurately.

Named Entity Recognition (NER): Cleaning and normalization help in standardizing the text, making it easier for models to identify and classify named entities correctly. Proper tokenization ensures that entities are not incorrectly split or merged, crucial for maintaining entity integrity across the text.

Sentiment Analysis: The sentiment often hinges on specific keywords or phrases. Normalization ensures that these sentiment indicators are consistently represented, enhancing the model's ability to gauge the text's sentiment accurately.

Question Answering and Chatbots: For systems designed to understand and respond to human queries, preprocessing ensures that the input text is in a suitable format for tokenization and subsequent analysis. Clean, normalized tokens enable more effective parsing of user queries, leading to more accurate and relevant responses.

Text preprocessing techniques - cleaning, normalization, and encoding - play a pivotal role in preparing text for tokenization, which in turn significantly impacts the performance of NLP tasks. These initial steps ensure that the text is in the most suitable form for generating meaningful tokens, which are the building blocks for all further NLP analysis and model training. By directly influencing the quality and consistency of the data fed into NLP models, these preprocessing steps are indispensable for achieving high accuracy and efficiency in a wide array of NLP applications. As the field of NLP evolves, the importance of rigorous text preprocessing remains constant, underlining its critical role in the success of NLP endeavors.

Conclusion

Through the detailed examination of text preprocessing techniques, "Natural Language Processing (NLP): The Complete Guide" equips readers with a thorough understanding of the essential groundwork required for any NLP project. By emphasizing the importance of cleaning, normalization, and encoding, the guide underscores the meticulous attention to detail necessary for transforming raw text into a valuable resource for analysis and insight generation in the field of natural language processing.

Tokenization Methods for Breaking Text:

The exploration of tokenization methods forms a cornerstone of understanding how to effectively break down text into analyzable components. Tokenization, the process of segmenting text into its constituent elements - words, sentences, or phrases - is a critical initial step in the NLP pipeline.

Tokenization Methods

Tokenization methods can be broadly categorized based on the unit of text they target: words, sentences, or phrases. The choice of method depends on the specific requirements of the NLP task at hand.

I. Word Tokenization

Word tokenization involves breaking down text into individual words or tokens. This method is fundamental for tasks that require analysis at the word level, such as part-of-speech tagging or word frequency analysis.

Whitespace Tokenization:

The simplest form, where text is split based on spaces. While straightforward, it may not accurately handle punctuation or complex cases like contractions (e.g., "don't" being split into "don" and "'t").

Among the various methods for word tokenization, whitespace tokenization stands out for its simplicity and straightforward application.

An Overview

Whitespace tokenization is a method where text is segmented into words by splitting it at whitespace characters, such as spaces, tabs, and newline characters. This approach is based on the assumption that in written language, words are generally separated by whitespace, making it a natural delimiter for word tokenization.

Methodology

The process of whitespace tokenization can be described in the following steps:

Input Text: The raw text data is taken as input for tokenization.

Identify Whitespace: The algorithm scans the text for whitespace characters. These characters serve as the points at which the text will be split.

Split Text: Once a whitespace character is identified, the text is split at that point, segmenting the text into individual words.

Output Tokens: The split segments, or tokens, are then outputted as the result of the tokenization process.

This method can be implemented with relative ease in most programming languages, often requiring only a few lines of code to achieve effective tokenization.

Advantages

Simplicity: Whitespace tokenization is straightforward to understand and implement, making it accessible for beginners and efficient for quick analysis tasks.

Speed: Due to its simplicity, it is fast and can process large volumes of text quickly, which is beneficial for time-sensitive applications.

Utility in Clean Data: In well-structured and cleanly formatted texts where words are consistently separated by spaces, whitespace tokenization can be surprisingly effective.

Limitations

However, whitespace tokenization is not without its limitations, which include:

Punctuation Handling: It does not account for punctuation. Words followed by punctuation (e.g., "Hello,") are treated as distinct from the same words without punctuation (e.g., "Hello"). This can lead to inaccuracies in word counts and other analyses.

Complex Text Structures: It struggles with texts that use non-standard spacing or have complex structures (e.g., URLs, email addresses, or compound words connected by hyphens) which are not effectively segmented by whitespace alone.

Language Variations: Not all languages use whitespace in the same way as English. For example, languages like Chinese or Japanese do not typically separate words with spaces, making whitespace tokenization ineffective.

Whitespace tokenization serves as an entry point into the broader domain of word tokenization, offering a simple yet effective method for segmenting text into words under specific conditions. While its advantages make it a useful tool for initial explorations of text data or applications where text is well-formatted, its limitations necessitate the consideration of more sophisticated tokenization methods for handling complex texts or languages without whitespace word delimiters. Understanding the capabilities and constraints of whitespace tokenization is crucial for NLP practitioners as they navigate the intricate process of preparing text for deeper analysis and model training. As such, it represents a foundational concept in the comprehensive study of text processing and tokenization in natural language processing.

Punctuation-Based Tokenization:

Enhances whitespace tokenization by considering punctuation. This method splits text at punctuation marks, treating them as separate tokens, which can be more accurate for certain languages and datasets.

The exploration of tokenization methods is critical for understanding how text is prepared for various NLP tasks. Among these methods, punctuation-based tokenization is a sophisticated technique that builds upon the simplicity of whitespace tokenization by incorporating the handling of punctuation marks.

Punctuation-Based Tokenization: An Overview

Punctuation-based tokenization extends beyond the basic premise of using whitespace to segment text into tokens. It recognizes that punctuation marks—such as commas, periods, semicolons, and question marks—play a significant role in the structure and meaning of sentences. This method aims to separate words from punctuation marks, treating them as individual tokens, thereby enabling a more nuanced analysis of text.

Methodology

The process of punctuation-based tokenization involves several key steps:

1. **Input Text:** As with other tokenization methods, the process begins with raw text data.

2. **Scan for Punctuation:** The algorithm scans the text for both whitespace and punctuation marks. Each is identified as a potential delimiter for tokenization.

3. **Split Text:** The text is split into tokens at each delimiter point. Unlike whitespace tokenization, this method creates separate tokens for punctuation marks, ensuring they are not attached to the adjacent words.

4. **Output Tokens:** The resulting tokens, including both words and punctuation marks as separate entities, are outputted for further processing.

This method requires a more complex algorithm than whitespace tokenization, as it must accurately identify a wide range of punctuation marks and understand their role as delimiters.

Advantages

Improved Text Structure Representation: By treating punctuation as separate tokens, this method preserves more of the original text's structure, facilitating tasks that rely on sentence composition and syntax.

Enhanced Accuracy for Certain Tasks: For NLP tasks like sentiment analysis or syntactic parsing, accurately identifying punctuation can improve model performance, as punctuation often carries significant syntactic and emotional weight.

Flexibility: Punctuation-based tokenization can be adapted or combined with other tokenization methods (e.g., rule-based tokenization) for even more nuanced text processing.

Limitations

Despite its advantages, punctuation-based tokenization faces challenges:

Complex Implementation: Accurately identifying and handling a wide range of punctuation marks increases the complexity of the tokenization algorithm.

Contextual Sensitivity: Punctuation marks can have different functions in different contexts (e.g., a period can signify an abbreviation, a decimal point, or the end of a sentence). Distinguishing these uses can be challenging.

Language Variability: The use and significance of punctuation vary across languages, which can complicate the application of a single punctuation-based tokenization approach to multilingual text processing.

Punctuation-based tokenization represents a significant advancement in the segmentation of text into analyzable components, addressing some of the limitations inherent in simpler tokenization methods. By separating punctuation from words, it allows for a deeper understanding of text structure and meaning, enhancing the capabilities of NLP systems across a range of tasks. However, its implementation complexity and sensitivity to context highlight the need for careful design and possibly the integration of additional linguistic knowledge or machine learning models. As such, punctuation-based tokenization is a powerful tool in the NLP toolkit, offering refined insights into the intricate dance of words and punctuation that constitute human language.

Rule-Based Tokenization:

Utilizes a set of predefined rules to handle complex tokenization scenarios, such as splitting contractions into their constituent words and correctly handling punctuation. It's more sophisticated but requires extensive language-specific rules.

Among the myriad approaches to word tokenization, rule-based tokenization emerges as a sophisticated method, designed to address the limitations of simpler tokenization techniques such as whitespace or punctuation-based methods.

An Overview

Rule-based tokenization is a method that applies a series of predefined linguistic rules to segment text into words. These rules are crafted based on the syntactic and morphological characteristics of the language being processed, making this method highly adaptable to the complexities and nuances of natural language.

Methodology

The process of rule-based tokenization typically involves the following steps:

1. **Analysis of Text:** The raw text is analyzed to identify linguistic patterns and elements that require specialized

handling, such as contractions (e.g., "don't" into "do" and "not"), compound words, and punctuation.

2. **Application of Rules:** A set of predefined rules is applied to the text. These rules might include guidelines for handling punctuation (e.g., separating punctuation from adjoining words), dealing with contractions, and recognizing word boundaries in complex cases.

3. **Segmentation:** Based on these rules, the text is segmented into individual words or tokens. This process is careful to distinguish between punctuation that signifies word boundaries and punctuation that is part of a word (e.g., periods within abbreviations).

4. **Output Tokens:** The final output is a series of tokens that accurately reflect the intended segmentation of the text into words, taking into account the identified linguistic features.

Advantages

Precision: By leveraging linguistic knowledge, rule-based tokenization can achieve a high level of precision, accurately handling cases that simpler methods might misinterpret.

Language Adaptability: The rules can be tailored to the specific characteristics of any language, making this method versatile across linguistic contexts.

Handling Complexity: This method excels in processing texts with complex linguistic features, such as contractions, abbreviations, and special punctuation usage, ensuring that the tokenization reflects the intended meaning of the text.

Challenges and Considerations

Rule Complexity: Developing a comprehensive set of rules that can handle all linguistic scenarios is challenging and time-consuming. The rules must be constantly refined and expanded to address new cases and variations in language use.

Language-Specific Rules: Each language has its unique characteristics, necessitating the development of language-specific rule sets. This can increase the effort required to adapt rule-based tokenization for multilingual applications.

Maintenance: As language evolves, the rules need to be updated to accommodate new linguistic trends and usage patterns, requiring ongoing maintenance and linguistic expertise.

Application in NLP Tasks

Rule-based tokenization is particularly valuable in NLP tasks that demand high accuracy in tokenization, such as syntactic parsing, where the precise identification of words and their boundaries is crucial for analyzing sentence structure. It's also beneficial in applications involving languages with complex syntactic rules or in processing texts with a high degree of linguistic variation.

Rule-based tokenization represents a powerful approach to word tokenization in NLP, offering precision and adaptability to linguistic complexities. While it requires significant effort in rule development and maintenance, its ability to accurately segment text makes it an invaluable tool in the NLP practitioner's arsenal. As NLP continues to advance, rule-based tokenization stands as a testament to the importance of linguistic knowledge in the processing and understanding of natural language, underscoring its critical role in the broader context of text processing and tokenization .

Regular Expression (Regex) Tokenization:

Employs regular expressions to define patterns for splitting text, offering flexibility to handle varied tokenization needs. It can be customized to the intricacies of the text being processed.

This technique employs regular expressions, a powerful tool for pattern matching, to segment text into words, offering a flexible approach to handle the diverse challenges of tokenizing natural language text.

An Overview

Regular Expression Tokenization leverages the pattern-matching capabilities of regex to define complex criteria for tokenizing text. Regular expressions can match sequences of characters based on specified rules, making them highly effective for dissecting text into tokens.

Methodology

The process of regex tokenization generally involves:

1. **Defining Patterns:** The first step is to define regex patterns that capture the linguistic elements of interest, such as words, punctuation, or specific text structures. These patterns dictate how the text will be segmented.

2. **Applying Patterns:** The defined patterns are then applied to the text, where they identify matches based on the regex criteria. This step can involve either splitting the text at pattern matches or extracting matches as tokens.

3. **Segmentation:** Through pattern matching, the text is segmented into tokens. This can include not only words but also punctuation and other textual elements, depending on the regex rules applied.

4. **Output Tokens:** The output is a list of tokens derived from the original text, segmented according to the defined regex patterns.

Advantages

Customizability: Regex tokenization offers unparalleled flexibility, allowing for the customization of tokenization rules to fit the specific needs of a task or the peculiarities of a dataset.

Complex Pattern Identification: It excels at identifying complex patterns and structures within text, making it suitable for languages and texts with intricate syntactic or formatting rules.

Efficiency: Regex can process large volumes of text quickly, especially when the patterns are well-defined and optimized.

Challenges and Considerations

Complexity: Crafting effective regex patterns requires a deep understanding of both regex syntax and the linguistic structure of the text, which can be complex and time-consuming.

Overfitting to Patterns: There's a risk of overfitting the tokenization to specific patterns, which may not generalize well across different texts or languages.

Performance Issues: Inefficient or overly complex regex patterns can lead to performance bottlenecks, especially with very large texts.

Application in NLP Tasks

Regex tokenization is particularly useful in scenarios where text follows a predictable structure or contains complex patterns not easily handled by simpler tokenization methods. It's widely used in preprocessing steps for tasks such as:

- **Text Cleaning:** Extracting or removing specific elements from text, such as URLs, email addresses, or code snippets.

- **Data Extraction:** Identifying and extracting structured data from unstructured text, such as dates, phone numbers, or specific identifiers.

- **Custom Text Segmentation:** Segmenting text based on specific linguistic or formatting criteria that standard tokenizers might miss.

Regular Expression Tokenization represents a potent and versatile approach to word tokenization in the domain of NLP, characterized by its customizability and precision in handling complex text patterns. While it requires a nuanced understanding of regex and careful pattern definition, its capacity to tailor tokenization to the intricate requirements of diverse texts makes it an invaluable asset in the NLP toolkit.

II. Sentence Tokenization

Sentence tokenization segments text into individual sentences, essential for tasks that operate on the sentence level, such as sentiment analysis or machine translation.

Simple Rule-Based Methods:

These rely on punctuation marks (e.g., periods, question marks) to identify sentence boundaries. However, they may struggle with abbreviations or other exceptions.

Sentence tokenization, the process of breaking down text into individual sentences, is a fundamental task in NLP that enables the analysis and understanding of text at a higher structural level.

Sentence Tokenization: Simple Rule-Based Methods

Simple rule-based methods for sentence tokenization rely on predefined rules to identify sentence boundaries. These rules often hinge on punctuation marks commonly used to denote the end of a sentence, such as periods (.), exclamation points (!), and question marks (?).

Methodology

The methodology behind simple rule-based sentence tokenization typically involves the following steps:

1. **Scan Text for Punctuation Marks:** The text is scanned for specific punctuation marks that are known to signify the end of a sentence. This is based on the linguistic convention that sentences are punctuated by periods, exclamation points, or question marks.

2. **Apply Sentence Boundary Rules:** Once potential sentence-ending punctuation is identified, additional rules are applied to determine whether these punctuation marks actually denote sentence boundaries. This can involve checking for whitespace after punctuation, capitalization of the subsequent word, or the presence of typical sentence starters.

3. **Segment Text into Sentences:** Based on these rules, the text is segmented at identified sentence boundaries, breaking the text into individual sentences.

4. **Output Sentence Tokens:** The segmented sentences are then outputted as individual tokens, each representing a single sentence from the original text.

Advantages

Simplicity and Speed: Simple rule-based methods are straightforward to implement and can quickly process large volumes of text, making them efficient for initial explorations or applications where speed is a priority.

Transparency: The rules used for sentence tokenization are explicit and easy to understand, allowing for clear insight into how sentences are being segmented.

Challenges and Considerations

Ambiguity of Punctuation: Punctuation marks like periods can serve multiple roles (e.g., sentence endings, decimal points, abbreviations), leading to potential misinterpretation of sentence boundaries.

Complex Text Structures: Texts with complex structures or unconventional punctuation usage can pose significant challenges for simple rule-based methods, leading to inaccurate sentence segmentation.

Language Variability: Different languages may have unique punctuation rules or use punctuation marks differently, requiring adjustments or entirely different sets of rules for effective sentence tokenization.

Application in NLP Tasks

Despite their limitations, simple rule-based methods for sentence tokenization are widely used in a variety of NLP tasks, including:

- **Text Summarization:** Breaking text into sentences to identify key sentences for inclusion in summaries.

- **Sentiment Analysis:** Analyzing sentiment at the sentence level to understand the nuances of sentiment in different parts of the text.

- **Machine Translation:** Segmenting text into sentences as a preprocessing step before translation, since translations often proceed on a sentence-by-sentence basis.

Simple rule-based methods for sentence tokenization offer a straightforward approach to breaking text into sentences, providing an essential tool for many NLP applications. While they may not capture the full complexity of natural language sentence boundaries, their speed and simplicity make them invaluable for tasks where efficiency is key or as a first pass in a multi-stage tokenization process.

Machine Learning-Based Methods:

Utilize trained models to more accurately predict sentence boundaries, considering contextual clues beyond mere punctuation. This approach is more robust, especially for complex texts with nuanced uses of punctuation.

Sentence tokenization is a pivotal process that segments text into its constituent sentences. This step is crucial for tasks that require an understanding of the text at the sentence level, such as sentiment analysis, machine translation, and summarization. Beyond the simple rule-based methods for sentence tokenization, machine learning-based methods offer sophisticated approaches that can handle the nuances and complexities of natural language more effectively.

Machine Learning-Based Methods for Sentence Tokenization

Machine learning-based methods employ statistical models that are trained on large corpora of text to learn the patterns and indicators of sentence boundaries. Unlike rule-based approaches that rely on predefined rules to identify punctuation marks as sentence delimiters, machine learning methods can consider a broader context, including the syntactic and semantic cues that signify sentence breaks.

Mechanisms

Training on Annotated Corpora: These methods involve training models on text corpora that have been annotated with sentence boundaries. The models learn to predict the likelihood of a sentence break at each point in the text.

Feature Extraction: During training, the models analyze various features of the text, such as punctuation, capitalization, word tokens, and the context around potential sentence-ending points. Advanced methods may also consider linguistic features such as part-of-speech tags or dependency structures.

Model Types: Various types of models can be used, including decision trees, support vector machines (SVM), and more recently, deep learning models such as recurrent neural networks (RNNs) and transformers. Deep learning models, in particular, excel at capturing the complex, contextual relationships between text elements.

Advantages

- **Contextual Understanding:** Machine learning methods can understand the context around potential sentence boundaries, reducing errors caused by punctuation used in non-terminal ways (e.g., abbreviations, dates).

- **Adaptability:** These methods can adapt to different writing styles and genres by learning from diverse training data, improving their accuracy across a wide range of texts.

- **Handling Complex Cases:** They are capable of handling cases where rule-based methods might struggle, such as dialogues in quotes or sentences with embedded clauses.

Impact on NLP Tasks

Machine learning-based sentence tokenization methods significantly enhance the performance of NLP tasks that depend on accurate sentence-level analysis. For instance:

Sentiment Analysis: Accurate sentence boundaries ensure that sentiment is correctly attributed to the relevant sentences, improving the accuracy of sentiment models.

Machine Translation: Proper sentence segmentation allows for better context understanding and translations that capture the intended meanings more faithfully.

Summarization: Identifying sentences accurately is crucial for extracting relevant information and generating coherent summaries.

Challenges

- **Resource Intensiveness:** Training machine learning models requires substantial computational resources and large annotated datasets.

- **Generalization:** While these models excel in contexts similar to their training data, their performance can degrade on texts with significantly different styles or structures.

Conclusion

Machine learning-based methods for sentence tokenization represent a significant advancement in the field of NLP, offering nuanced and adaptable approaches to understanding and segmenting text. By leveraging the power of statistical learning and deep learning, these methods provide a robust solution to the complexities of sentence tokenization, enhancing the foundation upon which sophisticated NLP applications are built. As NLP continues to evolve, the role of machine learning in accurately parsing and interpreting natural language will undoubtedly remain at the forefront, underscoring its critical importance in "Natural Language Processing (NLP): The Complete Guide."

III. Phrase Tokenization

Phrase tokenization, or chunking, involves breaking text into meaningful phrases or expressions. It's valuable for extracting specific information or understanding the structure of sentences.

Grammar-Based Chunking:

Uses predefined grammatical rules to identify phrases within sentences. This method requires a deep understanding of language syntax and grammar.

Phrase tokenization - or chunking - emerges as a nuanced and sophisticated approach to dissecting text beyond the level of words and sentences. Among the various strategies for phrase tokenization, grammar-based chunking holds a pivotal position. This method utilizes predefined grammatical rules to identify and extract meaningful phrases from text, offering a deeper insight into its structure and meaning.

An Overview

Grammar-based chunking, also known as syntactic chunking, involves breaking down text into syntactically correlated units like noun phrases, verb phrases, and prepositional phrases. Unlike simpler tokenization methods, chunking aims to preserve the semantic relationship within the text, offering a more structured representation that facilitates comprehensive linguistic analysis.

Methodology

The process of grammar-based chunking typically involves the following steps:

Defining Grammatical Rules: The first step in grammar-based chunking is to define a set of grammatical rules that determine how sentences should be segmented into phrases. These rules are often expressed in terms of regular expressions or patterns that match specific sequences of part-of-speech tags.

Part-of-Speech Tagging: Before chunking, the text is processed through a part-of-speech (POS) tagger that assigns tags to each word based on its role in the sentence (e.g., noun, verb, adjective).

Applying Rules to POS-Tagged Text: The predefined grammatical rules are then applied to the POS-tagged text. The rules identify patterns within the tagged text that correspond to the desired phrases.

Extracting Phrases: Based on these rules, phrases are identified and extracted from the text as distinct units, each representing a chunked syntactic component.

Advantages

- **Structural Insight:** Grammar-based chunking provides valuable insights into the syntactic structure of text, facilitating tasks that require an understanding of linguistic relationships.

- **Enhanced Text Analysis:** By identifying phrases, this method enables more nuanced analysis of text, such as identifying subjects and objects, which is crucial for semantic processing and information extraction.

- **Customizability:** The rules for chunking can be customized to target specific types of phrases, making this method highly adaptable to various linguistic analysis needs.

Applications in NLP

Grammar-based chunking is instrumental in a range of NLP tasks that benefit from an understanding of text structure, including:

Information Extraction: Chunking can be used to identify entities and their attributes within sentences, facilitating the extraction of structured information from unstructured text.

Relation Extraction: By identifying noun phrases and verb phrases, chunking helps in extracting relationships between entities, essential for building knowledge graphs and databases.

Sentiment Analysis: Understanding the structure of phrases can improve the accuracy of sentiment analysis by better capturing the sentiment associated with specific entities or aspects within the text.

Machine Translation: A deeper understanding of the phrase structure within sentences can enhance translation algorithms by preserving syntactic accuracy and meaning in the translated text.

Challenges

- **Complexity of Rule Definition:** Crafting effective grammatical rules for chunking requires deep linguistic expertise and can be time-consuming.

- **Language Dependency:** The effectiveness of grammar-based chunking is highly dependent on the language, as different languages have different syntactic structures and complexities.

• **Processing Overhead:** The need for POS tagging before chunking adds an additional processing step, which can increase the computational overhead for large datasets.

Grammar-based chunking represents a sophisticated approach to phrase tokenization in NLP, offering deep structural insights into text. By leveraging grammatical rules to dissect sentences into meaningful phrases, it enables a more nuanced understanding and processing of natural language. While the method presents challenges in terms of rule complexity and processing demands, its contributions to advancing NLP tasks like information extraction, relation extraction, and sentiment analysis are invaluable. As outlined, the adoption and refinement of grammar-based chunking techniques continue to propel the field of NLP forward, enhancing our ability to analyze, interpret, and leverage the wealth of information contained in natural language text.

Statistical Methods:

Machine learning models trained on annotated corpora can identify phrases based on patterns in the data. This approach can adapt to the nuances of language use in specific contexts.

The discussion on text processing and tokenization extends into the domain of phrase tokenization, a critical step for understanding and extracting meaningful information from text. Among the techniques employed for phrase tokenization, statistical methods stand out for their ability to leverage large datasets and machine learning models to identify phrases effectively.

An Overview

Statistical methods for phrase tokenization use probabilistic models and machine learning algorithms to identify and segment phrases within text. These methods analyze patterns in large corpora to learn the likelihood of certain word combinations forming meaningful phrases, beyond the simple adjacency of terms. This approach contrasts with grammar-based chunking by relying less on predefined rules and more on statistical evidence derived from text data.

Principles

Training on Large Corpora: Statistical models are trained on extensive collections of text data, from which they learn the frequency and distribution of word combinations. This training enables the models to predict the likelihood of a sequence of words constituting a phrase.

Probability and Co-occurrence: The core of these methods lies in calculating the probability of word co-occurrence within a given window of text. High co-occurrence rates suggest that the words likely form a phrase.

Machine Learning Algorithms: Various algorithms, including association rule mining, clustering, and neural networks, are employed to identify patterns and relationships between words. Techniques like pointwise mutual information (PMI) or latent semantic analysis (LSA) can also be applied to quantify the strength of association between words.

Advantages

- **Data-Driven Insights:** Statistical methods derive insights directly from data, making them adaptable to different languages, domains, and contexts without the need for extensive rule definition.

- **Scalability:** These methods can handle large volumes of text efficiently, benefiting from the scalability of machine learning models and computational resources.

- **Flexibility:** They can easily be integrated with other NLP processes, such as named entity recognition (NER) or part-of-speech (POS) tagging, to enhance phrase identification based on context.

Applications in NLP

Statistical methods for phrase tokenization find application in a variety of NLP tasks, including:

Information Extraction: By identifying phrases that represent entities or concepts, these methods enhance the extraction of structured information from unstructured text.

Topic Modeling: Identifying common phrases across documents can reveal latent topics and themes, improving the quality of topic models.

Text Summarization: Understanding the key phrases within text aids in generating concise summaries that capture the core information and context.

Search and Retrieval: Phrase tokenization improves search algorithms by enabling them to match on meaningful phrases rather than individual words, enhancing search relevance and accuracy.

Challenges

- **Complexity of Language:** Statistical methods may struggle with linguistic nuances, such as idiomatic expressions or phrases with variable word order, due to their reliance on statistical patterns.

- **Dependency on Training Data:** The effectiveness of these methods is closely tied to the quality and representativeness of the training data. Biases in the data can lead to biases in phrase identification.

- **Computational Demands:** Training and applying statistical models, especially deep learning algorithms, require significant computational resources, which can be a limiting factor for some applications.

Conclusion

Statistical methods for phrase tokenization represent a powerful and adaptable approach in the field of NLP, leveraging the vast amounts of text data available to uncover the statistical patterns that signify meaningful phrases. While they offer significant advantages in terms of scalability and flexibility, the challenges they present underscore the importance of careful data selection and model training.

Choosing the Right Tokenization Method

Selecting the appropriate tokenization method depends on several factors, including the nature of the text (formal vs. informal), the language (and its peculiarities), and the specific requirements of the NLP task. While simpler methods may suffice for straightforward tasks, complex analyses may benefit from more sophisticated approaches that consider the subtleties of language.

Understanding the Nature of Your Text

The first step in choosing the right tokenization method is to thoroughly understand the characteristics of the text at hand:

Language: The linguistic rules and syntax of the text's language significantly influence the choice of tokenization method. For instance, languages without clear word boundaries, like Chinese or Japanese, may require specialized word tokenization approaches.

Domain-Specific Language: Texts from specific domains (e.g., medical, legal, or technical fields) might contain jargon, abbreviations, or complex sentence structures that necessitate advanced tokenization methods to accurately capture the domain-specific meanings.

Informality and Text Type: Informal texts, such as social media posts or chat logs, often contain slang, emojis, and unconventional punctuation, requiring more nuanced tokenization strategies to handle the variability and context.

Matching the Tokenization Method to the NLP Task

Different NLP tasks may benefit from different levels and methods of tokenization:

Word Tokenization: Essential for tasks like part-of-speech tagging, word-level sentiment analysis, or term frequency analyses. The choice between whitespace, punctuation-based, rule-based, or regular expression (Regex) tokenization depends on the complexity of the text and the need for accuracy versus computational efficiency.

Sentence Tokenization: Crucial for sentence-level processing tasks such as machine translation or sentence-level sentiment analysis. Simple rule-based methods might suffice for well-structured texts, whereas machine learning-based methods offer advantages for texts with complex sentence structures or mixed-use of punctuation.

Phrase Tokenization: Important for extracting meaningful phrases for tasks like information extraction, topic modeling, or enhancing search and retrieval systems. Grammar-based chunking might be preferred for texts requiring deep syntactic analysis, while statistical methods can offer flexibility and adaptability across large datasets and varied text types.

Considerations for Implementation

- **Resource Availability:** The computational resources and available corpora for training can influence the choice of tokenization method, especially when considering machine learning-based approaches versus simpler rule-based methods.

- **Accuracy vs. Efficiency:** The trade-off between the need for high accuracy in tokenization and the computational efficiency of processing large volumes of text must be carefully weighed. In some cases, a simpler method might be preferred for its speed and lower resource consumption, even if it sacrifices some degree of accuracy.

- **Integration with Other NLP Processes:** The selected tokenization method should integrate seamlessly with subsequent steps in the NLP pipeline, such as parsing, named entity recognition, or machine learning modeling. Ensuring compatibility and smooth data flow between processes is essential for the overall success of the project.

Choosing the right tokenization method in NLP is a multifaceted decision that hinges on a deep understanding of the text, the specific requirements of the NLP task, and practical considerations around resources and integration.

Conclusion

stage for successful analysis and modeling. By carefully selecting and applying the appropriate tokenization method, practitioners can ensure that the text is accurately and effectively segmented into analyzable units. Whether the task requires understanding individual words, analyzing sentence structures, or identifying phrases, the choice of tokenization method significantly influences the outcome of NLP applications. As the field of NLP continues to evolve, so too will the methods and technologies for effective text tokenization, reflecting the ongoing refinement of our understanding and processing of natural language.

Handling Special Cases:

These special cases include contractions, abbreviations, and punctuation, each presenting unique challenges to the accuracy and efficiency of NLP tasks.

Contractions

Contractions are shortened forms of words or syllables, often created by omitting certain letters and sounds. In English, for example, "don't" is a contraction for "do not," and "I'm" for "I am."

- **Handling Strategy:** A robust NLP system must expand contractions to their full forms or recognize them as valid tokens in their own right. This can be achieved through rule-based methods, where a dictionary of common contractions and their expansions is used to preprocess the text. Alternatively, machine learning models can be trained to understand contractions within the context they are used, though this requires a significant amount of annotated training data.

Abbreviations

Abbreviations and acronyms condense longer phrases into shorter forms, often leading to ambiguity without contextual understanding. For example, "Dr." could stand for "Doctor" or "Drive" depending on the context.

- **Handling Strategy:** Addressing abbreviations effectively often requires a combination of dictionary-based lookup for common abbreviations and context-based disambiguation for those with multiple meanings. In some instances, specialized tokenization methods that account for the presence of periods and capitalization can help distinguish between abbreviations and sentence terminations.

Punctuation

Punctuation marks can serve multiple roles in text, such as indicating sentence boundaries, denoting possessives, or clarifying the structure of complex sentences. However, punctuation can also introduce challenges in tokenization, especially when the same symbol serves different functions.

- **Handling Strategy:** The key to managing punctuation is to incorporate rules or models that understand its usage within different contexts. For sentence tokenization, machine learning-based methods can learn the nuanced roles of punctuation from training data, improving the accuracy of sentence boundary detection. For word tokenization, strategies may include treating punctuation as separate tokens or, in some cases, incorporating punctuation into adjacent tokens based on linguistic rules.

Cross-cutting Strategies for Handling Special Cases

Across all these special cases, a few cross-cutting strategies emerge:

Lexical Databases and Rule-based Systems: Utilizing comprehensive lexical databases and rule-based systems can provide immediate solutions for expanding contractions, resolving abbreviations, and managing punctuation. However, these systems require regular updates to accommodate evolving language use.

Contextual Analysis: Leveraging context is essential for correctly interpreting the function and meaning of words, abbreviations, and punctuation. Machine learning models, especially those based on deep learning architectures like Transformers, are particularly adept at understanding context.

Hybrid Approaches: Often, the most effective strategy involves combining rule-based and machine learning methods. For instance, initial processing could expand known contractions and abbreviations using a rule-based system, followed by a machine learning model to handle ambiguous cases or context-dependent punctuation usage.

Handling special cases such as contractions, abbreviations, and punctuation is pivotal in refining the text processing and tokenization steps of NLP workflows. The strategies chosen to address these challenges directly impact the accuracy and reliability of downstream NLP tasks, from sentiment analysis to machine translation. "Natural Language Processing (NLP): The Complete Guide" emphasizes that a nuanced approach, often combining rule-based methods with advanced machine learning techniques, is essential for navigating the complexities of natural language. By effectively managing these special cases, NLP systems can achieve a deeper and more accurate understanding of text data, unlocking new possibilities in language modeling and processing.

Python Libraries for Text Processing:

In Natural Language Processing (NLP), Python stands out as a leading language due to its simplicity and the powerful ecosystem of libraries it supports. We delve into the core Python libraries that have become indispensable tools for text processing and tokenization: NLTK (Natural Language Toolkit), spaCy, and TextBlob. Each of these libraries offers unique features and capabilities, making them suitable for different NLP tasks and workflows.

NLTK (Natural Language Toolkit)

NLTK is one of the most widely used Python libraries for natural language processing. It provides easy-to-use interfaces to over 50 corpora and lexical resources such as WordNet, along with a suite of text processing libraries for classification, tokenization, stemming, tagging, parsing, and semantic reasoning.

<u>Key Features:</u>

- Extensive collection of corpora and lexical resources

- Support for classical NLP tasks such as tokenization, part-of-speech tagging, and parsing

- Comprehensive documentation and tutorials, making it ideal for educational purposes and research

Strengths:

- Highly versatile and comprehensive in its scope of NLP functionalities

- Well-documented, with a plethora of tutorials and guides available

Use Cases:

- Academic and educational projects

- Initial exploration and prototyping of NLP applications

- Research in computational linguistics and language modeling

spaCy

spaCy is designed for production use and offers fast, efficient, and practical features for real-world NLP tasks. It excels in tasks such as tokenization, part-of-speech tagging, named entity recognition, and dependency parsing.

Key Features:

- Highly optimized and efficient algorithms for text processing

- Pre-trained statistical models for various languages

- Easy integration with deep learning frameworks like TensorFlow and PyTorch

- Extensible and customizable pipeline components

Strengths:

- Focus on performance and practicality for real-world applications

- Offers pre-trained models for several languages, facilitating multilingual NLP tasks

- Streamlined API and workflow for deploying NLP models in production environments

Use Cases:

- Developing production-ready NLP applications

- Large-scale text processing tasks requiring efficiency and speed

- Projects requiring deep learning integration and advanced text analysis

TextBlob

TextBlob is built on top of NLTK and Pattern, aiming to provide a simple API for common NLP tasks. It is particularly user-friendly, making it accessible for beginners and convenient for rapid prototyping.

Key Features:

- Simplified interface for common NLP tasks such as part-of-speech tagging, noun phrase extraction, sentiment analysis, classification, and translation

- Extensibility to use NLTK's extensive resources and functionalities

- Intuitive object-oriented approach, making it easy to work with for beginners

Strengths:

- Ease of use and simplicity, with minimal setup required

- Suitable for educational purposes and introductory NLP projects

- Provides a gentle introduction to NLP concepts without sacrificing functionality

Use Cases:

- Rapid prototyping and development of NLP applications

- Educational projects and tutorials for beginners in NLP

- Small to medium-scale text processing tasks requiring straightforward implementations

Conclusion

Choosing the right Python library for text processing and tokenization depends on several factors, including the specific requirements of the NLP task, the scale of the project, and the level of complexity involved. NLTK offers a comprehensive toolkit ideal for education and research, spaCy delivers high-performance and production-ready features, and TextBlob provides a simple, user-friendly interface for common NLP tasks.

Chapter 3: Text Representation

In text representation and feature extraction, the processes by which textual data is transformed into a format that machine learning algorithms can understand and analyze. This transformation is pivotal for the success of NLP applications, as it directly affects the ability of models to learn from text data.

Text Representation: The Foundation

Text representation refers to the method of converting text data into numerical or symbolic formats that encapsulate the essential information in a way that computational models can process. The choice of representation significantly impacts the performance of NLP tasks such as classification, sentiment analysis, and machine translation.

Key Approaches to Text Representation

Bag of Words (BoW): The BoW model represents text as an unordered collection of words, disregarding grammar and word order but maintaining multiplicity. It's a simple yet effective way to transform text into a vector format, where each dimension corresponds to a unique word in the vocabulary, and the value represents the frequency of the word.

TF-IDF (Term Frequency-Inverse Document Frequency): This model improves upon BoW by considering not just the frequency of a word in a document but also how unique the word is across all documents in the corpus. It helps to highlight words that are important for a particular document, thereby enhancing the model's ability to discern relevant information.

Word Embeddings: Word embeddings provide a dense representation of words in a continuous vector space where semantically similar words are mapped to proximate points. Models like Word2Vec, GloVe, and FastText capture the context and semantic relationships between words, offering a powerful tool for a wide range of NLP applications.

Contextual Embeddings: Advances in NLP introduced contextual embeddings, such as those generated by BERT (Bidirectional Encoder Representations from Transformers) and GPT (Generative Pre-trained Transformer), which produce word representations that consider the context in which a word appears. This approach allows for the dynamic representation of words, capturing nuances and variations in meaning based on surrounding text.

Feature Extraction: Capturing the Essence

Feature extraction involves selecting and transforming the variables (features) in the text data that are most relevant for the task at hand. It's about distilling the vast amount of information contained in text into a concise set of features that can effectively train machine learning models.

Strategies for Feature Extraction

- **Statistical Features:** Include basic metrics like word frequencies, sentence lengths, and part-of-speech distributions. These features can provide foundational insights into the text's structure and content.

- **Syntactic Features:** Parsing and syntactic analysis can extract features related to the grammatical structure of sentences, such as dependency trees, which can be crucial for understanding complex linguistic relationships.

- **Semantic Features:** Advanced techniques aim to capture the meaning of text, utilizing semantic networks, ontologies, or context-based embeddings to represent the underlying concepts and relationships within the text.

Importance in NLP Tasks

The effectiveness of text representation and feature extraction directly influences the performance of subsequent NLP tasks:

- **Classification and Clustering:** The choice of features and their representation determines how well models can differentiate between categories or clusters of text.

- **Sentiment Analysis:** The sentiment conveyed in text often hinges on specific word choices and their semantic relationships, necessitating a nuanced representation of text.

- **Machine Translation and Summarization:** Capturing the syntactic and semantic intricacies of language is essential for generating accurate translations and coherent summaries.

Representing Text Data as Numerical Features:

A fundamental concept that bridges the gap between raw text and actionable insights is the representation of text data as numerical features. This transformation is crucial because, while humans can intuitively understand and process text, computers require numerical data to perform any form of analysis.

Importance of Numerical Representation

The representation of text as numerical features allows algorithms to "understand" and manipulate text by quantifying patterns, relationships, and structures inherent in the language. This numerical transformation facilitates a wide range of tasks in NLP, from simple classification to complex natural language understanding (NLU) and generation (NLG) tasks.

Methodologies for Representing Text as Numerical Features

Several methodologies have been developed to convert text into numerical form, each with its strengths and use cases. These include:

Bag of Words (BoW)

Overview:

BoW is one of the simplest forms of text representation. It involves creating a vocabulary of all the unique words in a corpus and representing each document as a vector indicating the presence or frequency of these words.

The transformation of text data into numerical features is underscored as a fundamental step for enabling computational methods to interpret and analyze language.

Importance of Numerical Representation

The numerical representation of text data is crucial in NLP for several reasons:

- **Enabling Computational Analysis:** Computers process numbers, not text. Transforming text into numerical form allows for the application of mathematical and statistical models to analyze and understand natural language.

- **Quantifying Textual Information:** Numerical representation allows for the quantification of information in text, such as the frequency of words, the significance of specific terms within a document, or the similarity between texts.

- **Facilitating Machine Learning:** Most machine learning algorithms require numerical input to perform tasks such as classification, clustering, and prediction. Numerical representation of text is essential for training these algorithms on language data.

- **Supporting Scalability:** By converting text to numbers, NLP systems can efficiently process and analyze large datasets, making it possible to scale applications to meet real-world demands.

Methodologies for Representing Text as Numerical Features: Bag of Words (BoW)

The Bag of Words (BoW) model is one of the simplest and most widely used methods for text representation in NLP. It involves the following steps:

1. **Tokenization:** The text is broken down into individual elements, typically words or terms.

2. **Vocabulary Building:** A vocabulary is created from all unique words in the corpus.

3. **Vectorization:** Each document is represented as a vector within the vocabulary space. The elements of this vector correspond to the vocabulary's words, with the value in each position representing the presence or frequency of the word in the document.

Key Characteristics of BoW

*   **Simplicity:** BoW is straightforward to understand and implement, making it accessible for beginners in NLP.

*   **Unordered Representation:** The model disregards the order of words, considering only the occurrence or frequency of terms within the text. This simplification can be both a strength and a limitation.

*   **High Dimensionality:** The dimensionality of the vector space can be very large, especially for extensive vocabularies, leading to sparse representations where most values are zero.

*   **Customizability:** The model can be adjusted to include weighting schemes such as Term Frequency-Inverse Document Frequency (TF-IDF) to highlight the importance of terms within documents relative to the entire corpus.

Strengths

*   **Effectiveness for Certain Tasks:** BoW can perform remarkably well for tasks where the presence of specific words is highly indicative of the text's meaning or category, such as spam detection or topic classification.

- **Ease of Implementation:** Its simplicity allows for quick development cycles and serves as a good starting point for text analysis projects.

Limitations

- **Loss of Context:** Ignoring the order of words means the loss of contextual information, which can be crucial for understanding the meaning of sentences.

- **Sparsity and Dimensionality:** The high dimensionality of the BoW vectors, most of which are zeros, can lead to computational inefficiency and necessitates dimensionality reduction techniques for large datasets.

The Bag of Words model plays a foundational role in the numerical representation of text, facilitating a wide range of NLP applications by transforming text into a format amenable to computational analysis. Despite its limitations, especially concerning the loss of contextual information, BoW remains a valuable tool in the NLP toolkit, particularly for tasks where the presence of specific terms is more critical than their order or proximity.

Term Frequency-Inverse Document Frequency (TF-IDF)

Overview:

TF-IDF builds upon BoW by weighting each word's frequency by its inverse document frequency. This approach reduces the influence of common words that appear frequently across documents and highlights words that are unique to specific documents. A detailed exploration of the methodologies for transforming text into numerical features reveals the pivotal role of Term Frequency-Inverse Document Frequency (TF-IDF).

Importance of Numerical Representation

The transformation of text into a numerical format is essential in the field of NLP for several key reasons:

- **Facilitates Machine Learning:** Numerical representation allows text data to be inputted into machine learning algorithms, enabling a wide array of NLP tasks, from classification to clustering.

- **Enables Quantitative Analysis:** Converting text to numbers makes it possible to apply statistical and mathematical operations to analyze patterns, trends, and relationships within the text.

- **Supports Scalability:** Numerical data can be efficiently processed and analyzed by computers, allowing NLP systems to handle large volumes of text data.

- **Improves Interpretability:** By representing text numerically, it becomes easier to understand and interpret the significance of different features within the text.

Methodologies for Representing Text as Numerical Features: Term Frequency-Inverse Document Frequency (TF-IDF)

TF-IDF stands as a refined technique for text representation, improving upon the simpler Bag of Words (BoW) model by considering not only the frequency of words within a document but also their relevance across a collection of documents.

Mechanism

- **Term Frequency (TF):** This component measures the frequency of a word in a document, indicating its importance within that specific document.

- **Inverse Document Frequency (IDF):** This component evaluates the importance of the word across a set of documents. Words that appear in many documents are deemed less significant, and their scores are adjusted accordingly.

The TF-IDF score of a word in a document is calculated by multiplying its TF and IDF scores, thus balancing the word's local importance with its uniqueness across the corpus.

Key Features

- **Relevance over Frequency:** TF-IDF prioritizes words that are not only frequent in a document but also provide distinctive information, distinguishing between common and meaningful terms.

- **Automatic Feature Selection:** By emphasizing words that offer the most information about a document's content, TF-IDF acts as a form of automatic feature selection, highlighting terms that are likely to be more relevant for analysis or classification tasks.

- **Customizable and Scalable:** TF-IDF can be adapted to various NLP tasks and scaled to accommodate large datasets, making it a versatile tool for text representation.

Strengths

- **Enhanced Document Discrimination:** TF-IDF effectively differentiates documents based on their unique content, improving the performance of algorithms in tasks such as search, document clustering, and information retrieval.

- **Reduction of Noise:** By de-emphasizing common words that appear across many documents, TF-IDF reduces the noise in the dataset, focusing the analysis on more meaningful features.

Limitations

- **Loss of Word Order:** Similar to BoW, TF-IDF does not capture the order of words or the context in which they appear, which can be crucial for understanding the semantics of text.

- **Requires a Corpus:** The calculation of IDF values necessitates a corpus of documents. The choice of this corpus can affect the TF-IDF scores and, consequently, the analysis outcomes.

Practical Applications

- **Information Retrieval:** TF-IDF enhances the relevance of search results by ranking documents based on the significance of query terms within them.

- **Document Clustering:** By highlighting distinctive terms, TF-IDF facilitates the grouping of documents with similar content, aiding in the organization and categorization of large text collections.

- **Text Classification:** The weighted features generated by TF-IDF can improve the accuracy of classifiers by emphasizing terms that are predictive of the document's category.

Term Frequency-Inverse Document Frequency (TF-IDF) represents a sophisticated approach to representing text as numerical features, addressing some of the limitations inherent in simpler models like BoW. By considering both the local and global importance of words, TF-IDF provides a nuanced and effective method for encoding text, enhancing the capabilities of NLP systems to analyze, understand, and derive insights from textual data.

Word Embeddings

Overview:

Word embeddings are dense vector representations of words generated using neural networks. Techniques like Word2Vec, GloVe, and FastText map words to vectors in such a way that the spatial relationships between vectors capture semantic relationships between words.

The transformation of text into numerical features is pivotal for the advancement and application of NLP technologies. Among the various methodologies for text representation, Word Embeddings represent a significant leap forward, offering a nuanced and powerful approach to understanding the semantic and syntactic nuances of language.

Importance of Numerical Representation

The conversion of text to numerical form is foundational in NLP for several key reasons:

Algorithm Compatibility:

Machine learning algorithms, at their core, operate on numerical data. Representing text as numbers enables the application of these algorithms to natural language tasks.

The core premise of numerical representation in NLP is to make textual data comprehensible and actionable for algorithms. This process involves converting text - a complex, highly variable form of data - into a structured, fixed-length set of numerical features. The necessity of this transformation arises from several computational and analytical needs:

Algorithm Compatibility

Machine learning algorithms, at their heart, manipulate numerical values to discern patterns, make predictions, or generate new data. These algorithms are designed to operate on vectors, matrices, and higher-dimensional tensors, all of which are numerical entities. For these algorithms to process natural language:

- **Quantitative Input Requirement:** Algorithms require input data to be expressed quantitatively. Since natural language is inherently qualitative, representing words, sentences, or documents as numerical vectors is a prerequisite for any form of computational analysis.

- **Feature Engineering:** Transforming text into numerical form allows for the extraction of features that capture relevant aspects of the data for specific tasks. Features might include the frequency of certain words, the presence of specific phrases, or more complex properties encoded by techniques like Word Embeddings.

- **Dimensionality and Structure:** Numerical representation provides a structured, fixed-length format for input data, aligning with the requirements of many machine learning models. This structure facilitates consistent and efficient processing of text data across diverse datasets and tasks.

Word Embeddings and Algorithm Compatibility

Word Embeddings offer a sophisticated approach to meeting the demands of algorithm compatibility in NLP. By representing words as dense vectors in a continuous, high-dimensional space, embeddings encapsulate a wealth of linguistic information in a format amenable to algorithmic manipulation:

- **Semantic and Syntactic Information:** Unlike simpler methods of numerical representation, Word Embeddings capture both semantic meaning and syntactic relationships. This rich encoding allows algorithms to perform more nuanced and effective analysis of text data, from understanding context and sentiment to detecting similarities and relationships between words and phrases.

- **Improved Model Performance:** The detailed and context-sensitive nature of Word Embeddings often leads to significant improvements in the performance of NLP models. Algorithms trained on data represented by embeddings can achieve higher accuracy and more insightful results across a wide range of tasks, including classification, translation, and sentiment analysis.

- **Flexibility and Generalization:** Word Embeddings are derived from the statistical properties of language as observed in large corpora. This means they are not tied to specific tasks but can be applied broadly across different NLP applications, enhancing the versatility and generalization capability of models.

The compatibility of algorithms with numerical representations of text is a foundational aspect of NLP, enabling the application of advanced machine learning techniques to the analysis and understanding of natural language. Word Embeddings represent a pinnacle in the evolution of text representation methodologies, offering deep insights into language's semantic and syntactic dimensions.

Semantic Analysis:

Numerical representation allows for the encoding of semantic relationships between words, facilitating tasks that require an understanding of meaning, such as sentiment analysis and machine translation.

The discourse on text representation and feature extraction underscores the transformative role of numerical representation in analyzing and interpreting natural language. Among the various methodologies for converting text into numerical features, word embeddings stand out for their depth and sophistication, particularly in their capacity for semantic analysis.

Importance of Numerical Representation in NLP

Numerical representation forms the crux of machine learning and NLP, serving as a bridge between the rich, nuanced domain of natural language and the precise, logical realm of algorithms. Without converting text into a numerical format, the subtleties and complexities of language remain inaccessible to computational models, hindering our ability to automate understanding and generation of natural language.

Semantic Analysis with Word Embeddings

Word embeddings revolutionize semantic analysis by providing a nuanced, high-dimensional representation of words that captures much more than their surface meanings or syntactic roles.

Capturing Semantic Relationships

Word embeddings are trained on large corpora of text, allowing them to capture a wide array of semantic relationships. For instance, synonyms tend to be located close to each other in the embedding space, while antonyms are positioned in a manner that reflects their opposition. This spatial arrangement extends to capturing a spectrum of semantic relations, including analogies (e.g., "man" is to "king" as "woman" is to "queen").

Understanding Context

One of the most significant advantages of word embeddings over previous methods of text representation is their ability to understand the context in which a word is used. Traditional methods like Bag of Words (BoW) or TF-IDF treat each occurrence of a word identically, irrespective of its context. In contrast, word embeddings, especially those derived from models like BERT or ELMo, offer contextualized representations. This means that the same word can have different embeddings based on its surrounding words, enabling a deeper understanding of its use in specific sentences or phrases.

Enhancing NLP Applications

The semantic richness of word embeddings has led to substantial improvements across a wide range of NLP tasks:

- **Sentiment Analysis:** By understanding the nuanced meanings of words in context, models can more accurately gauge the sentiment of texts.

- **Text Classification:** Embeddings allow for the classification of documents not just based on the presence of keywords but on the overall semantic content.

- **Question Answering and Chatbots:** The ability to parse queries and respond in a contextually appropriate manner is greatly enhanced by the semantic understanding provided by embeddings.

Overcoming Limitations

Despite their advantages, word embeddings are not without limitations. The need for large volumes of training data, computational resources, and the challenge of interpreting high-dimensional vectors are notable challenges. However, the ongoing development in NLP methodologies continues to address these challenges, making word embeddings increasingly accessible and effective.

The numerical representation of text, particularly through word embeddings, marks a significant advance in the field of NLP. By facilitating a deeper semantic analysis of language, word embeddings enhance the ability of algorithms to engage with natural language in a meaningful way. We've position word embeddings as a pivotal technology in NLP, essential for developing applications that require an understanding of the intricate web of meanings that constitute human language. As the field evolves, the exploration and refinement of word embeddings and their applications will continue to be a central theme in pushing the boundaries of what's possible in NLP.

Efficiency and Scalability:

Numerical data can be processed efficiently, allowing for the analysis of large text corpora in ways that are computationally feasible and scalable.

The discussion on text representation and feature extraction emphasizes the critical role of converting text into numerical features for processing and analysis. Among the diverse methodologies available, word embeddings represent a paradigm shift in how text is numerically represented, particularly highlighting the aspects of efficiency and scalability.

Importance of Numerical Representation in NLP

The transformation of text into a numerical format is a foundational step in NLP that allows algorithms to perform a wide array of language-related tasks. This numerical representation is crucial for several reasons:

- **Algorithm Compatibility:** Most machine learning and deep learning algorithms require numerical input to function. Numerical representation translates the inherently qualitative aspects of language into a quantitative format that these algorithms can manipulate and learn from.

- **Pattern Recognition:** Numerical representation enables the identification of patterns within text data, such as the frequency of specific words or the relationships between terms, which are essential for understanding and generating language.

- **Data Manipulation:** Once text is represented numerically, a wide range of mathematical and statistical operations become possible, facilitating tasks such as clustering, classification, and regression on text data.

Word Embeddings: Enhancing Efficiency and Scalability

Word embeddings, as a method of representing text as dense vectors of real numbers, offer significant advantages in terms of efficiency and scalability, making them particularly suited to large-scale NLP applications.

Efficiency

- **Dense Representation:** Unlike sparse representations like the Bag of Words (BoW) model, which might result in high-dimensional vectors with many zeros, word embeddings are dense, containing more information in a smaller number of dimensions. This compactness improves the efficiency of computations involving text data.

- **Reduced Dimensionality:** Word embeddings significantly reduce the dimensionality of text representation while retaining semantic richness. This reduction eases the computational load on NLP systems, enabling faster processing and analysis.

Scalability

- **Handling Large Vocabularies:** Word embeddings can effectively represent large vocabularies, including rare words, through pre-trained models on extensive corpora. This capability is vital for scaling NLP applications to handle real-world datasets that encompass diverse topics and languages.

- **Transfer Learning:** The use of pre-trained word embeddings allows for transfer learning, where embeddings trained on one large dataset can be applied to a different task with minimal re-training. This approach significantly scales NLP applications by leveraging existing learned representations, saving on training time and computational resources.

- **Parallel Processing:** The numerical nature of word embeddings lends itself well to parallel processing techniques. Modern computing architectures, particularly GPUs, can process these embeddings in parallel, drastically reducing the time required for tasks such as training deep learning models on text data.

Word embeddings transform the landscape of NLP by providing a method for representing text that marries semantic depth with computational efficiency and scalability. These characteristics are essential for developing robust, high-performing NLP applications that can handle the vast and growing volumes of text data encountered in various domains. As NLP continues to evolve, the efficiency and scalability offered by word embeddings will remain critical in pushing the boundaries of what's possible in understanding and leveraging natural language.

Word Embeddings: A Methodology for Text Representation

Word Embeddings are a class of techniques for representing words in a continuous vector space, where semantically similar words are mapped to proximate points. This approach contrasts sharply with earlier, more simplistic methods like Bag of Words (BoW) or TF-IDF, offering a deeper understanding of language.

How Word Embeddings Work

- **Dense Vector Representation:** Each word is represented by a dense vector of floating-point numbers, typically of much lower dimensionality than the size of the vocabulary. Unlike sparse representations, where most elements are zero, dense embeddings capture a wealth of information in a compact form.

- **Contextual Similarity:** Word Embeddings are trained on large text corpora, learning representations that reflect the contexts in which words appear. Words used in similar contexts are embedded close to each other in the vector space, capturing their semantic and syntactic similarities.

- **Training Models:** Techniques such as Word2Vec, GloVe (Global Vectors for Word Representation), and FastText are popular models for generating word embeddings. These models use different approaches to learn the vector representation of words based on their co-occurrence patterns.

Strengths of Word Embeddings

- **Semantic Richness:** Word embeddings capture subtle semantic relationships between words, such as synonyms, antonyms, and more complex linguistic patterns.

- **Dimensionality Reduction:** Embeddings provide a way to represent words in a lower-dimensional space compared to the vocabulary size, mitigating the curse of dimensionality.

- **Versatility:** Word embeddings can be used across a wide range of NLP tasks and models, providing a standardized method for inputting text data.

Applications of Word Embeddings

Word embeddings have revolutionized several areas of NLP, including:

- **Semantic Text Similarity:** Assessing the similarity between texts based on the semantic closeness of their constituent words.

- **Named Entity Recognition (NER):** Improving the identification of named entities by understanding the context in which words appear.

- **Machine Translation:** Enhancing translation accuracy through better representations of source and target language vocabularies.

- **Sentiment Analysis:** Capturing the sentiment of texts more accurately by understanding the nuances of language used.

Word Embeddings represent a profound advancement in the representation of text as numerical features within NLP. By capturing the semantic and syntactic essence of words in dense vector spaces, embeddings facilitate a deeper understanding of language, enabling more sophisticated and accurate NLP models. As NLP continues to evolve, the methodologies and technologies surrounding Word Embeddings will remain at the forefront, driving forward the capabilities and applications of natural language understanding and processing.

Contextual Embeddings

Overview:

Contextual embeddings, generated by models like BERT and GPT, provide word representations that take into account the context in which a word appears. Each occurrence of a word can has a different representation based on its surrounding words.

A significant emphasis is placed on the evolution and sophistication of methodologies for representing text data as numerical features. Among these, contextual embeddings emerge as a groundbreaking advancement, building on the foundation laid by word embeddings to introduce a deeper level of linguistic understanding.

Importance of Numerical Representation in NLP

The numerical representation of text is a fundamental prerequisite for applying machine learning algorithms to natural language data. It translates the intricate and nuanced forms of human language into a structured format that computational models can process, enabling a wide array of applications, from machine translation to sentiment analysis. This transformation is not merely a technical requirement but a bridge to unlocking the potential of algorithms to "understand" and generate human language.

Evolution to Contextual Embeddings

While traditional word embeddings offer a robust method for capturing semantic relationships between words, they fall short in representing the dynamic nature of language—the way the meaning of a word can shift based on its context. Contextual embeddings address this limitation by providing word representations that vary dynamically according to the word's context in a sentence, offering a more nuanced and comprehensive understanding of language.

How Contextual Embeddings Work

- **Dynamic Representation:** Unlike static word embeddings, where a word has a single, fixed representation regardless of its usage, contextual embeddings generate unique representations for each occurrence of a word, based on the surrounding words.

- **Deep Learning Models:** Contextual embeddings are typically produced by deep learning models, such as Bidirectional Encoder Representations from Transformers (BERT), GPT (Generative Pre-trained Transformer), and ELMo (Embeddings from Language Models). These models are trained on vast corpora of text, learning to predict words based on their context or generate text by understanding the preceding content.

- **Layered Understanding:** These models capture not just surface-level patterns but also deeper syntactic and semantic nuances, reflecting the complexity of human language. The embeddings encapsulate this rich linguistic information, making them incredibly powerful for a wide range of NLP tasks.

Importance of Contextual Embeddings

- **Enhanced Semantic Precision:** By capturing the context-specific meanings of words, contextual embeddings allow for a more accurate representation of text, leading to significant improvements in NLP tasks that rely on nuanced understandings of language.

- **Flexibility Across Tasks:** The dynamic nature of contextual embeddings makes them highly versatile, enabling their application across diverse NLP tasks without the need for task-specific tuning.

- **Deeper Language Models:** The use of contextual embeddings has led to the development of more sophisticated language models that can generate coherent and contextually relevant text, understand complex queries, and provide answers that are contextually appropriate.

Applications

Contextual embeddings have revolutionized various NLP applications, including:

- **Machine Translation:** By understanding the context of words and phrases, models can produce more accurate and natural translations.

- **Question Answering Systems:** These systems can comprehend the nuances of questions and retrieve or generate more accurate answers.

- **Sentiment Analysis:** Analyzing the sentiment of text with contextual nuances, recognizing how the same word can convey different sentiments in different contexts.

Contextual embeddings represent a significant leap forward in the numerical representation of text for NLP, offering an unparalleled depth of linguistic understanding. As NLP continues to advance, the role of contextual embeddings in facilitating more sophisticated and nuanced language understanding remains a central theme, marking a new era in the exploration of natural language by computational means.

Strengths of Contextual Embeddings

Contextual embeddings, such as those generated by BERT (Bidirectional Encoder Representations from Transformers), ELMo (Embeddings from Language Models), and GPT (Generative Pre-trained Transformer), have fundamentally altered the landscape of NLP by offering dynamic, context-aware representations of text. Their strengths include:

- **Context-Awareness:** Unlike static embeddings, contextual embeddings consider the surrounding words, allowing the same word to have different representations based on its context. This leads to a more nuanced understanding of language, capturing variations in meaning that depend on sentence structure and word usage.

- **Deeper Linguistic Understanding:** These models capture a broad spectrum of linguistic features, including syntax and semantics, by analyzing text at different layers. This layered approach allows for a richer representation of language nuances, significantly improving performance on complex NLP tasks.

- **Versatility Across Tasks:** The flexibility of contextual embeddings enables their application across a diverse range of NLP tasks without task-specific tuning. Whether it's question answering, text summarization, or sentiment analysis, contextual embeddings provide a solid foundation for models to understand and generate human-like text.

- **Transfer Learning Capability:** Contextual embeddings are often derived from models pre-trained on vast amounts of data, allowing for transfer learning. This means that the knowledge gained from one task can be applied to others, reducing the need for extensive training data for specific applications and speeding up the development process.

Limitations of Contextual Embeddings

Despite their significant advantages, contextual embeddings are not without their challenges:

- **Computational Resources:** The training of models like BERT or GPT requires substantial computational resources, including powerful GPUs or TPUs. This can be a barrier for organizations or individuals with limited access to such resources.

- **Model Complexity:** The complexity of these models, while a strength, can also be a limitation. Fine-tuning and deploying these models requires a deep understanding of their architecture and functioning, which can be a steep learning curve for practitioners new to the field.

- **Inference Time:** The complexity and depth that allow contextual embeddings to capture nuanced meanings also mean that generating these embeddings can be time-consuming. This can impact the latency of applications, especially those requiring real-time processing.

- **Data Bias and Ethical Considerations:** Models trained on large, uncurated datasets may inadvertently learn and perpetuate biases present in the training data. This necessitates careful consideration and potential mitigation strategies to ensure that applications using these embeddings do not amplify societal biases.

Contextual embeddings represent a significant advancement in the numerical representation of text, offering unparalleled depth and flexibility for a wide range of NLP applications. The strengths of contextual embeddings - particularly their ability to understand the nuanced meanings of words in context - have the potential to drive forward the capabilities of NLP systems. However, the limitations, particularly in terms of computational resource requirements and potential biases, underscore the need for ongoing research and development in the field. Balancing these strengths and limitations is crucial for harnessing the full potential of contextual embeddings in advancing the state of NLP.

Applications in NLP

The numerical representation of text is a foundational step that enables numerous NLP applications, including but not limited to:

- **Text Classification:** Categorizing documents into predefined classes.

- **Sentiment Analysis:** Determining the sentiment expressed in a piece of text.

- **Machine Translation:** Translating text from one language to another.

- **Named Entity Recognition (NER):** Identifying and classifying key elements in text into predefined categories.

- **Question Answering:** Building systems that can answer questions posed in natural language.

Bag-of-Words (BoW) and (TF-IDF):

A detailed examination of text representation and feature extraction methodologies is crucial for understanding the foundation of NLP. Among the various techniques for transforming text into numerical features, the Bag-of-Words (BoW) and Term Frequency-Inverse Document Frequency (TF-IDF) models stand out for their simplicity and effectiveness.

Bag-of-Words (BoW) Model

The Bag-of-Words model is a fundamental approach to text representation, treating text as an unordered collection of words. The primary focus is on the vocabulary of known words and their occurrence frequencies in the document.

Principles and Implementation

- **Vocabulary Creation:** BoW starts by building a vocabulary of all unique words across the documents in the corpus.

- **Document Representation:** Each document is then represented as a vector in this vocabulary space, where each dimension corresponds to a word in the vocabulary, and the value in each dimension represents the frequency or presence (binary) of that word in the document.

Applications

- **Text Classification:** BoW vectors can serve as features for classifying documents into categories, such as spam detection in emails or sentiment analysis.

- **Information Retrieval:** The model can be used to retrieve documents similar to a query by comparing the BoW vectors using similarity measures.

Strengths

- **Simplicity:** The model is straightforward to understand and implement, making it accessible for beginners in NLP.

- **Efficiency:** Due to its simplicity, BoW can be efficiently computed, even for large datasets.

Limitations

- **Loss of Context:** BoW ignores the order of words, losing valuable contextual information that can affect the meaning of the text.

- **High Dimensionality:** The vocabulary can become very large, leading to sparse and high-dimensional vectors, which can be computationally challenging to manage.

Term Frequency-Inverse Document Frequency (TF-IDF) Model

The TF-IDF model builds upon the BoW concept by weighting the word frequencies in a document against the word's importance across the corpus. This approach helps to highlight words that are more relevant for a specific document.

Principles and Implementation

- **Term Frequency (TF):** Measures the frequency of a word in a document, indicating its importance in that specific document.

- **Inverse Document Frequency (IDF):** Calculates the log of the number of documents in the corpus divided by the number of documents containing the word. This reduces the weight of commonly occurring words across documents.

- **TF-IDF Score:** The TF-IDF score for a word in a document is the product of its TF and IDF scores, giving higher weight to words that are unique to a particular document.

Applications

- **Feature Weighting:** TF-IDF provides a way to weight the importance of words for tasks like text classification and clustering.

- **Search Engine Ranking:** It can be used to rank the relevance of documents to a query, highlighting documents that contain rare terms found in the query.

Strengths

- **Contextual Relevance:** TF-IDF weighting emphasizes words that are distinctive to a document, providing a measure of word relevance.

- **Reduction of Noise:** Common words across documents receive lower weights, helping to reduce the impact of frequent but less informative words.

Limitations

- **Still Ignores Word Order:** Like BoW, TF-IDF does not capture the sequence of words, missing out on contextual meanings that can arise from word order.

- **Document-Length Bias:** TF-IDF can be biased towards longer documents, which might have higher term frequencies by virtue of their length, rather than relevance.

Both the Bag-of-Words and Term Frequency-Inverse Document Frequency models offer foundational methods for representing text as numerical features in NLP. Understanding these models is essential for anyone venturing into NLP, providing the tools to transform raw text into structured formats suitable for analysis. While they have limitations, particularly in capturing contextual and syntactic nuances, their simplicity and effectiveness make them invaluable for a wide range of NLP applications.

Word Embeddings:

The exploration of text representation and feature extraction delves into the advanced domain of word embeddings, a significant leap beyond traditional models like Bag-of-Words (BoW) and Term Frequency-Inverse Document Frequency (TF-IDF). Word embeddings offer dense, continuous vector representations of words, capturing semantic and syntactic nuances. Among the most influential word embedding models are Word2Vec, GloVe (Global Vectors for Word Representation), and FastText.

Word2Vec

Developed by a team led by Tomas Mikolov at Google, Word2Vec is a predictive model for generating word embeddings. It operates on the principle that words appearing in similar contexts tend to have similar meanings.

Methodologies

- **Continuous Bag of Words (CBOW):** This approach predicts a target word from a window of surrounding context words. It is particularly efficient in terms of its use of context.

- **Skip-Gram:** In contrast, the Skip-Gram model predicts surrounding context words from a target word, effectively capturing a broad range of contextual information, especially for less frequent words.

Strengths

- **Semantic Similarity:** Word2Vec excels at capturing semantic similarity, where semantically similar words are located close to each other in the embedding space.

- **Efficiency:** It is computationally efficient, making it suitable for working with large datasets.

Applications

- **Similarity and Analogy Tasks:** Word2Vec embeddings are used to find similar words or to solve word analogies, such as "king is to queen as man is to woman."

- **Feature Generation for Deep Learning Models:** The embeddings serve as input features for various deep learning models in NLP tasks like sentiment analysis and named entity recognition.

GloVe

GloVe, developed by researchers at Stanford, combines the benefits of the matrix factorization techniques used in latent semantic analysis (LSA) with the local context window methods of Word2Vec.

Methodologies

- **Co-occurrence Matrix:** GloVe builds a global matrix of word co-occurrence counts from a corpus. The matrix provides a comprehensive picture of how words co-occur in the entire corpus, capturing their relationships.

- **Dimensionality Reduction:** The model then applies matrix factorization to reduce the dimensionality of the co-occurrence matrix, resulting in dense word embeddings.

Strengths

- **Global Context:** By incorporating global statistics of word co-occurrences, GloVe captures both the semantic and statistical relationships between words.

- **Robust and Scalable:** The model is effective across a variety of datasets and scales well with corpus size.

Applications

- **Text Categorization:** GloVe embeddings are adept at categorizing texts based on their overall thematic content.

- **Information Retrieval:** They improve the relevance of results in search queries by leveraging semantic relationships between words.

FastText

Developed by researchers at Facebook AI Research (FAIR), FastText extends Word2Vec to represent each word as an n-gram of characters, enabling it to capture morphological information.

Methodologies

- **Subword Information:** FastText represents words as bags of character n-grams, plus the whole word itself, allowing it to capture subword information such as prefixes and suffixes.

- **Skip-Gram Model:** It applies a modified skip-gram model over these n-grams, effectively learning representations for short sequences of characters within words.

Strengths

- **Handling of Rare Words:** By breaking words down into subword units, FastText can generate meaningful representations for rare words, or even words not seen during training.

- **Morphological Richness:** The model captures morphological information, making it particularly useful for languages with rich morphology.

Applications

- **Language Modeling:** FastText's nuanced understanding of morphology and syntax enhances performance in language modeling tasks.

- **Text Classification:** Its ability to understand rare and out-of-vocabulary words improves classification tasks, especially in languages other than English.

Word embeddings, particularly through Word2Vec, GloVe, and FastText, represent a cornerstone of modern NLP, providing dense, meaningful representations of text. Each model offers unique strengths and capabilities, from capturing semantic and syntactic nuances with Word2Vec and GloVe to addressing morphological complexity with FastText, underscoring the diverse approaches to understanding and leveraging the power of natural language.

Document Embeddings:

A deep dive into the methodologies for representing text data reveals the significance of document embeddings as a pivotal advancement in capturing the essence of textual information. Unlike word embeddings, which focus on individual word representations, document embeddings aim to encapsulate the meaning of entire documents, paragraphs, or sentences in dense vector spaces. This section explores three influential approaches to document embeddings: Doc2Vec, BERT, and ELMo, detailing their mechanisms, applications, and impacts on the field of NLP.

Doc2Vec

Building on the principles of Word2Vec, Doc2Vec (also known as Paragraph Vector) extends the idea to entire documents, producing a fixed-length feature vector for documents of any length.

Mechanism

- **Training:** Doc2Vec modifies the Word2Vec architecture by adding a document token (a unique identifier for each document) to the input. This document token acts alongside words to predict the surrounding words in texts. During training, the model learns vector representations for words and the document token, effectively embedding the entire document in the same vector space as words.

Applications

- **Document Similarity:** Doc2Vec vectors can be used to compute similarities between documents, supporting tasks such as document classification, clustering, and recommendation systems.

- **Information Retrieval:** By representing documents as dense vectors, Doc2Vec facilitates efficient retrieval of documents relevant to a query.

Impact

- **Versatility:** Doc2Vec provides a straightforward method for embedding texts of varying lengths, from sentences to entire documents, making it a versatile tool in the NLP toolkit.

BERT (Bidirectional Encoder Representations from Transformers)

BERT represents a significant leap in document embeddings, utilizing a deep learning approach based on the Transformer architecture to generate context-sensitive embeddings for words, sentences, and documents.

Mechanism

- **Bidirectional Context:** BERT processes text in both directions (left-to-right and right-to-left), capturing the context around each word comprehensively. This allows BERT to understand the nuanced meanings of words based on their use in sentences and documents.

- **Fine-Tuning:** BERT is pre-trained on a large corpus of text using tasks like masked word prediction and next sentence prediction. For specific applications, BERT models can be fine-tuned with additional layers to adapt to particular NLP tasks.

Applications

- **Natural Language Understanding (NLU):** BERT's deep contextual embeddings excel in tasks requiring an understanding of complex language structures, such as question answering, named entity recognition, and sentiment analysis.

- **Text Generation:** While primarily used for NLU, BERT's understanding of context and language can also enhance text generation tasks.

Impact

- **State-of-the-Art Performance:** BERT has set new benchmarks across a range of NLP tasks, showcasing the power of contextual embeddings in understanding language.

ELMo (Embeddings from Language Models)

ELMo introduces the concept of deep contextualized word representations, where the meaning of a word can change based on its surrounding text, offering significant improvements over traditional word embeddings.

Mechanism

- **Dynamic Word Representations:** ELMo generates embeddings for words by considering their entire context within a sentence, using a bidirectional LSTM trained on a language modeling objective. This results in word representations that reflect their varied meanings across different contexts.

Applications

- **Enhancing Existing Models:** ELMo embeddings can be incorporated into existing NLP models to improve their performance on tasks like text classification, sentiment analysis, and more.

- **Polysemy Resolution:** ELMo is particularly effective at handling words with multiple meanings, disambiguating based on context.

Impact

- **Improved Understanding of Context:** ELMo paved the way for subsequent developments in contextual embeddings, highlighting the importance of context in understanding language.

As NLP continues to evolve, the exploration and application of document embeddings remain central to advancing the field, driving forward the capabilities of machines to comprehend and interact with human language in ever more complex and meaningful ways.

Conclusion

Text representation and feature extraction are foundational elements in the NLP pipeline, setting the stage for the successful application of machine learning models to natural language data. With ongoing advancements in machine learning and computational linguistics, the methods and technologies for text representation and feature extraction continue to evolve, offering ever more sophisticated tools for unlocking the wealth of information contained within natural language.

Chapter 4: Text Classification and Sentiment Analysis

The exploration of text classification and sentiment analysis represents a crucial domain where the computational treatment of language seeks to categorize text and discern its underlying sentiment. These tasks leverage the advancements in NLP methodologies to interpret and classify textual data, enabling machines to understand human language in a way that is insightful and actionable for various applications.

Text Classification: Overview

Text classification involves categorizing text into predefined groups or classes. It is a fundamental NLP task with a wide range of applications, from spam detection in emails to categorizing news articles.

Methodologies

- **Feature Extraction:** This step involves transforming text into a set of usable features using techniques like Bag-of-Words, TF-IDF, word embeddings, or contextual embeddings. The choice of feature extraction method significantly impacts the classification performance.

- **Machine Learning Models:** A variety of machine learning models can be applied to the feature vectors for classification, including Naive Bayes, Support Vector Machines (SVM), Random Forests, and neural network models. The advent of deep learning has introduced models like Convolutional Neural Networks (CNNs) and Recurrent Neural Networks (RNNs), which can directly process text data and capture complex patterns for more accurate classification.

- **Evaluation:** The performance of text classification models is typically evaluated using metrics such as accuracy, precision, recall, and F1 score, depending on the specific requirements of the task.

Sentiment Analysis: Overview

Sentiment analysis, or opinion mining, seeks to determine the emotional tone behind a body of text. This is crucial for understanding consumer sentiments in reviews, social media posts, and more.

Methodologies

- **Polarity Detection:** The basic form of sentiment analysis involves classifying the sentiment of a text as positive, negative, or neutral. This can be achieved using predefined sentiment lexicons or machine learning models trained on labeled sentiment data.

- **Aspect-Based Sentiment Analysis:** A more advanced form, aspect-based sentiment analysis, involves identifying specific aspects or features mentioned in the text and determining the sentiment expressed towards each aspect.

- **Deep Learning Approaches:** Recent advances utilize deep learning models, such as LSTM or BERT, to capture the contextual nuances of language, improving the ability to discern sentiment accurately even in complex or ambiguous texts.

Challenges

- **Contextual Ambiguity:** The meaning of words can change based on context, making it challenging to accurately classify texts or determine sentiment. Sarcasm and irony present particular challenges for sentiment analysis.

- **Data Sparsity and Imbalance:** The lack of labeled data for training, or imbalanced datasets with uneven class distributions, can affect the performance of models, requiring techniques like data augmentation or transfer learning to address.

- **Language and Domain Variability:** The effectiveness of text classification and sentiment analysis models can vary across different languages and domains, necessitating domain-specific models or transfer learning approaches to adapt to new contexts.

Real-World Applications

- **Customer Feedback Analysis:** Businesses use sentiment analysis to gauge customer satisfaction and improve products or services based on feedback from reviews and social media.

- **Content Moderation:** Text classification helps in automating the moderation of user-generated content, filtering out inappropriate or irrelevant material.

- **Market Research:** Sentiment analysis provides insights into public opinion on products, services, or topics, aiding in market research and strategy formulation.

Introduction To Text Classification Tasks:

The exploration of text classification encompasses a variety of tasks that are central to understanding and organizing textual data. Among these, sentiment analysis, topic classification, and spam detection stand out as fundamental applications that leverage NLP techniques to decipher, categorize, and respond to the vast amounts of text generated daily.

Sentiment Analysis

Sentiment analysis, often referred to as opinion mining, involves determining the emotional tone behind a body of text. This is a key aspect of understanding human communication, allowing businesses and researchers to gauge public opinion, brand reputation, or market trends from online discussions, reviews, and social media.

Methodologies:

- **Lexicon-based Approaches:** Utilize a predefined list of words associated with positive or negative sentiments. The overall sentiment of a text is determined based on the presence and combination of these words.

- **Machine Learning Approaches:** Employ algorithms to learn from a dataset containing texts with predefined sentiments, enabling the model to predict the sentiment of new, unseen texts. Techniques range from traditional models like Naive Bayes and SVM to more advanced neural network models.

Challenges:

- **Context and Sarcasm:** Understanding the context and detecting sarcasm or irony in text can be difficult, often leading to misinterpretation of sentiment.

- **Subtlety of Language:** Sentiments can be expressed through subtle cues in language, which can be challenging for algorithms to capture accurately.

Topic Classification

Topic classification (or categorization) is the process of identifying the main topic or category of a text document, enabling the organization and retrieval of information based on content. Applications include news article categorization, content recommendation systems, and organizing academic papers.

Methodologies:

- **Supervised Learning:** Involves training a classifier on a labeled dataset where each document is tagged with a topic. Upon training, the classifier can categorize new documents into one of the learned topics.

- **Unsupervised Learning:** Techniques like clustering are used to group documents into topics without pre-labeled training data, based on the similarity of their content.

Challenges:

- **Overlapping Topics:** Texts often cover multiple topics or contain aspects of topics that are closely related, complicating clear categorization.

- **Evolution of Topics:** Topics can evolve over time, requiring classifiers to adapt to new terminology and concepts.

Spam Detection

Spam detection focuses on identifying and filtering out unwanted or unsolicited messages, particularly in emails and social media platforms. Effective spam detection helps in improving user experience by minimizing exposure to irrelevant or potentially harmful content.

Methodologies:

- **Rule-based Filtering:** Defines explicit rules or patterns that are typically found in spam messages, such as certain keywords or sender characteristics.

- **Machine Learning Models:** Trained on datasets of spam and non-spam messages, these models learn to distinguish between the two based on features extracted from the text.

Challenges:

- **Adaptive Spammers:** Spammers continuously evolve their tactics to bypass detection systems, necessitating constant updates to spam detection models.

- **False Positives/Negatives:** Balancing the sensitivity of spam detection to minimize false positives (legitimate messages marked as spam) and false negatives (spam messages not detected).

Text classification tasks like sentiment analysis, topic classification, and spam detection illustrate the diverse applications of NLP in extracting actionable insights from text data. Mastering these tasks requires not only an understanding of the underlying linguistic and computational principles but also a continuous engagement with the dynamic nature of language and communication. Through the development and refinement of NLP methodologies, researchers and practitioners can enhance the accuracy and effectiveness of text classification, contributing to advancements in information retrieval, content analysis, and digital communication.

Supervised Learning Algorithms for Text Classification:

A significant focus is given to the application of supervised learning algorithms for text classification, including sentiment analysis. Supervised learning, where models are trained on a labeled dataset to learn the relationship between input texts and their corresponding labels (e.g., categories, sentiments), is foundational in NLP. Among the plethora of algorithms available, Naive Bayes, Support Vector Machines (SVM), and Logistic Regression are prominently featured due to their effectiveness and widespread use in text classification tasks. This section explores these algorithms, their application in text classification and sentiment analysis, and their strengths and limitations.

Naive Bayes

Naive Bayes classifiers are based on Bayes' theorem, with the 'naive' assumption that the features (e.g., words) in a text are independent of each other given the document's category. This simplicity makes Naive Bayes particularly suited for text classification, where it performs remarkably well despite the assumption of independence often being violated in real-world text data.

Applications:

- **Spam Detection.** One of the hallmark applications of the Naive Bayes classifier is in spam detection, particularly for filtering email. By analyzing the frequency and distribution of words in emails, Naive Bayes calculates the probability of an email being spam or not spam. Its effectiveness in this domain stems from its ability to handle large feature sets inherent in text data, making it an efficient and reliable choice for distinguishing spam from legitimate messages.

- **Sentiment Analysis.** Naive Bayes plays a significant role in sentiment analysis, where the objective is to classify text according to the sentiment expressed— typically as positive, negative, or neutral. The algorithm assesses the probabilities of sentiment-laden words and phrases within the text, providing a basis for determining the overall sentiment. Its application in sentiment analysis extends to product reviews, social media monitoring, and customer feedback, enabling businesses and researchers to gauge public opinion and emotional trends.

Topic Classification

documents to predefined topics based on their content. The model learns the likelihood of words appearing in documents of each topic and uses this information to classify new documents. This application is vital in organizing and managing large datasets, such as news articles, academic papers, and web content, facilitating easier access to information and insights.

Language Detection

The Naive Bayes classifier is effectively applied in language detection, identifying the language of a given piece of text. By training on text samples from multiple languages, the model learns the distribution of words and characters unique to each language, allowing it to predict the language of new texts. This capability is crucial for multilingual applications and content management systems that need to process and categorize content in various languages.

Authorship Attribution

Another intriguing application of Naive Bayes is in authorship attribution, where the goal is to identify the author of a text based on stylistic and linguistic features. By analyzing the usage patterns of words, phrases, and syntactic structures, Naive Bayes can help in forensic linguistics, literary studies, and historical text analysis to ascertain authorship of disputed or anonymous texts.

The Naive Bayes classifier, with its straightforward implementation and statistical underpinnings, offers a powerful approach to various text classification and sentiment analysis tasks. The ability of Naive Bayes to handle high-dimensional text data efficiently, coupled with its adaptability to different classification problems, underscores its enduring value in the NLP field. Despite its assumption of feature independence, the practical success of Naive Bayes in these applications highlights its significance as a versatile tool in the text analysis and NLP toolkit.

Strengths:

- **Simplicity and Ease of Implementation.** One of the most significant strengths of Naive Bayes is its simplicity. The algorithm's foundation on Bayes' theorem allows for an intuitive understanding and straightforward implementation. This accessibility makes it an excellent starting point for those new to NLP and machine learning, providing a gentle introduction to the concepts of text classification and sentiment analysis without the complexity associated with more advanced models.

- **Efficiency in Handling Large Datasets.** Naive Bayes excels in processing and classifying large volumes of text data efficiently. Its computational efficiency stems from the algorithm's ability to make classification decisions based on the conditional probability of each feature independently, avoiding the computational complexity of feature interdependencies. This characteristic makes Naive Bayes particularly well-suited for applications where speed and scalability are crucial, such as real-time spam detection and large-scale document categorization.

Strong Performance with Small Training Sets

Despite its simplicity, Naive Bayes can achieve remarkably high accuracy with relatively small training datasets. This efficiency in learning from limited data is particularly valuable in scenarios where annotated training examples are scarce or expensive to obtain. The algorithm's ability to generalize from minimal data while maintaining competitive performance is a testament to its robustness and effectiveness in text classification tasks.

Good Baseline for Comparison

Given its ease of implementation and strong baseline performance, Naive Bayes serves as an excellent benchmark for evaluating more complex models. In practice, it's common to first apply Naive Bayes to a text classification problem to establish a baseline performance level. Subsequent models can then be assessed against this baseline to determine if the added complexity offers significant improvements in accuracy or other relevant metrics.

Adaptability to Multiclass Classification

Naive Bayes naturally extends to multiclass classification problems, where documents need to be categorized into one of several possible classes. This adaptability makes it a versatile tool for a wide range of NLP applications beyond binary classification tasks, such as topic identification, sentiment analysis across multiple sentiment categories, and more.

Robustness to Irrelevant Features

The probabilistic nature of Naive Bayes lends it a degree of robustness against irrelevant or noisy features. By considering the contribution of each feature to the overall probability of a class, the model can often maintain high performance even in the presence of features that do not contribute significantly to the classification decision. This characteristic is especially beneficial in text classification, where the feature space can be vast and not all features may be equally informative.

The Naive Bayes algorithm, with its compelling blend of simplicity, efficiency, and robustness, occupies a critical position in the toolbox of NLP techniques for text classification and sentiment analysis. Whether used on its own or as a benchmark for more complex models, Naive Bayes remains an indispensable algorithm in the field of natural language processing.

Limitations:

- **Assumption of Feature Independence.** The fundamental limitation of Naive Bayes lies in its core assumption: the independence of features. In text classification, this translates to the assumption that the presence or absence of a word in a document is independent of the presence or absence of any other word. While this simplification contributes to the algorithm's efficiency and simplicity, it is often unrealistic in natural language, where words frequently exhibit dependence (e.g., "not good" vs. "good").

- **Handling of Rare and Unseen Features.** Naive Bayes can struggle with rare and unseen features. When a feature (word) that has not been seen during training appears in a test document, the algorithm might incorrectly estimate its contribution to the probability of the document belonging to a certain class. This issue, known as the "zero-frequency problem," can significantly impact classification accuracy, particularly in datasets with a wide vocabulary or in domains where new terminology frequently emerges.

- **Difficulty with Long Document.** The performance of Naive Bayes can degrade with long documents. As the length of a document increases, the likelihood scores calculated by the algorithm can become extremely small, leading to numerical underflow issues. Additionally, the effect of irrelevant or less informative features is amplified in longer texts, potentially skewing classification decisions.

- **Limited Contextual Understanding.** While Naive Bayes is effective for many text classification tasks, its limited ability to understand context and semantics is a notable drawback. Since the algorithm treats each word independently, it cannot capture the meaning conveyed by word order, syntax, or semantics. This limitation is particularly evident in sentiment analysis, where the same words might convey different sentiments depending on their context (e.g., "This movie is predictably good" vs. "This movie is good, predictably").

- **Bias Toward More Frequent Classes.** Naive Bayes classifiers can exhibit a bias toward classes that are more frequent in the training dataset. If the class distribution is imbalanced, the algorithm might show a preference for the majority class, potentially reducing its effectiveness in identifying instances of less frequent classes. This issue requires careful handling, such as by balancing the class distribution in the training set or adjusting the model's class prior probabilities.

Despite these limitations, Naive Bayes remains a widely used and highly valuable tool in the NLP practitioner's arsenal, particularly for text classification and sentiment analysis tasks. Its limitations underscore the importance of selecting the right tool for the task at hand, considering the specific characteristics and requirements of the dataset and the problem domain. Understanding both the strengths and limitations of algorithms like Naive Bayes is crucial for effectively applying NLP techniques to the vast and varied landscape of natural language data. In many cases, the choice to use Naive Bayes, or any algorithm, is informed by a trade-off between simplicity, efficiency, and the need for nuanced language understanding.

Support Vector Machines (SVM)

Support Vector Machines are a powerful class of algorithms for classification and regression. In text classification, SVM aims to find the optimal hyperplane that separates the different classes in the feature space with the maximum margin.

Applications:

- **Topic Identification:** SVM is widely used to automatically classify documents into topics. For example, it can distinguish between articles related to politics, sports, technology, and health efficiently, even when the distinction between topics is subtle.

- **Spam Detection:** In the realm of email filtering, SVM has been effectively utilized to differentiate between spam and legitimate emails. It analyzes the frequency and distribution of words to learn the characteristics that distinguish spam from non-spam.

- **News Categorization:** SVM helps news agencies automatically tag articles with appropriate categories, facilitating easier navigation and improving reader experience.

Sentiment Analysis

Another significant application of SVM in NLP is sentiment analysis, where the objective is to determine the sentiment expressed in a piece of text, typically categorizing it as positive, negative, or neutral.

Applications:

- **Product Reviews:** SVM models are trained on labeled datasets of product reviews to automatically identify the sentiment expressed in new reviews. This application is crucial for businesses seeking insights into customer satisfaction and product perception.

- **Social Media Monitoring:** Companies use SVM to monitor social media platforms, analyzing posts and comments to gauge public sentiment towards brands, products, or events. This real-time sentiment analysis enables companies to respond swiftly to customer opinions and trends.

Advantages of SVM in Text Classification and Sentiment Analysis

- **Effectiveness in High-Dimensional Spaces:** SVM excels in environments where the number of dimensions (features) exceeds the number of samples, which is often the case with text data.

- **Versatility:** The ability to use different kernel functions makes SVM adaptable to a variety of text classification tasks, including linear and non-linear separations.

- **Robustness:** SVM is relatively less prone to overfitting, especially in high-dimensional spaces. This robustness is partly due to the regularization parameters that control the trade-off between achieving a low error on the training data and minimizing the norm of the coefficients.

Support Vector Machines (SVM) represent a cornerstone technique in the supervised learning algorithms used for text classification and sentiment analysis within NLP. The broad applicability, robustness, and effectiveness of SVM in handling text data make it an indispensable tool for practitioners and researchers alike. Whether it's categorizing vast amounts of text data, detecting spam, or deciphering the sentiment behind words, SVM provides a powerful approach to making sense of the complex and high-dimensional world of natural language, underscoring its pivotal role in advancing the field of NLP.

Strengths:

- **High-Dimensional Space Performance.** One of the most significant strengths of SVM is its exceptional performance in high-dimensional spaces, which is typical of text data. Text data, when converted into numerical form (e.g., TF-IDF vectors), often results in a feature space with thousands to millions of dimensions. SVM thrives in such environments by effectively handling the curse of dimensionality, making it well-suited for text classification tasks where the number of features far exceeds the number of samples.

- **Margin Maximization Principle.** SVM operates on the principle of margin maximization, aiming to find the hyperplane that separates different classes with the maximum margin. This approach not only helps in achieving high accuracy but also enhances the model's generalization ability to new, unseen data. The emphasis on margin maximization makes SVM robust against overfitting, a critical advantage when working with complex text datasets.

- **Versatility Through Kernel Trick.** The kernel trick is a pivotal feature of SVM that allows it to solve not only linearly separable problems but also non-linear ones without explicitly transforming data into a higher dimensional space. By using different kernel functions (linear, polynomial, radial basis function, etc.), SVM can adapt to various text classification tasks, ranging from linear separations in spam detection to more complex non-linear separations in sentiment analysis across different contexts and genres.

- **Robustness to Overfitting.** SVM's inherent regularization parameter controls the balance between achieving a low error on the training data and minimizing the norm of the coefficients, thereby avoiding overfitting. This regularization is particularly beneficial in text classification, where models might encounter noisy or irrelevant features. SVM's ability to focus on the most informative features contributes to its robustness and reliability.

- **Effective Handling of Unbalanced Data.** Text classification tasks often involve unbalanced datasets, where some classes are significantly more frequent than others. SVM's optimization objective and the ability to adjust class weights make it adept at handling unbalanced data, ensuring that minority classes are not overshadowed by majority classes. This capacity is crucial for applications like sentiment analysis, where the distribution of sentiments can vary widely across different datasets.

- **Scalability and Computational Efficiency.** While SVM can be computationally intensive, especially during the training phase, advances in optimization algorithms and the development of linear SVMs have significantly improved its scalability and computational efficiency. These improvements enable SVM to be applied to large-scale text datasets, a common scenario in many NLP applications, without prohibitive increases in training time or resource consumption.

Support Vector Machines (SVM) stand out as a powerful and versatile tool for text classification and sentiment analysis within the field of NLP. Despite challenges in scalability and parameter selection, the strategic advantages of SVM, including its robustness, versatility, and effectiveness in high-dimensional spaces, solidify its status as a cornerstone algorithm in the NLP practitioner's toolkit.

Limitations:

- **Computational Complexity in Training.** One of the primary limitations of SVM, particularly when dealing with large datasets, is the computational complexity involved in training the model. The training time for SVM can grow substantially as the size of the dataset increases, primarily due to the quadratic optimization problem that SVM needs to solve to find the optimal hyperplane. This aspect can make SVM less practical for applications that require processing vast amounts of text data or necessitate frequent re-training.

- **Parameter Tuning and Model Selection.** The performance of SVM heavily depends on the selection of the kernel function and the tuning of hyperparameters, such as the regularization parameter (C) and kernel-specific parameters (e.g., gamma in the RBF kernel). Finding the optimal set of parameters often requires exhaustive search techniques like grid search or random search, which can be time-consuming and computationally expensive. The need for careful parameter tuning can be a significant hurdle, particularly for practitioners without extensive experience in machine learning.

- **Handling of Non-linearly Separable Data.** While the kernel trick enables SVM to effectively handle non-linearly separable data, choosing the appropriate kernel function is not always straightforward. The decision largely depends on the specific characteristics of the dataset and the underlying problem. Furthermore, the use of complex kernel functions can lead to increased model complexity and overfitting, especially if the chosen kernel maps the data into a much higher dimensional space.

- **Scalability to Large Datasets.** SVM's scalability to large datasets is limited by its training algorithm's computational demands. Although linear SVMs and some optimizations can mitigate this issue to an extent, SVM can still struggle with very large text corpora compared to some other algorithms that are inherently more scalable, such as stochastic gradient descent (SGD) classifiers.

- **Interpretability of the Model.** The interpretability of SVM models, particularly those using non-linear kernels, can be challenging. Unlike some other models that might offer more insight into the contribution of individual features to the classification decision, SVM models, especially with complex kernels, do not readily provide such interpretability. This limitation can be a drawback in applications where understanding the rationale behind predictions is important.

- **Sensitivity to Feature Scaling.** SVM's performance can be sensitive to the scaling of input features. Inconsistent feature scaling can disproportionately influence the model's decision boundary, leading to suboptimal classification performance. Proper pre-processing of text data to ensure uniform scaling is a necessary step, which adds to the preprocessing overhead.

Support Vector Machines (SVM) remain a powerful tool for text classification and sentiment analysis within NLP. However, understanding the limitations of SVM is crucial for its effective application. The challenges associated with computational complexity, parameter tuning, scalability, interpretability, and data preprocessing underscore the importance of careful algorithm selection and optimization in NLP projects. By acknowledging these limitations, practitioners can make informed decisions, potentially combining SVM with other techniques or selecting alternative algorithms better suited to the specific requirements of their NLP tasks.

Logistic Regression

Logistic Regression is a statistical method that estimates probabilities using a logistic function, making it suitable for binary classification tasks, including text classification where the objective is to categorize texts into two classes (e.g., spam or not spam, positive or negative).

Applications:

Sentiment Analysis:

One of the primary applications of Logistic Regression in NLP is sentiment analysis, where the goal is to categorize a piece of text according to the sentiment it expresses—typically positive, negative, or neutral. Logistic Regression is well-suited for this task due to its ability to model probabilities; it can predict the likelihood of a text expressing a certain sentiment based on its features (e.g., word occurrences or TF-IDF scores).

- **Product Reviews:** Logistic Regression is used to analyze customer reviews across various platforms, helping businesses gauge consumer sentiment towards products or services.

- **Social Media Monitoring:** Companies employ Logistic Regression to monitor social media for public sentiment about brands, campaigns, or events, enabling real-time marketing and customer service responses.

Topic Classification:

Topic classification involves assigning a document or piece of text to one or more predefined categories or topics. Logistic Regression can effectively handle this task, leveraging word frequencies or embeddings as predictive features to determine the most likely topic for a given text.

- **News Article Sorting:** Media outlets and content aggregators use Logistic Regression to automatically categorize news articles into topics such as sports, politics, entertainment, etc., streamlining content organization and retrieval.

- **Content Tagging:** Online platforms and content management systems apply Logistic Regression to tag blog posts, articles, and other content with relevant topics, enhancing searchability and user engagement.

Spam Detection

Spam detection is a crucial application of Logistic Regression in identifying and filtering out unwanted or malicious content, especially in emails and online forums. By analyzing text features, Logistic Regression models learn to distinguish between spam and legitimate messages, helping to protect users from unsolicited content.

- **Email Filtering:** Email services implement Logistic Regression to classify messages as spam or not spam, based on characteristics derived from the email text and metadata.

- **Comment Moderation:** Online platforms utilize Logistic Regression to automatically moderate comments, identifying and removing spam or inappropriate content from forums, social media, and websites.

Language Identification

Logistic Regression is also employed in language identification tasks, where the objective is to determine the language in which a given text is written. This application is particularly relevant in multilingual datasets or platforms, enabling content localization and targeted language processing.

- **Multilingual Content Management:** Websites and content platforms that cater to a global audience use Logistic Regression to automatically detect the language of user-generated content, directing it to the appropriate language-specific processing pipeline.

Logistic Regression, with its applications ranging from sentiment analysis and topic classification to spam detection and language identification, demonstrates its versatility and reliability as a supervised learning algorithm for text classification in NLP. The strength of Logistic Regression lies in its simplicity, interpretability, and efficiency, making it an invaluable tool for practitioners looking to extract insights from textual data. Whether applied to analyzing customer sentiment, organizing content, safeguarding digital communication, or bridging language gaps, Logistic Regression offers a robust foundation for addressing a wide array of challenges in the field of natural language processing.

Strengths:

- **Mathematical Simplicity and Efficiency.** Logistic Regression is grounded in a straightforward mathematical framework, modeling the probabilities of different classes based on a linear combination of input features. This simplicity facilitates a fast and efficient training process, especially valuable for large datasets often encountered in NLP. Moreover, the efficiency of Logistic Regression extends to its prediction phase, making it suitable for applications requiring real-time analysis.

- **High Interpretability.** One of the most significant strengths of Logistic Regression is its interpretability. Unlike more complex models such as deep neural networks, the output of a Logistic Regression model can be directly understood in terms of the influence of input features on the predicted probabilities. This attribute is particularly advantageous in text classification and sentiment analysis tasks, where understanding the contribution of specific words or phrases to the classification decision can provide valuable insights and allow for more transparent decision-making processes.

- **Flexibility in Feature Engineering.** Logistic Regression's performance can be significantly enhanced with thoughtful feature engineering, making it a versatile tool adaptable to a wide range of text data. Whether working with basic bag-of-words models, TF-IDF vectors, or more sophisticated word embeddings, Logistic Regression can incorporate these diverse feature representations, enabling practitioners to tailor the model to the specific nuances of their text classification task.

- **Robustness to Irrelevant Features.** Despite its simplicity, Logistic Regression demonstrates a remarkable robustness to irrelevant or less informative features. Its regularization mechanisms, such as L1 and L2 regularization, help prevent overfitting by penalizing large weights, thereby discouraging the model from relying too heavily on any single feature. This characteristic is particularly beneficial in the high-dimensional feature spaces common in text data, where many features may have little to no predictive value.

- **Efficacy in Binary and Multiclass Classification.** Logistic Regression naturally handles binary classification problems, a common scenario in sentiment analysis (positive vs. negative). However, it is also effectively adapted for multiclass classification tasks, such as topic classification, through strategies like the One-vs-Rest (OvR) scheme. This flexibility ensures that Logistic Regression can be applied across a broad spectrum of text classification challenges.

- **Scalability to Large Datasets.** While inherently efficient, Logistic Regression can be further scaled to accommodate very large datasets—a frequent requirement in NLP. Techniques such as stochastic gradient descent enable Logistic Regression models to be trained on massive corpora of text data, ensuring that the model remains practical for real-world applications that involve extensive textual content.

Logistic Regression's strengths in mathematical simplicity, interpretability, flexibility, robustness, and scalability render it an indispensable tool in the NLP practitioner's toolkit, its adaptability to different feature representations and efficacy in both binary and multiclass text classification tasks ensure its continued relevance in the evolving landscape of NLP. Whether used on its own or as part of an ensemble of models, Logistic Regression provides a solid foundation for developing insightful and effective text classification and sentiment analysis solutions.

Limitations:

- **Linear Decision Boundaries.** Logistic Regression inherently assumes a linear relationship between the input features and the log odds of the output class probabilities. This assumption can be a significant limitation in text classification tasks where the relationship between features (words or phrases) and classes (such as sentiments or topics) is complex and non-linear. While feature engineering and the use of polynomial features can mitigate this to some extent, capturing the intricate patterns in language data often requires more sophisticated, non-linear models.

- **Feature Independence Assumption.** Similar to the Naive Bayes algorithm, Logistic Regression performs best when features are independent of each other. However, this assumption rarely holds in natural language, where words and phrases often exhibit strong contextual dependencies. The model's inability to account for these dependencies can lead to suboptimal performance, especially in tasks requiring a deep understanding of context, such as sentiment analysis in nuanced or sarcastic text.

- **Difficulty with High-Dimensional Data.** Text data is typically transformed into high-dimensional feature vectors (e.g., through one-hot encoding or TF-IDF), resulting in a feature space where the number of features far exceeds the number of samples. Logistic Regression can struggle in these high-dimensional spaces, particularly if not regularized properly. Overfitting becomes a considerable risk, where the model performs well on training data but fails to generalize to unseen data.

- **Sensitivity to Imbalanced Data.** Text classification tasks often involve imbalanced datasets, where some classes are much more frequent than others. Logistic Regression can exhibit a bias towards the majority class in such scenarios, leading to poor classification performance for minority classes. While techniques like oversampling, undersampling, or adjusting class weights can help, they require careful tuning and validation.

- **Limited Capture of Contextual Information.** One of the most notable limitations of Logistic Regression in NLP is its limited ability to capture contextual information and the sequential nature of language. Traditional implementations of Logistic Regression treat text as a bag of features, ignoring the order of words and the contextual relationships that critically determine meaning. Advanced models like recurrent neural networks (RNNs) or transformers are better equipped to understand these dynamics.

- **Computational Efficiency in Large-Scale Applications.** Although Logistic Regression is generally efficient, the need for feature engineering and selection can become a computational bottleneck in large-scale applications. The process of creating and selecting the right features from massive text corpora can be computationally intensive and time-consuming, potentially making Logistic Regression less suitable for projects with tight performance or timing constraints.

Despite these limitations, Logistic Regression remains a valuable tool in the arsenal of NLP techniques for text classification and sentiment analysis. Its simplicity, interpretability, and efficiency make it an attractive option, especially when used with appropriate preprocessing, feature engineering, and regularization techniques. However, awareness of its limitations is crucial for deploying Logistic Regression effectively, ensuring that practitioners select the most suitable algorithm for their specific NLP tasks and data characteristics. In many cases, combining Logistic Regression with other models or leveraging it as part of an ensemble approach can help mitigate its limitations, leveraging its strengths while compensating for its weaknesses.

Deep Learning Approaches for Text:

The exploration of text classification and sentiment analysis extends into the realm of deep learning, a subset of machine learning that leverages neural networks with many layers to model complex patterns in data. Among the various deep learning architectures, Convolutional Neural Networks (CNNs) and Recurrent Neural Networks (RNNs) have emerged as particularly influential in advancing the capabilities of NLP.

Convolutional Neural Networks (CNNs) for Text Classification

Traditionally associated with image processing and computer vision, CNNs have also proven highly effective for text classification tasks. By applying convolutional layers to text data, CNNs can capture local patterns within sentences or documents, such as the co-occurrence of words or phrases, making them powerful tools for NLP.

Methodology

Embedding Layer

The initial step in using CNNs for text classification involves transforming words into vectors using an embedding layer. Word embeddings, such as Word2Vec, GloVe, or those learned during the training process, serve as dense representations of words, capturing semantic relationships in a continuous vector space. This embedding layer converts input text—typically a sequence of tokens—into a matrix where each row corresponds to the vector representation of a word, laying the groundwork for convolutional operations.

Convolutional Layers.

The core of a CNN's methodology for text classification lies in its convolutional layers. These layers apply filters (or kernels) of varying sizes to the embedded word vectors, sliding across the entire sequence to capture local patterns within the text. Each filter size can be thought of as focusing on a different 'n-gram' length, allowing the model to learn important features from single words (unigrams) to longer phrases (bigrams, trigrams, etc.).

- **Feature Maps:** The application of a filter across the text generates a feature map, which represents the response of that filter at every position. The convolution operation effectively detects specific patterns or sequences of words that the filter has learned to recognize as important for classification.

Activation Functions

After the convolutional layers capture local patterns within the text, activation functions are applied to introduce non-linearity into the model, enabling it to learn complex relationships. The Rectified Linear Unit (ReLU) is a common activation function used in CNNs for text classification, helping the model differentiate relevant signals from noise in the feature maps.

Pooling Layers

Pooling layers follow the convolutional layers and activation functions to reduce the dimensionality of the feature maps. Max pooling is frequently used, which involves downsampling the feature maps by taking the maximum value in a region, thereby retaining the most salient features detected by the convolutions. This process reduces computational complexity and helps to make the model more generalizable by focusing on the most important features regardless of their position in the text.

Fully Connected Layers and Output

The final stages of a CNN for text classification typically involve one or more fully connected (dense) layers that integrate the features learned by the convolutional and pooling layers across the text. These layers culminate in an output layer designed to match the classification task such as a single neuron with a sigmoid activation function for binary classification or multiple neurons with a softmax activation for multiclass classification.

- **Classification Decision:** The output layer provides the probabilities that the input text belongs to each class. In training, these predictions are compared to the actual labels using a loss function, and the model's parameters are adjusted to minimize this loss.

The methodology of utilizing Convolutional Neural Networks for text classification, reveals the sophisticated interplay of embedding, convolutional, and pooling layers in processing textual data. By capturing local patterns within sentences or documents and integrating these features into a coherent classification decision, CNNs offer a potent tool for understanding and categorizing text. This deep learning approach not only enhances the accuracy of text classification tasks but also extends the boundaries of what is achievable in sentiment analysis and beyond, marking a significant evolution in the capabilities of NLP technologies.

Applications

- **Sentiment Analysis.** One of the hallmark applications of CNNs in NLP is sentiment analysis, where the goal is to determine the emotional tone (e.g., positive, negative, neutral) of a given text. CNNs excel in this domain by identifying patterns and features in text data that are indicative of sentiment, such as the presence of specific adjectives or phrases. Their ability to process input text in segments, capturing local semantic features, enables the accurate classification of text according to sentiment, making them invaluable for analyzing customer reviews, social media posts, and other user-generated content.

- **Topic Classification.** CNNs are also widely used for topic classification, where the objective is to categorize documents or articles into predefined topics or genres. Through the application of multiple filters that capture different n-gram patterns, CNNs can learn the characteristic features of various topics, from sports and politics to technology and entertainment. This capability allows for the automated organization and tagging of large volumes of text, facilitating content discovery and management across digital platforms.

- **Spam Detection.** In the realm of email filtering and online moderation, CNNs have been employed to detect and filter out spam or unwanted content. By learning the textual patterns commonly associated with spam, such as specific keywords, phrases, or formatting cues, CNNs can effectively distinguish between legitimate messages and spam. This application not only improves user experience by reducing exposure to irrelevant or malicious content but also enhances security by identifying potentially harmful communications.

- **Language Identification.** CNNs can be applied to the task of language identification, determining the language in which a text is written. This is particularly challenging in contexts where multiple languages are present or in texts containing a mix of languages. The convolutional layers of CNNs, designed to pick up on specific character or word patterns, enable the accurate classification of text by language, supporting applications in content localization, multilingual content management, and automatic translation services.

- **Fake News Detection.** The proliferation of misinformation and fake news has made the ability to automatically identify and flag unreliable content increasingly important. CNNs contribute to this effort by analyzing the linguistic features and writing styles characteristic of fake news, distinguishing them from credible sources. This application leverages CNNs' strength in pattern recognition to support the integrity of information disseminated across news platforms and social media.

The diverse applications of Convolutional Neural Networks in text classification, underscore their adaptability and effectiveness in deciphering complex textual phenomena. From sentiment analysis and topic classification to spam detection, language identification, and beyond, CNNs offer a powerful approach to understanding and organizing the vast expanses of textual data generated in the digital age. Their continued development and integration into NLP systems promise to further advance the capabilities of machines in interpreting human language, opening new avenues for research and application in the field of natural language processing.

Recurrent Neural Networks (RNNs) for Text Classification

RNNs are specifically designed to handle sequential data, making them ideal for text processing where the order of words and the context play crucial roles in determining meaning. RNNs' ability to maintain information across inputs (words or characters) through hidden states allows them to model the entire context of a sentence or document.

Methodology

Fundamental Concept of RNNs

RNNs are a class of neural networks designed to handle sequential information. Unlike traditional neural networks, which assume all inputs (and outputs) are independent of each other, RNNs perform the same task for every element of a sequence, with the output being dependent on the previous computations. This characteristic makes RNNs ideal for processing text data, where the meaning of a word often depends on the words that precede or follow it.

RNN Architecture for Text Classification

Embedding Layer

The first step in using RNNs for text classification typically involves converting words into dense vectors using an embedding layer. This layer maps each word in the text to a high-dimensional vector space, where semantically similar words are positioned closer to each other. These word embeddings can either be pre-trained (using models like Word2Vec or GloVe) or learned from scratch during the training process.

Sequential Processing

At the core of RNNs is their ability to process sequences one element at a time, maintaining a hidden state that acts as a memory of the information seen so far. In the context of text classification:

- The RNN reads each word (as an embedding vector) sequentially.

- For each word, it updates its hidden state based on the current word's embedding and the previous hidden state, effectively capturing information from the entire sequence up to that point.

Capturing Long-term Dependencies

Traditional RNNs can struggle with long-term dependencies due to issues like vanishing or exploding gradients. To address this, variants such as Long Short-Term Memory (LSTM) units and Gated Recurrent Units (GRUs) introduce mechanisms to better capture information from long sequences without losing relevance over time.

- **LSTM units** incorporate gates that control the flow of information, allowing the network to retain or forget information selectively.

- **GRUs** simplify the LSTM architecture while maintaining its ability to handle long-term dependencies.

Classification Layer

After processing the sequence, the final hidden state of the RNN (which encapsulates information from the entire text) is often used as a representation of the document. This representation is then passed through one or more fully connected layers, culminating in an output layer designed for classification (e.g., using softmax activation for multiclass classification).

RNNs in Practice

In practice, RNNs for text classification might involve:

- Preprocessing text data into sequences of a fixed length.

- Utilizing dropout or other regularization techniques to prevent overfitting.

- Experimenting with different architectures (e.g., stacking multiple LSTM or GRU layers) to enhance model capacity.

The methodology of using Recurrent Neural Networks for text classification, showcases the adaptability and depth of RNNs in capturing the sequential and contextual nature of language. By leveraging their architecture to model the dependencies between words in a text, RNNs offer a nuanced approach to understanding and categorizing textual data. Whether applied to sentiment analysis, topic identification, or other classification tasks, RNNs represent a cornerstone of modern NLP, enabling more sophisticated and accurate interpretations of text through deep learning.

Applications

Sentiment Analysis

RNNs have significantly advanced sentiment analysis, offering nuanced understanding and classification of textual sentiments. Their architecture, inherently designed to process sequences, allows them to consider the order of words and their contextual relationships, crucial for capturing the sentiment expressed in text. RNNs are adept at analyzing customer reviews, social media posts, and other user-generated content, providing insights into public opinion, customer satisfaction, and emotional trends.

Topic Classification

In the domain of topic classification, RNNs excel by leveraging their sequential processing to understand the thematic structure of texts. They can classify news articles, academic papers, and other documents into predefined categories or topics based on the flow and development of ideas within the text. This ability is particularly beneficial for content management systems, news aggregators, and educational platforms seeking to automatically organize and categorize large volumes of textual information.

Spam Detection

RNNs contribute to enhancing email security and online moderation through their application in spam detection. By learning from sequences of words and their context, RNNs can distinguish between legitimate messages and spam with high accuracy. This application not only improves user experience by filtering out unwanted content but also aids in the detection of phishing attempts and malicious communications.

Language Identification

The task of identifying the language of a given piece of text benefits from the sequential processing capabilities of RNNs. They are capable of recognizing patterns and structures unique to specific languages, even in texts with mixed-language content. Language identification serves as a foundational step in multilingual NLP applications, including automatic translation systems, multilingual content analysis, and global content management strategies.

Machine Translation

RNNs have been pivotal in machine translation, where the goal is to automatically translate text from one language to another. Their ability to process text sequences and maintain contextual information across sentences allows for the generation of coherent and contextually appropriate translations. While newer architectures like transformers have set new benchmarks, RNNs, especially those with attention mechanisms, continue to be valuable in research and applications focused on sequential data processing and translation.

Text Summarization

The application of RNNs in text summarization involves condensing a longer document into a shorter version that retains the original text's key points and meaning. RNNs manage this by capturing the progression and salience of information throughout the document, enabling the generation of concise summaries. This is crucial for news outlets, content aggregators, and information retrieval systems aimed at providing quick insights without the need for reading entire documents.

Recurrent Neural Networks (RNNs) have emerged as a cornerstone technology in the deep learning approaches to text classification and sentiment analysis. Their unique ability to process text sequentially and recognize patterns over time has unlocked new possibilities in understanding and categorizing textual data. Despite challenges such as handling long-term dependencies, the diverse applications of RNNs - from sentiment analysis and topic classification to spam detection, language identification, machine translation, and text summarization

- highlight their indispensable role in advancing NLP methodologies and applications. As the field continues to evolve, RNNs and their variants will undoubtedly remain integral to the development of sophisticated natural language understanding and processing systems.

Strengths and Unique Contributions

- **Contextual Understanding:** Both CNNs and RNNs offer a deep understanding of text data. CNNs excel in identifying local patterns within text, while RNNs are adept at modeling the sequential nature and context of language.

- **Feature Learning:** Unlike traditional machine learning models that require manual feature engineering, CNNs and RNNs automatically learn to identify the most predictive features directly from the text data, simplifying the modeling process and potentially uncovering new insights.

- **Versatility:** These deep learning models can be adapted and extended for a wide range of NLP tasks beyond classification, including text generation, machine translation, and more, demonstrating their flexibility and power.

The deep learning approaches embodied by CNNs and RNNs represent a significant advancement in text classification and sentiment analysis. By leveraging these models, practitioners can tap into the rich, contextual, and sequential information embedded in text, enabling more accurate and nuanced analysis. As NLP continues to evolve, the exploration and application of deep learning models like CNNs and RNNs will undoubtedly remain at the forefront of innovation, driving forward the capabilities of machines to understand and interact with human language in ever more sophisticated ways.

Sentiment Analysis Techniques:

The sentiment analysis is underscored as a pivotal component of understanding human language through computational means. Sentiment analysis, or opinion mining, is the process of determining the emotional tone behind a body of text. This is crucial for a myriad of applications, from gauging public sentiment on social media platforms to understanding consumer opinions about products and services. An essential aspect of sentiment analysis is the utilization of sentiment lexicons, which are comprehensive lists of words and phrases with associated sentiment scores.

Sentiment Analysis Techniques

Sentiment analysis techniques can broadly be categorized into machine learning-based approaches and lexicon-based approaches, each with its own set of strategies for analyzing text sentiment.

Machine Learning-Based Approaches

Machine learning methods for sentiment analysis involve training algorithms to classify the sentiment of text as positive, negative, or neutral based on features extracted from the text. This can be further divided into supervised and unsupervised learning techniques:

- **Supervised Learning:** Requires a labeled dataset where each text is associated with a sentiment. Models such as Naive Bayes, SVM, Logistic Regression,

CNNs, and RNNs are trained on this dataset to learn the correlation between text features and sentiment.

- **Unsupervised Learning:** Does not rely on labeled data but instead uses algorithms to identify patterns and structures in the data that might indicate sentiment. Techniques include clustering based on sentiment-related features and dimensionality reduction.

Lexicon-Based Approaches

Lexicon-based sentiment analysis relies on sentiment lexicons, dictionaries of words that have been manually or algorithmically assigned sentiment scores. These approaches evaluate the overall sentiment of a text based on the presence and combination of positive and negative words.

- **Simple Count-Based:** The most straightforward lexicon-based method involves counting the number of positive and negative words in a text and calculating the overall sentiment based on these counts.

- **Score-Based:** More sophisticated lexicon-based methods calculate sentiment by aggregating the sentiment scores of words found in the text, taking into account intensifiers (words that may amplify or dampen sentiment) and negations.

Sentiment Lexicons

Sentiment lexicons are at the heart of lexicon-based sentiment analysis, providing the necessary resources to assess the sentiment value of words and phrases within a text. Several well-known sentiment lexicons include:

- **AFINN:** Contains words rated for valence with an integer between minus five (negative) and plus five (positive).

- **SentiWordNet:** An extension of WordNet with sentiment scores for each term, providing separate scores for positivity, negativity, and objectivity.

- **VADER (Valence Aware Dictionary and sEntiment Reasoner):** Specifically tuned to sentiments expressed in social media, incorporating emojis, slang, and acronyms into its lexicon.

Applications of Sentiment Analysis Techniques and Lexicons

The combination of machine learning techniques and lexicon-based approaches enables a wide range of applications:

- **Market Analysis and Consumer Sentiment:** Businesses analyze customer reviews and social media mentions to gauge sentiment towards products, services, or brands.

- **Social Media Monitoring:** Organizations and individuals monitor social media platforms to understand public sentiment towards events, topics, or trends.

- **Political Sentiment Analysis:** Analysis of public opinion on political issues, campaigns, or figures based on news articles, speeches, and social media discourse.

Sentiment analysis techniques, particularly when augmented with sentiment lexicons, offer a nuanced understanding of the emotional undertones in textual data.

The intersection of machine learning algorithms and lexicon-based methods provides a comprehensive toolkit for practitioners to extract, analyze, and interpret sentiment from vast and varied text sources. As sentiment analysis continues to evolve, the integration of these techniques will remain central to advancements in NLP, enabling deeper insights into human language and emotion.

Conclusion

Text classification and sentiment analysis are pivotal components of NLP, offering the means to organize and interpret vast quantities of text data. The advancement of these tasks relies on sophisticated methodologies, from feature extraction to the application of cutting-edge machine learning models. Overcoming challenges related to context, data quality, and variability remains a central focus, driving forward innovations that enhance the accuracy and applicability of text classification and sentiment analysis across diverse domains.

Chapter 5: Named Entity Recognition (NER)

Named Entity Recognition (NER) and Part-of-Speech (POS) Tagging are presented as foundational components of NLP, enabling machines to understand and interpret the structure and meaning of text at a granular level. Both processes are critical for a myriad of applications, from information extraction and content classification to question answering and machine translation.

Named Entity Recognition (NER)

Named Entity Recognition involves identifying and classifying named entities within text into predefined categories such as persons, organizations, locations, dates, and other specific data types. NER is crucial for understanding the context and relationships within textual data, making it a key step in information extraction and knowledge graph construction.

Methodologies

- **Rule-Based Approaches:** Utilize hand-crafted linguistic rules to identify named entities based on patterns, such as capitalization and context (e.g., "President" preceding a person's name).

- **Statistical and Machine Learning Approaches:** Employ algorithms like Conditional Random Fields (CRFs), Support Vector Machines (SVMs), and Hidden Markov Models (HMMs) trained on annotated corpora to recognize entities based on features extracted from the text.

- **Deep Learning Approaches:** Leverage neural network architectures, particularly Recurrent Neural Networks (RNNs), Convolutional Neural Networks (CNNs), and more recently, Transformer models like BERT, to learn entity recognition from large datasets without explicit rule-based feature engineering.

Applications

- **Information Extraction:** Automatically extract structured information from unstructured text for database population, knowledge base construction, or content summarization.

- **Content Categorization and Recommendation:** Enhance content discovery and recommendation systems by tagging entities, enabling more precise filtering and search functionality.

- **Sentiment Analysis:** Improve sentiment analysis by identifying entities and attributing sentiments to specific organizations, individuals, or products.

Part-of-Speech (POS) Tagging

Part-of-Speech Tagging involves assigning word classes or parts of speech (such as nouns, verbs, adjectives, etc.) to each word in a sentence, based on both its definition and context. POS tagging is essential for parsing sentences, understanding grammatical structure, and supporting deeper linguistic analysis and natural language understanding tasks.

Methodologies

- **Rule-Based Approaches:** Use predefined grammatical rules to assign parts of speech based on word suffixes, prefixes, and contextual clues.

- **Statistical and Machine Learning Approaches:** Implement algorithms like HMMs and CRFs, which consider the likelihood of a word belonging to a certain part of speech based on its position and context within a sentence.

- **Deep Learning Approaches:** Apply neural networks, especially RNNs and Transformers, to model the sequential nature of language, learning POS tagging from large annotated datasets with high accuracy.

Applications

- **Syntactic Parsing:** Serve as a preliminary step for parsing, where understanding the role of each word in a sentence aids in constructing parse trees and analyzing sentence structure.

- **Word Sense Disambiguation:** Help determine the meaning of words with multiple senses based on their parts of speech in context.

- **Text-to-Speech Systems:** Improve pronunciation in text-to-speech systems by identifying the grammatical role of words, influencing intonation and stress patterns.

Named Entity Recognition (NER):

Named Entity Recognition (NER) is highlighted as a critical task that focuses on identifying and categorizing key information elements in text into predefined categories such as person names, organizations, locations, dates, and other specific data types. NER is fundamental to the semantic processing of natural language, enabling the extraction of structured information from unstructured text, which is essential for numerous applications in NLP.

Importance of NER

Named Entity Recognition serves as a cornerstone for understanding the context and meaning within textual data. By identifying entities, NER facilitates a deeper understanding of the content, context, and relationships present in the text, making it indispensable for:

Information Retrieval:

Enhancing search functionality by allowing users to query based on specific entities such as names or locations.

Enhancing Search Functionality

NER contributes to the sophistication of search engines and information retrieval systems by enabling entity-based search queries. Users can perform searches specifically for entities such as people, organizations, or places, rather than relying solely on keyword matching. This distinction allows for more precise search results, reducing the volume of irrelevant information returned and improving user satisfaction.

Facilitating Semantic Search

By identifying entities within documents, NER supports semantic search capabilities, where the intent and contextual meaning of the query are considered, beyond the literal match of query terms. Semantic search can interpret the nuance of natural language queries, connect them with relevant entities, and retrieve documents that are contextually related, even if they don't contain the exact query terms.

Improving Document Indexing

NER aids in the indexing process of information retrieval systems by tagging documents with identified entities. This tagging enriches the metadata of documents, enabling more sophisticated indexing strategies that take into account the presence of specific entities. As a result, the retrieval process becomes more efficient, as the system can quickly access and return documents based on entity relevance, in addition to traditional keyword-based approaches.

Supporting Query Expansion

NER can be instrumental in query expansion, a technique used to enhance information retrieval by automatically enlarging the original query with synonyms or related terms. By recognizing entities within a query, NER can help to expand it with additional relevant entities or attributes. For instance, if a user searches for a specific company, NER can identify it as an organization and suggest related entities, such as subsidiaries, competitors, or key personnel, thereby broadening the search to capture more relevant documents.

Personalization and User Context Understanding

Information retrieval systems can leverage NER to personalize search results based on the user's context or previous interactions. By understanding the entities involved in a user's search history or preferences, the system can tailor future search results to align more closely with the user's likely interests or needs. For example, identifying a preference for news articles related to certain locations or organizations can refine the relevance of the content presented to the user.

As NLP continues to evolve, the role of NER in enhancing information retrieval will undoubtedly expand, driving innovations that further bridge the gap between human language and machine understanding.

Knowledge Graph Construction:

Populating knowledge bases with entities and their relationships extracted from text, which can be used for semantic search, question answering, and recommendation systems.

Content Analysis:

Providing insights into documents by highlighting the key entities, enabling content summarization and categorization.

Enhancing Content Discoverability

NER dramatically improves content discoverability by tagging entities within texts, thereby enabling more efficient indexing and search capabilities. For digital libraries, news archives, and content management systems, NER facilitates the automated categorization of vast amounts of text based on identified entities. This categorization allows users to filter and search content not just by keywords but by specific entities, such as finding all articles mentioning a particular person, organization, or location, significantly narrowing down search results to the most relevant documents.

Enriching Semantic Understanding

Beyond mere identification, NER contributes to the semantic understanding of text by recognizing the types of entities present and their potential relationships. In content analysis, understanding these relationships is crucial for tasks such as summarization, where the goal is to distill the most important information, including key entities, from a document or collection of documents. NER helps highlight the principal actors (persons, organizations) and locations, providing a clearer picture of the document's content and context.

Supporting Content Recommendation Systems

In the realm of personalized content recommendation systems, NER plays a vital role by extracting entities that reflect user interests and preferences. By analyzing the entities present in content that a user engages with, systems can tailor recommendations to include similar or related entities, enhancing the user experience with more targeted and relevant suggestions. For instance, if a user frequently reads articles about certain companies or technologies, NER can identify these interests and recommend new content featuring the same or related entities.

Facilitating Content Summarization and Categorization

NER aids in the automatic summarization and categorization of content by identifying the most salient entities within a text. This process is invaluable for quickly understanding the main topics or themes of large datasets, enabling the grouping of documents by common entities or the generation of concise summaries that capture the essential named entities and their actions or attributes. Such capabilities are especially beneficial for news organizations, research institutions, and businesses that need to process and synthesize information from numerous sources efficiently.

Empowering Sentiment Analysis

In sentiment analysis, NER enhances the granularity of insights by allowing sentiments to be attributed to specific entities rather than the text as a whole. This entity-specific sentiment analysis is crucial for understanding public opinions about products, services, individuals, or organizations. For businesses and marketers, analyzing sentiment at the entity level provides a nuanced view of consumer perceptions, informing decision-making and strategy development.

Named Entity Recognition's role in content analysis. Underscores its value in transforming unstructured text into structured, actionable knowledge. By enabling the precise identification and categorization of entities, NER lays the groundwork for a myriad of applications, from enhancing content discoverability and semantic understanding to supporting personalized recommendations, summarization, and sentiment analysis. As NLP technologies evolve, the integration of NER in content analysis will continue to be a critical factor in unlocking deeper insights from textual data, shaping the future of information retrieval, content management, and beyond.

Sentiment Analysis:

Associating sentiments with specific entities rather than the text as a whole, offering more granular sentiment insights.

The intersection of Named Entity Recognition (NER) with sentiment analysis is highlighted as a significant advancement in the field of NLP. NER's ability to accurately identify and categorize entities such as names, organizations, and locations within text plays a crucial role in enhancing sentiment analysis, a process aimed at determining the emotional tone behind words. This section delves into the importance of NER in the context of sentiment analysis, showcasing how it enriches the process by providing deeper insights into textual data.

Enabling Entity-Specific Sentiment Analysis

One of the primary contributions of NER to sentiment analysis is its ability to enable entity-specific sentiment assessment. Traditional sentiment analysis often focuses on understanding the overall sentiment of a piece of text, which, while valuable, can miss nuances related to specific entities mentioned within the text. By employing NER, sentiment analysis models can attribute sentiments to particular entities, allowing for a more granular understanding of how sentiments are directed towards different subjects within the same document.

Enhancing Precision in Sentiment Attribution

Sentiment analysis can sometimes suffer from inaccuracies in sentiment attribution, especially in complex sentences where multiple entities and sentiments are present. NER helps mitigate this issue by clearly identifying entities, thereby reducing the likelihood of misattributing sentiments to the wrong subjects. This precision is particularly important in analyzing customer feedback, news articles, and social media posts, where understanding the specific targets of positive or negative sentiments can provide actionable insights.

Improving Aspect-Based Sentiment Analysis

Aspect-based sentiment analysis, which aims to identify sentiments related to specific aspects or attributes of a product or service, benefits significantly from NER. By identifying entities and categorizing them into aspects (e.g., "battery life" in a smartphone review), NER enhances the model's ability to analyze sentiments with respect to these aspects. This detailed analysis is invaluable for businesses seeking to understand consumer opinions on various product features or services.

Supporting Cross-Document Sentiment Analysis

In scenarios involving the aggregation of sentiments across multiple documents, such as tracking public opinion on a political figure or a brand over time, NER is instrumental. It ensures that sentiments are accurately associated with the correct entities across different texts, facilitating a coherent analysis of sentiment trends. NER's role in disambiguating entities (e.g., distinguishing between a company and a product with the same name) is crucial for maintaining the integrity of cross-document sentiment analysis.

Enhancing Sentiment Analysis in Multilingual Contexts

NER systems that are capable of recognizing entities across languages play a vital role in multilingual sentiment analysis. They allow models to identify and categorize entities in texts of different languages, providing a consistent framework for sentiment analysis in a global context. This capability is essential for international brands, global media monitoring, and multilingual social media analysis, where understanding sentiments across language barriers is crucial.

The integration of Named Entity Recognition (NER) into sentiment analysis processes, significantly enriches the depth and accuracy of sentiment analysis. By enabling entity-specific, aspect-based, and cross-document sentiment assessments, NER enhances the ability of models to extract nuanced insights from textual data. Moreover, NER's contribution to sentiment analysis in multilingual contexts underscores its importance in today's globally connected world. As NLP continues to evolve, the synergy between NER and sentiment analysis will undoubtedly remain a focal point, driving advancements in how machines understand and interpret human emotions and opinions expressed through language.

Methodologies for NER

Named Entity Recognition approaches can be broadly classified into rule-based, statistical/machine learning, and deep learning methods, each with its advantages and challenges.

Rule-Based Methods

Rule-based NER systems rely on a set of hand-crafted linguistic rules and dictionaries to identify entities. These rules might include patterns for capitalization, affiliation words (e.g., "Corp.", "Inc."), and context (e.g., "President" before a person's name). While rule-based approaches can be highly accurate for well-defined and narrow domains, they are less flexible and require significant manual effort to create and maintain.

Statistical and Machine Learning Methods

These methods use algorithms such as Hidden Markov Models (HMMs), Support Vector Machines (SVMs), and Conditional Random Fields (CRFs) to model the likelihood of sequences of words being entities based on features extracted from the text. Such models are trained on annotated corpora and can generalize well to unseen text, though their performance heavily depends on the quality and representativeness of the training data.

Foundation of Statistical NER Methods

Statistical methods for NER rely on the probabilistic modeling of language to identify named entities. Techniques such as Hidden Markov Models (HMMs) and Conditional Random Fields (CRFs) have been instrumental in this regard.

- **Hidden Markov Models (HMMs):** HMMs model the sequence of words in a text as a series of hidden states (representing the entity types) with transition probabilities. They utilize the observed data (words or tokens) to infer the most likely sequence of hidden states that generated the observed sequence, thus identifying entities based on statistical likelihood.

- **Conditional Random Fields (CRFs):** CRFs are a type of discriminative model used to predict sequences of labels for sequences of input samples. Unlike HMMs, CRFs do not assume the independence of input features and can model the conditional probability of the output labels given the input sequence, making them particularly effective for NER. CRFs take into account the context and dependencies between labels, offering more accurate entity recognition.

Machine Learning Approaches

Supervised machine learning models have also been applied to NER tasks, leveraging annotated corpora to learn the characteristics of different entity types. Models such as Support Vector Machines (SVMs) and decision trees have been used, often in combination with feature engineering to capture the linguistic cues relevant to named entity identification.

- **Feature Engineering:** The success of traditional machine learning models in NER heavily relies on the extraction of informative features from text. Features might include word-level information (e.g., the word itself, prefixes, and suffixes), syntactic information (e.g., POS tags), and context features (e.g., neighboring words). The choice and design of these features are critical for the model's ability to recognize entities accurately.

- **Supervised Learning Models:** Techniques like SVMs have been utilized for NER by treating it as a classification problem where each token is classified as part of an entity or not. The use of feature vectors representing tokens and their context allows these models to learn from examples and generalize to unseen data.

Importance in NER Evolution

- **Flexibility and Adaptability:** Statistical and machine learning methods for NER provided a flexible and adaptable framework for entity recognition, capable of handling various languages and domains with appropriate feature engineering and model tuning.

- **Foundation for Advanced Models:** These methods laid the groundwork for the development of more advanced NER systems, including those based on deep learning. Insights gained from the use of statistical and machine learning models have informed the design and implementation of neural network architectures tailored for NER.

- **Bridging the Gap:** Before the widespread adoption of deep learning, statistical and machine learning methods bridged the gap between rule-based systems and the current state-of-the-art, providing scalable and effective solutions for named entity recognition across a wide range of applications.

Statistical and machine learning methods have played a crucial role in the development and success of Named Entity Recognition (NER). Their ability to model linguistic patterns and dependencies statistically paved the way for sophisticated NER systems capable of automatically extracting and classifying named entities from text. While deep learning approaches have since taken the forefront in NER research and application, the importance of statistical and traditional machine learning methods remains evident, both as a historical foundation and as a comparative benchmark for evaluating newer methodologies in the ever-evolving field of NLP.

Deep Learning Methods

Deep learning approaches to NER employ neural networks, particularly Recurrent Neural Networks (RNNs), Convolutional Neural Networks (CNNs), and Transformers, to automatically learn features from large amounts of text data. These models, especially those based on the Transformer architecture (e.g., BERT), have achieved state-of-the-art performance in NER by capturing complex patterns and dependencies in the data. They benefit from being able to learn contextual representations of words, significantly improving the accuracy of entity recognition.

Evolution to Deep Learning in NER

The transition to deep learning methods in NER was driven by the need to overcome limitations associated with earlier approaches, such as the intensive labor required for rule crafting and the challenges in capturing contextual nuances with statistical models. Deep learning methods, with their ability to learn hierarchical representations and understand context through data-driven learning, offer a powerful alternative for automating and enhancing NER tasks.

Methodologies in Deep Learning for NER

Recurrent Neural Networks (RNNs) and LSTM

RNNs, and specifically their variant Long Short-Term Memory (LSTM) networks, have been widely adopted for NER due to their capability to process sequential data, maintaining information about previous tokens in a sentence to inform the classification of subsequent tokens. This sequential processing is crucial for understanding the context in which an entity appears, significantly improving the recognition accuracy.

Convolutional Neural Networks (CNNs)

Although more commonly associated with image processing, CNNs have also been applied to NER tasks. Their ability to extract local and position-invariant features from text data makes them useful for identifying patterns indicative of named entities, especially when combined with word embeddings that encapsulate semantic information.

Transformer Models

The advent of Transformer models, such as BERT (Bidirectional Encoder Representations from Transformers) and its variants (e.g., RoBERTa, ALBERT), has set new benchmarks in NER. Transformers employ self-attention mechanisms to capture contextual relationships between words in a sentence, regardless of their distance from each other. This comprehensive understanding of context has led to remarkable improvements in NER performance, enabling more accurate and nuanced entity recognition.

Advantages of Deep Learning Methods in NER

- **Contextual Understanding:** Deep learning models excel at capturing the context in which words appear, a critical factor for accurate entity recognition.

- **Data-Driven Feature Learning:** Unlike traditional methods that rely on manual feature engineering, deep learning models automatically learn the most predictive features from data, reducing the need for domain-specific knowledge and extensive preprocessing.

- **Scalability:** Deep learning models, particularly those pre-trained on large corpora, can be fine-tuned on specific NER tasks with relatively small datasets, offering scalability and adaptability to a wide range of domains and languages.

Transformative Impact on NER

The application of deep learning methods to NER has transformed the field, enabling more sophisticated and automated extraction of named entities across diverse datasets and domains. These advancements have broadened the applicability of NER, supporting complex applications in information extraction, content analysis, sentiment analysis, and beyond, where the accurate identification of entities is paramount.

The incorporation of deep learning methods into Named Entity Recognition represents a significant milestone in NLP. By leveraging the strengths of RNNs, CNNs, and Transformer models, NER systems have achieved unprecedented levels of accuracy and efficiency. As deep learning continues to evolve, its application to NER promises further innovations, enhancing the ability of machines to understand and interact with human language in more meaningful ways.

Named Entity Recognition (NER) is an essential process in the extraction and analysis of information from natural language texts. By identifying and categorizing entities, NER systems unlock the potential for machines to understand the semantics of language, facilitating advanced applications such as information retrieval, knowledge graph construction, and content analysis. As NLP technology advances, the methodologies for NER continue to evolve, with deep learning approaches leading the way in achieving high accuracy and flexibility. NER remains a vibrant area of research and application in NLP, reflecting its critical role in bridging the gap between unstructured text and structured understanding.

Part-Of-Speech (POS) Tagging:

Tagging is presented as a fundamental task that forms the bedrock of understanding natural language through computational methods. POS tagging involves labeling each word in a text with its appropriate grammatical category, such as noun, verb, adjective, etc. This process is crucial for numerous downstream NLP tasks, as it provides essential information about the grammatical structure of sentences, which in turn aids in understanding their meaning.

Significance of POS Tagging

POS tagging is vital for parsing the syntactic structure of language, facilitating a deeper understanding of text semantics. By determining the parts of speech of words within their specific contexts, POS tagging helps disambiguate words that can serve multiple grammatical roles, thus clarifying their functions and meanings in sentences. This clarification is essential for accurate syntactic parsing, word sense disambiguation, and numerous other NLP applications that require an understanding of language beyond mere word tokens.

POS tagging, the task of labeling each word in a text with its corresponding grammatical category, such as noun, verb, adjective, etc., serves as a foundational step in understanding and analyzing language computationally.

Foundation for Syntactic Parsing

POS tagging is crucial for syntactic parsing, where the structure of sentences is analyzed to determine the relationships between words. By identifying the parts of speech, POS tagging provides the necessary preliminary information that parsing algorithms use to construct parse trees. These trees are vital for understanding sentence structure, enabling further linguistic analysis and supporting complex NLP tasks like natural language understanding and machine translation.

Enhancing Semantic Analysis

The ability to accurately identify parts of speech is indispensable for semantic analysis. Knowing the grammatical role of words in sentences helps in disambiguating word meanings and understanding sentence semantics. For instance, POS tagging can help distinguish between the noun "bear" (an animal) and the verb "bear" (to carry or support), which is critical for tasks such as word sense disambiguation, sentiment analysis, and entity recognition.

Improving Language Modeling

Language models, which predict the likelihood of sequences of words, benefit significantly from the nuanced understanding of language that POS tagging offers. By incorporating knowledge of grammatical categories, language models can generate more syntactically coherent and contextually appropriate text, enhancing applications in text generation, autocomplete features, and conversational AI.

Supporting Information Extraction

POS tagging aids in the extraction of structured information from unstructured text, a key capability in numerous applications like knowledge base construction, question answering, and summarization. For example, identifying verbs and their subjects and objects can help extract actionable information about events described in text, while adjectives can provide insights into sentiments and opinions.

Facilitating Machine Translation

In machine translation, the accuracy of translating a sentence from one language to another can be greatly enhanced by understanding the grammatical structure of the source text. POS tagging allows translation models to grasp the syntactic roles of words, contributing to more grammatically accurate and semantically faithful translations.

Enabling Part-of-Speech-Specific Processing

Certain NLP tasks may require focusing on specific parts of speech. For example, extracting adjectives and adverbs can be particularly useful in sentiment analysis, while focusing on nouns and proper nouns might be more relevant for named entity recognition and topic modeling. POS tagging enables this targeted processing, allowing for more efficient and effective analysis.

Part-of-Speech tagging's significance in NLP extends beyond mere grammatical labeling. It underpins the syntactic and semantic understanding of language, serving as a critical step in virtually all complex NLP tasks. The process of POS tagging enables machines to parse, interpret, and generate human language with a higher degree of accuracy and sophistication. As NLP technologies continue to advance, the role of POS tagging in enabling a deeper understanding of text and facilitating nuanced language processing remains indispensable, laying the groundwork for future innovations in the field.

Methodologies for POS Tagging

Rule-Based Approaches

Rule-based POS tagging utilizes a set of predefined linguistic rules developed by experts. These rules might involve grammatical relationships between words, specific suffixes or prefixes indicative of certain parts of speech, and contextual cues within a sentence. While rule-based approaches can achieve high accuracy in well-defined domains, they lack flexibility and scalability, especially across languages and diverse linguistic contexts.

Design and Implementation of Rule-Based POS Tagging

Rule-based POS tagging systems are built upon a comprehensive set of linguistic rules crafted by experts. These rules often incorporate patterns observed in the language, such as:

Morphological Cues: Rules may consider word endings or prefixes that are indicative of certain parts of speech. For example, words ending in "-ed" in English are often tagged as past-tense verbs.

Syntactic Clues: The syntactic structure of a sentence provides context for POS tagging. For instance, a word following a determiner ("the," "a") is likely to be a noun.

Contextual Information: Rule-based systems can utilize the context surrounding a word to disambiguate its part of speech. For example, if a word can be both a noun and a verb, its position relative to other parts of speech in the sentence can determine the correct tag.

These rules are applied sequentially or through a decision tree structure to analyze sentences and assign the most likely part of speech to each word based on the rule set.

Advantages of Rule-Based POS Tagging

- **Transparency:** Rule-based systems offer high transparency in their tagging decisions, as each decision can be traced back to specific linguistic rules. This makes rule-based tagging appealing for applications where explainability is important.

- **No Need for Annotated Corpora:** Unlike statistical or machine learning methods, rule-based POS tagging does not require large annotated corpora for training, making it suitable for languages or domains where such resources are scarce.

- **Consistency:** The application of consistent rule sets ensures uniform tagging across texts, which is beneficial for maintaining consistency in linguistic research and language teaching applications.

Limitations of Rule-Based POS Tagging

- **Complexity in Rule Creation:** Developing a comprehensive set of rules that can accurately capture the nuances of a language is a complex and time-consuming process, requiring deep linguistic expertise.

- **Lack of Scalability:** Rule-based systems can become unwieldy as the number of rules grows to cover the linguistic diversity of a language, impacting maintainability and performance.

- **Limited Generalization:** These systems may struggle to accurately tag ambiguous or context-dependent cases that are not explicitly covered by the rules, limiting their flexibility and adaptability to new texts or domains.

Rule-based approaches to Part-of-Speech tagging represent a critical step in the evolution of POS tagging methodologies. While these approaches have been largely supplanted by statistical and machine learning methods in many applications, their influence persists, particularly in the form of hybrid systems that incorporate rule-based logic to refine and improve tagging accuracy. Understanding the design, advantages, and limitations of rule-based POS tagging provides foundational knowledge essential for advancing NLP technologies and highlights the ongoing need for linguistic expertise in the development of automated language processing systems.

Statistical and Machine Learning Approaches

Statistical methods, such as Hidden Markov Models (HMMs), rely on the probabilities of tag sequences to assign parts of speech to words based on their distribution in a tagged corpus. Machine learning models, including decision trees and Support Vector Machines (SVMs), learn from features extracted from the training data to predict POS tags. These approaches can generalize better to unseen text compared to rule-based systems but require substantial annotated corpora for training.

Statistical Approaches

The advent of statistical methods marked a significant advancement in POS tagging, moving beyond the constraints of rule-based systems. Statistical POS taggers utilize probabilistic models to predict the most likely tag for a word based on its context within a sentence. These approaches rely on annotated corpora, using the patterns found in these datasets to infer the grammatical categories of words.

Hidden Markov Models (HMMs)

One of the earliest and most influential statistical approaches is the Hidden Markov Model (HMM). HMMs treat POS tagging as a sequence modeling problem, where the observable sequence consists of the words in the text, and the hidden sequence represents their corresponding POS tags. The model calculates the probability of a given tag sequence given the observed sequence of words, using this information to choose the most probable sequence of tags for new texts.

- **Training:** During the training phase, HMMs learn the transition probabilities between tags (how likely a tag is to follow another) and the emission probabilities (how likely a word is to be associated with a tag).

- **Viterbi Algorithm:** The Viterbi algorithm is commonly used for decoding, determining the most likely sequence of tags for a given sentence based on the probabilities learned during training.

Maximum Entropy Models

Maximum Entropy (MaxEnt) models represent another statistical approach, focusing on making predictions that are consistent with the constraints imposed by the training data while assuming nothing beyond this. MaxEnt models calculate the probability distribution of tags for a given word that best fits the training data, optimizing to prevent any additional assumptions about the data.

Machine Learning Approaches

As machine learning technologies evolved, they began to play a pivotal role in POS tagging, offering methods that could automatically learn features from data, reducing the need for manual rule creation and allowing for more flexibility and accuracy.

Support Vector Machines (SVMs)

SVMs have been applied to POS tagging by treating it as a classification problem where each word is classified into one of the possible tags. This method benefits from SVMs' ability to handle high-dimensional feature spaces, making it well-suited for text data.

Conditional Random Fields (CRFs)

CRFs, a type of discriminative probabilistic model, have become a popular choice for POS tagging. Unlike HMMs, CRFs do not assume independence between output tags, allowing them to model the conditional relationships between tags in a sequence directly. This feature makes CRFs particularly effective at capturing the dependencies and constraints inherent in linguistic structures.

Deep Learning Approaches

With the rise of deep learning, neural network models have increasingly been used for POS tagging. Recurrent Neural Networks (RNNs), and specifically Long Short-Term Memory (LSTM) networks, are well-suited for handling the sequential nature of text. More recently, Transformer-based models like BERT have set new standards for POS tagging accuracy, benefiting from their ability to capture contextual information from large unannotated corpora and fine-tune on smaller annotated datasets for specific tasks.

Statistical and machine learning approaches have revolutionized POS tagging, providing robust, flexible, and accurate methods for determining the grammatical structure of text. The ongoing development of machine learning models, particularly in deep learning, continues to push the boundaries of what is possible in POS tagging, contributing to the overall advancement of natural language understanding and processing.

Deep Learning Approaches

Deep learning models, particularly Recurrent Neural Networks (RNNs) and more recently, Transformer-based models like BERT, have set new standards for POS tagging accuracy. These models benefit from their ability to learn complex, contextual representations of words from large amounts of unannotated text, supplemented by fine-tuning on smaller annotated datasets. The capacity of deep learning models to capture long-range dependencies and nuances in word usage has significantly advanced POS tagging performance.

Recurrent Neural Networks (RNNs)

Recurrent Neural Networks (RNNs) marked the initial foray of deep learning into POS tagging. RNNs are particularly suited for sequential data like text, as they maintain a form of memory that captures information about what has been processed so far. In POS tagging, this allows RNNs to consider the context of a word within a sentence, leading to more accurate tag predictions.

Term Memory (LSTM) Networks:

A specialized type of RNN, LSTMs, are designed to overcome the limitations of traditional RNNs in learning long-range dependencies within text. LSTMs can remember important information over long sequences, making them highly effective for POS tagging across complex sentence structures.

Convolutional Neural Networks (CNNs)

While primarily known for their applications in image processing, Convolutional Neural Networks (CNNs) have also been adapted for POS tagging. CNNs can capture local dependencies in data through their convolutional layers. In the context of text, this translates to effectively identifying relevant patterns in word usage and sentence syntax that are indicative of specific grammatical categories.

- **Feature Extraction:** CNNs automatically learn to extract features from word embeddings (dense vector representations of words) that are useful for POS tagging, reducing the need for manual feature engineering.

Transformer Models

The introduction of Transformer models, such as BERT (Bidirectional Encoder Representations from Transformers), has set new benchmarks in POS tagging accuracy. Transformers utilize self-attention mechanisms to weigh the importance of different words in a sentence when predicting a tag for each word. This allows for a nuanced understanding of context, both from preceding and following words, which is a significant advantage over unidirectional models.

- **Contextualized Word Embeddings:** Transformer models generate embeddings that are context-dependent, meaning that the representation of a word can change based on its surrounding words. This is particularly beneficial for POS tagging, where the grammatical role of a word can vary widely with context.

Transfer Learning and Fine-tuning

A key strength of deep learning approaches, especially Transformer models, is their capacity for transfer learning. Models pre-trained on large corpora of text on general language understanding tasks can be fine-tuned on smaller, task-specific datasets for POS tagging. This process leverages the rich linguistic knowledge the models have acquired during pre-training, leading to improved performance even with limited labeled data for POS tagging.

Challenges and Solutions

While deep learning methods have dramatically improved POS tagging accuracy, they also present challenges, such as the need for large annotated datasets for training and substantial computational resources. However, innovations in model architecture, training techniques, and the availability of pre-trained models have helped mitigate these challenges, making advanced POS tagging accessible for a wide range of applications.

Deep learning approaches to Part-of-Speech tagging represent a significant advancement in the ability of machines to understand the grammatical structure of language by leveraging RNNs, CNNs, and especially Transformer models, NLP practitioners can achieve unparalleled accuracy in POS tagging, unlocking new possibilities for text analysis and interpretation. As deep learning continues to evolve, its application to POS tagging promises further insights into the complexities of language, enhancing the breadth and depth of NLP research and applications.

Applications of POS Tagging

Syntactic Parsing

POS tags are instrumental in constructing syntactic parse trees, which represent the grammatical structure of sentences. Parsing relies on POS tags to identify subjects, verbs, objects, and other sentence elements, facilitating the analysis of sentence syntax and structure.

Syntactic Parsing: An Overview

Syntactic parsing involves analyzing a sentence's grammatical structure to identify its constituent parts, such as nouns, verbs, adjectives, and adverbs, and how these parts are organized into larger phrases and clauses. The ultimate goal is to build a parse tree or a syntactic structure that represents the hierarchical organization of the sentence, revealing the relationships between words and phrases. This understanding is crucial for a wide range of NLP tasks, including machine translation, question answering, and natural language generation.

The Role of POS Tagging in Syntactic Parsing

POS tagging is instrumental in syntactic parsing for several reasons:

Disambiguation: Many words in natural languages can serve as more than one part of speech, depending on their context in a sentence. POS tagging helps disambiguate these words, providing crucial information for correctly parsing their grammatical roles. For instance, the word "run" can be a verb ("I will run") or a noun ("This is a long run"), and identifying the correct POS is essential for parsing the sentence structure accurately.

Grammar Rule Application: Syntactic parsers often rely on grammatical rules to construct parse trees. These rules are usually defined in terms of POS tags (e.g., a noun phrase might be defined as an optional determiner followed by adjectives and a noun). Accurate POS tagging is thus critical for the correct application of these rules and the successful construction of parse trees.

Improving Parsing Efficiency: By providing an initial layer of linguistic analysis, POS tagging can streamline the parsing process. Knowing the parts of speech of words allows parsers to narrow down the possible grammatical structures and apply more targeted parsing strategies, thereby improving both the speed and accuracy of syntactic parsing.

Applications and Implications

The accurate syntactic parsing facilitated by POS tagging has profound implications for various NLP applications:

Machine Translation: Understanding the syntactic structure of sentences is essential for translating text between languages that may have different word orders and grammatical rules. POS tagging enables more accurate syntactic parsing, which in turn supports the development of translation models that can better preserve the meaning and structure of the original text.

Information Extraction: Syntactic parsing, supported by POS tagging, allows for the extraction of structured information (such as subjects, objects, and actions) from unstructured text, enabling the automated population of databases and knowledge bases with information from documents, web pages, and other textual sources.

Natural Language Understanding: At a broader level, syntactic parsing contributes to the machine's ability to understand the meaning of text. By revealing the grammatical relationships between words, parsing helps computational models grasp the nuances of language, supporting more sophisticated understanding and generation of natural language.

Part-of-Speech tagging's contribution to syntactic parsing highlights its indispensable role in the NLP pipeline. By enabling accurate syntactic parsing, POS tagging lays the groundwork for deeper linguistic analysis and understanding, facilitating advancements in machine translation, information extraction, and beyond. As NLP technologies continue to evolve, the interplay between POS tagging and syntactic parsing will remain a key area of focus, driving progress in the field's quest to bridge the gap between human language and machine comprehension.

Text-to-Speech Conversion

In text-to-speech systems, POS tagging helps determine the correct pronunciation of words based on their parts of speech, particularly for words with multiple pronunciations. It also aids in generating appropriate intonation and rhythm, enhancing the naturalness of synthesized speech.

Enhancing Pronunciation Accuracy

One of the fundamental ways in which POS tagging contributes to TTS conversion is by improving pronunciation accuracy. English and many other languages contain words that are spelled the same but pronounced differently depending on their grammatical roles in sentences (i.e., heteronyms). POS tags help disambiguate these words, ensuring that the TTS system applies the correct pronunciation. For example, the word "lead" can be pronounced as /lɛd/ when used as a verb in the present tense ("I will lead the way") and /lid/ when used as a noun referring to a metal ("The pipes are made of lead"). POS tagging allows the TTS system to identify the grammatical category of each word and apply the appropriate pronunciation rule.

Improving Prosody and Intonation

Beyond pronunciation, POS tagging is instrumental in enhancing the prosody and intonation of synthesized speech. Prosody refers to the rhythm, stress, and intonation patterns in speech, which are crucial for conveying meaning, emotion, and emphasis. By analyzing the POS tags of words in a sentence, TTS systems can infer which words should be emphasized (e.g., adjectives and nouns often carry more semantic weight than articles and prepositions) and adjust the speech melody accordingly. This leads to synthesized speech that sounds more natural and expressive, closely mimicking human speech patterns.

Facilitating Syntactic Disambiguation

POS tagging aids in syntactic disambiguation, helping TTS systems navigate sentences with complex structures. By understanding the grammatical roles of words, TTS systems can better predict the syntactic boundaries within sentences, which in turn informs appropriate pausing and phrasing in speech synthesis. This is particularly important for long sentences or those with embedded clauses, where incorrect pausing can significantly alter the intended meaning or reduce the intelligibility of the speech output.

Supporting Multilingual TTS Systems

In multilingual TTS systems, POS tagging plays a vital role in adapting the speech synthesis process to the grammatical structures of different languages. Since grammatical categories and their implications for pronunciation, stress, and intonation vary across languages, POS tagging provides the necessary linguistic information to tailor the TTS conversion process to each language's specific characteristics. This enables the development of TTS systems that can effectively support a wide range of languages, enhancing accessibility and user experience for speakers of different linguistic backgrounds.

The application of Part-of-Speech tagging in text-to-speech conversion exemplifies the critical role of POS tagging in bridging the gap between textual data and spoken language. By informing pronunciation, prosody, intonation, and syntactic disambiguation, POS tagging contributes to the generation of synthesized speech that is not only accurate but also engaging and natural-sounding. As TTS technologies continue to advance, the integration of sophisticated POS tagging methodologies will remain a cornerstone in the quest to create more lifelike and effective speech synthesis systems, further expanding the capabilities and applications of natural language processing.

Information Extraction and Named Entity Recognition

POS tags provide cues for identifying potential named entities and extracting structured information from unstructured text. For instance, proper nouns tagged as such can be candidates for further analysis in NER systems.

Enhancing Information Extraction

Information Extraction involves processing text to extract structured data from unstructured sources. It encompasses tasks such as identifying specific facts, relationships, events, or entities from text. POS tagging contributes to this process by providing a deeper understanding of the grammatical structure of sentences, which is crucial for accurately identifying the components that constitute relevant information.

Facilitating Pattern Recognition: Many IE systems rely on linguistic patterns that often include specific parts of speech. For instance, a simple pattern might involve extracting noun phrases as potential entities and verbs as possible relations between entities. POS tags help in accurately identifying these phrases and their grammatical roles, thereby facilitating more precise pattern recognition.

Improving Relation Extraction: Relation extraction, a subtask of IE, benefits from POS tagging by identifying verbs and prepositions that often indicate relationships between entities. By understanding the grammatical structure through POS tags, IE systems can more accurately detect and categorize these relationships.

Empowering Named Entity Recognition

Named Entity Recognition aims to locate and classify entities within text into predefined categories such as person names, organizations, locations, etc. POS tagging significantly enhances NER by providing insights into the likely categories of words based on their grammatical context, thereby improving the identification and classification process.

- **Identifying Entity Candidates:** POS tags help in narrowing down potential named entity candidates. For example, proper nouns (tagged as NNP in many tagging schemes) are more likely to be names of people, organizations, or locations. This information allows NER systems to focus on more likely entity candidates, improving both accuracy and efficiency.

- **Supporting Contextual Analysis:** The context in which a word appears is crucial for determining its role as a named entity. POS tags contribute to understanding this context by delineating the grammatical structure of sentences. Verbs, adjectives, and other POS tags provide cues about the possible nature of neighboring nouns or proper nouns, aiding in the disambiguation and accurate classification of entities.

Synergizing with Other NLP Tasks

The integration of POS tagging with NER and IE is emblematic of the interconnected nature of NLP tasks, where the output of one process enriches the input of another. POS tagging not only facilitates entity recognition and information extraction directly but also synergizes with syntactic parsing, dependency analysis, and other linguistic processing steps to create a comprehensive understanding of text structure and meaning.

The application of Part-of-Speech tagging in Information Extraction and Named Entity Recognition underscores its critical role in the NLP ecosystem. By providing essential insights into the grammatical structure of text, POS tagging enhances the accuracy and efficiency of extracting and classifying valuable information from vast and varied textual datasets. As NLP continues to advance, the integration of POS tagging with IE and NER will remain a cornerstone of efforts to mine, analyze, and interpret the wealth of knowledge contained within natural language, driving forward innovations in information retrieval, data analysis, and artificial intelligence.

Language Learning and Linguistic Research

POS tagging is a valuable tool in language learning applications and linguistic research, offering insights into the grammatical composition of texts. It facilitates the study of language patterns, grammatical trends, and the development of educational tools.

Facilitating Language Learning

POS tagging significantly aids in the process of language learning by providing clear examples of how words function in various grammatical contexts. Understanding the role of words in sentences is crucial for language learners, as it helps in mastering syntax, expanding vocabulary, and improving writing and speaking skills.

Grammar Teaching: By illustrating the grammatical categories of words within real-life sentence examples, POS tagging helps learners grasp complex grammatical concepts. Automated tagging can support interactive learning platforms, offering instant feedback on sentence construction exercises.

Reading Comprehension: POS-tagged texts can enhance reading comprehension by allowing learners to analyze sentence structure and understand the role of each word in conveying meaning. This analysis can be particularly beneficial for advanced learners delving into more complex texts.

Language Proficiency Assessment: Automated POS tagging can assist in evaluating language proficiency by analyzing learners' written or spoken outputs. The accuracy and appropriateness of word usage in different grammatical contexts serve as indicators of language mastery.

Advancing Linguistic Research

POS tagging has revolutionized linguistic research by enabling the automated analysis of large corpora of text. This capability allows researchers to uncover patterns, trends, and anomalies in language use that would be difficult, if not impossible, to detect manually.

Corpus Linguistics: POS tagging is essential in corpus linguistics, where researchers study the frequency and distribution of words and their parts of speech across large text corpora. These analyses can reveal insights into language evolution, dialectical variations, and genre-specific language use.

Syntax and Grammar Analysis: Linguists utilize POS-tagged data to investigate syntactic structures and grammatical phenomena. This research can lead to refined grammatical theories and enhance understanding of complex linguistic constructs.

Computational Models of Language: POS tagging contributes to the development of computational models that simulate human language understanding. These models rely on accurately tagged data to learn the rules and patterns of language, which can then be applied in machine translation, text generation, and other AI-driven language tasks.

Part-of-Speech tagging emerges as a pivotal technology bridging computational methods with the nuanced study of language. Its application in language learning opens up new pathways for interactive and effective education, while its role in linguistic research pushes the boundaries of our understanding of language structure and use. By automating the labor-intensive process of grammatical tagging, POS technology enables a more in-depth and broad-scale analysis of language than ever before, driving forward both academic inquiry and practical language acquisition efforts. As NLP technologies evolve, the integration of POS tagging into language learning platforms and linguistic research methodologies will undoubtedly continue to offer profound insights and innovative solutions to age-old challenges in the study and teaching of language.

Rule-Based and Machine Learning:

The exploration of Named Entity Recognition (NER) and Part-of-Speech (POS) tagging is presented through the lens of both rule-based and machine learning-based approaches. These methodologies underpin the evolution and effectiveness of NER and POS tagging within the domain of Natural Language Processing (NLP), each contributing unique strengths and facing distinct challenges. This comprehensive overview delves into the specifics of these approaches, elucidating their application, advantages, and limitations in the context of NER and POS tagging tasks.

Rule-Based Approaches

Rule-based systems for NER and POS tagging rely on a set of predefined linguistic rules. These rules are crafted by experts to identify entities and grammatical categories based on patterns in the text, such as word endings, capitalization, context, and placement within a sentence.

Application in NER and POS Tagging

NER: Rule-based NER systems might use lexicons of person names, organization names, and location names, along with patterns that frequently indicate named entities (e.g., titles like "Mr." or "Dr." preceding names).

POS Tagging: For POS tagging, rules may include identifying verbs by their placement relative to subjects or objects in a sentence, recognizing adjectives by their position adjacent to nouns, or using suffixes that are common to certain parts of speech.

Advantages

- **High Precision:** When the rules are well-defined and the domain is limited, rule-based systems can achieve high precision.

- **Interpretability:** The transparent nature of rule-based systems allows for easy interpretation and debugging of the tagging process.

- **No Need for Annotated Data:** Rule-based approaches do not require large corpora of annotated data for training, making them useful in scenarios where such data is scarce.

Limitations

Scalability and Flexibility: Developing and maintaining a comprehensive set of rules for large or diverse datasets is labor-intensive and often impractical.

Domain-Specificity: Rule-based systems are typically tailored to specific domains or languages and may not generalize well across different contexts.

Complexity of Language: Capturing the nuances and variations of natural language through a finite set of rules is inherently challenging.

Machine Learning-Based Approaches

Machine learning-based approaches for NER and POS tagging learn to identify entities and parts of speech from annotated training data, using statistical patterns and features extracted from the text.

Application in NER and POS Tagging

- **NER:** Machine learning models for NER learn from examples of text annotated with named entities to identify patterns and features indicative of entities in new texts.

- **POS Tagging:** Similarly, machine learning models for POS tagging are trained on corpora where each word is labeled with its part of speech, allowing the models to learn the contextual and morphological cues that predict grammatical categories.

Advantages

Generalization: Machine learning models can generalize from the training data to accurately tag new, unseen texts, adapting to variations and nuances in language use.

Scalability: Once trained, machine learning models can process large volumes of text efficiently, making them suitable for large-scale NLP tasks.

Language and Domain Adaptability: With sufficient annotated data, machine learning models can be adapted to different languages and domains.

Limitations

- **Dependence on Annotated Data:** The performance of machine learning models is heavily reliant on the quantity and quality of the annotated data used for training.

- **Model Complexity:** Some machine learning models, especially deep learning models, can be complex and opaque, making it difficult to understand the basis for specific tagging decisions.

- **Computational Resources:** Training sophisticated machine learning models for NER and POS tagging can require significant computational resources and expertise.

The juxtaposition of rule-based and machine learning-based approaches for tasks such as NER and POS tagging illuminates the broad spectrum of methodologies available in NLP. While rule-based systems offer precision and interpretability, especially in constrained domains, machine learning approaches provide scalability, adaptability, and the ability to capture the complexities of natural language through data-driven learning. As NLP continues to advance, the integration and evolution of both rule-based and machine learning-based strategies will remain central to developing more sophisticated, accurate, and efficient tools for language understanding and processing.

Deep learning models for NER and POS:

The evolution of Named Entity Recognition (NER) and Part-of-Speech (POS) tagging is marked by the adoption of deep learning models, significantly enhancing the capability and accuracy of these tasks. Among these models, Bidirectional Long Short-Term Memory networks (BiLSTMs), Conditional Random Fields (CRFs), and Transformers stand out as pivotal technologies.

Bidirectional Long Short-Term Memory Networks (BiLSTMs)

BiLSTMs extend the architecture of traditional LSTM units to efficiently process sequences from both directions. This bidirectional approach enables the model to capture context more comprehensively, considering both past and future input features for each element in the sequence.

NER and POS Tagging Applications

Contextual Understanding: BiLSTMs excel in understanding the context surrounding each word, making them exceptionally well-suited for tasks like POS tagging and NER, where the meaning and categorization of words can significantly depend on surrounding words.

Sequence Modeling: The ability to model sequences makes BiLSTMs ideal for NER and POS tagging, as they can learn the dependencies and relationships between words in a sentence or document.

Conditional Random Fields (CRFs)

CRFs are statistical modeling methods tailored for structured prediction. While CRFs themselves are not deep learning models, their integration with deep learning architectures like BiLSTMs creates a powerful combination for sequence tagging tasks.

Enhancing Deep Learning Models

Tagging Coherence: CRFs, when used as the final layer in deep learning models, ensure coherent and contextually consistent tagging outputs by considering the entire sequence of tags simultaneously, thereby optimizing the sequence of predicted labels.

Transformers

The introduction of Transformer models has significantly shifted the landscape of NLP, including NER and POS tagging. These models utilize self-attention mechanisms to process all parts of the input data simultaneously, offering a departure from the sequential processing inherent in RNNs and LSTMs.

Revolutionizing NER and POS Tagging

Contextualized Word Representations: Transformer models like BERT provide deep, contextualized word representations, capturing subtle nuances of language usage and meaning from extensive pre-training on large corpora. These representations serve as a robust foundation for fine-tuning on specific NLP tasks, including NER and POS tagging.

Efficiency and Scalability: By processing input data in parallel rather than sequentially, Transformers achieve remarkable efficiency and scalability, handling longer sequences and larger datasets more effectively than previous models.

Transfer Learning: The ability to transfer learning from pre-trained models to specific NER and POS tagging tasks with relatively small amounts of task-specific data reduces the barrier to entry for these advanced models, democratizing access to state-of-the-art NLP capabilities.

Synergy and Integration

The integration of CRFs with deep learning models like BiLSTMs and the advent of Transformer models represent a confluence of technologies that bolster the accuracy and efficiency of NER and POS tagging. BiLSTMs provide a robust mechanism for understanding sequential data, CRFs ensure the coherence of tagging sequences, and Transformers offer unparalleled contextual awareness and efficiency.

Combining BiLSTMs and CRFs: A common approach for NER and POS tagging is to use a BiLSTM to capture sequential and contextual information, followed by a CRF layer to optimize the sequence of tags based on the entire sequence's context.

Leveraging Transformers: Transformer models, with their pre-trained, contextualized embeddings, serve as a powerful stand-alone solution for NER and POS tagging, often surpassing models that combine BiLSTMs and CRFs in terms of accuracy and efficiency.

Deep learning models for NER and POS tagging underscore the rapid advancements in NLP technologies. BiLSTMs, CRFs, and Transformers each play distinct yet complementary roles in pushing the boundaries of what's possible in understanding and processing natural language. As NLP continues to evolve, the ongoing development and application of these models will undoubtedly lead to even more sophisticated and nuanced language understanding capabilities, marking a new era in the field of natural language processing.

Conclusion

Named Entity Recognition and Part-of-Speech Tagging are indispensable processes in NLP, laying the groundwork for sophisticated linguistic analysis and natural language understanding, as detailed in "Natural Language Processing (NLP): The Complete Guide." By accurately identifying entities and grammatical structures within text, these techniques enable a wide array of applications, from enhancing search and discovery to powering complex conversational agents. As NLP continues to evolve, the methodologies and applications of NER and POS tagging will remain central to unlocking the rich semantic and syntactic layers of language, driving forward innovations in machine understanding of human communication.

Chapter 6: Text Summarization and Generation

The realms of text summarization and generation are explored as pivotal areas that leverage the advancements in NLP to condense and create textual content, respectively. These tasks not only demonstrate the practical applications of NLP technologies but also underscore the evolving relationship between humans and machines in processing and generating language.

Text Summarization

Text summarization aims to produce a concise and coherent summary of a longer text document or a collection of documents. The goal is to retain the most critical information and present it in a condensed form. Summarization techniques can be broadly categorized into extractive and abstractive approaches.

Extractive Summarization

Extractive summarization involves selecting significant sentences or phrases from the original text and compiling them to form a summary. This method relies on algorithms to score and rank text segments based on features such as frequency, relevance, and the structure of the text.

- **Methodologies:** Traditional approaches include heuristic methods, where the importance of sentences is determined by specific criteria, and machine learning methods that learn to identify key sentences based on annotated datasets. More recently, deep learning models like recurrent neural networks (RNNs) and transformers have been applied to better capture the context and significance of text segments.

Abstractive Summarization

Abstractive summarization goes beyond merely extracting sentences; it involves generating new text that conveys the essential information in the original document. This approach aims to produce summaries that are more coherent and readable, often resembling how a human might summarize text.

- **Methodologies:** Early attempts at abstractive summarization relied on natural language generation techniques based on linguistic rules. The advent of deep learning, particularly sequence-to-sequence (Seq2Seq) models and transformers like GPT (Generative Pre-trained Transformer) and BERT, has significantly advanced abstractive summarization. These models can generate summaries by understanding and paraphrasing the content of the source text.

Text Generation

Text generation involves automatically creating coherent and contextually relevant text based on given inputs. This task encompasses a wide range of applications, from writing assistance to content creation and conversational agents.

Methodologies

- **Rule-Based Systems:** Initial text generation systems were based on sets of rules designed to produce text from structured data. While these systems could generate grammatically correct text, they often lacked flexibility and creativity.

- **Statistical and Machine Learning Approaches:** Statistical models, including n-gram models and hidden Markov models (HMMs), offered improvements by learning to generate text based on the probability of sequences of words. The introduction of machine learning and particularly deep learning models, such as Seq2Seq models and transformers, has revolutionized text generation. These models can learn complex patterns in large datasets, enabling the generation of text that is not only coherent and contextually relevant but also creative and varied.

Applications

- **Automated Reporting:** Both summarization and generation are used in automated reporting systems for finance, sports, and weather, where structured data is translated into narrative text.

- **Content Creation:** AI-driven content creation tools use text generation to produce articles, stories, and marketing copy, often starting from simple prompts or outlines.

- **Conversational Agents:** Chatbots and virtual assistants use text generation to produce natural-sounding responses based on user inputs, improving human-computer interaction.

- **Assistive Technologies:** Summarization helps distill critical information from lengthy texts for users with reading difficulties or for those needing quick insights.

Extractive And Abstractive Text Summarization Techniques:

A significant emphasis is placed on text summarization, a fundamental task in NLP aimed at distilling the most important information from a source text into a shorter form. Text summarization techniques are broadly classified into two categories: extractive and abstractive summarization. Each approach employs distinct methodologies to achieve the goal of summarization, catering to different needs and applications within the realm of NLP.

Extractive Text Summarization

Extractive summarization involves identifying key sentences or segments in the source text and compiling them into a summary without altering the original text. This technique hinges on the ability to assess the importance of each sentence and select those that encapsulate the core information or themes of the text.

Methodologies

Frequency-Based Methods:

Early approaches often relied on the frequency of significant words or phrases to determine sentence importance, assuming that sentences containing a higher number of key terms are more likely to be relevant to the main topic.

Frequency-based methods for extractive text summarization operate on the principle that the recurrence of certain words and phrases within a text is indicative of their importance to the overall theme or subject matter. These methods employ statistical measures to identify and rank sentences based on the presence of frequently occurring terms.

Term Frequency (TF)

- **Definition:** Term Frequency measures how frequently a term appears in a document. The underlying assumption is that terms appearing more often are more relevant to the document's main topic.

- **Application in Summarization:** In extractive summarization, sentences containing a higher number of high-frequency terms are deemed more important and are thus more likely to be included in the summary.

Term Frequency-Inverse Document Frequency (TF-IDF)

- **Definition:** TF-IDF extends the concept of TF by also considering the term's frequency across a set of documents (corpus). The idea is to reduce the weight of terms that are common across documents (and thus less informative) while highlighting terms that are frequent in a specific document but rare in others.

- **Application in Summarization:** TF-IDF can be used to score sentences based on the weighted importance of their terms, selecting those with higher scores for the summary. This approach helps in identifying sentences that contain terms unique and central to the document.

Stop Words Removal and Filtering

- **Process:** Frequency-based summarization often involves preprocessing steps such as the removal of stop words (commonly used words of little value in deciding sentence importance, like "the," "is," "at," etc.) and filtering based on part-of-speech tags to focus on nouns and verbs primarily.

- **Impact:** These preprocessing steps ensure that the frequency counts and subsequent rankings are not skewed by common but uninformative words, thereby improving the relevance of selected sentences for the summary.

Advantages and Challenges

Advantages

- **Simplicity and Efficiency:** Frequency-based methods are relatively straightforward to implement and do not require complex computational resources, making them accessible for a wide range of applications.

- **No Need for Annotated Data:** These methods do not require training on annotated corpora, contrasting with machine learning approaches that necessitate large datasets of pre-summarized texts.

Challenges

- **Lack of Contextual Awareness:** Frequency-based methods may overlook the nuanced context and semantic relationships between terms, potentially affecting the coherence and quality of the summary.

- **Overemphasis on Common Themes:** There's a risk that these methods might favor sentences that reflect the most common themes, possibly at the expense of important but less frequently mentioned details or viewpoints.

   While their simplicity and efficiency are notable advantages, the evolution of summarization techniques—especially those incorporating advanced statistical models and deep learning—continues to expand the toolkit available for extractive summarization. These advancements aim to address the inherent limitations of frequency-based methods, pushing towards summaries that better capture the depth and breadth of source texts.

Graph-Based Models:

Techniques such as TextRank use the relationships between sentences, modeled as a graph, to compute sentence importance based on centrality measures, treating sentences as nodes and their similarities as edges.

Principles of Graph-Based Models

Graph-based models for extractive text summarization construct a graph where nodes represent text units (typically sentences), and edges denote the relationships or similarities between these units. The core idea is to use graph theory to analyze the text structure, leveraging metrics like centrality to determine the importance of each node (sentence) in the overall text network.

Text Representation as Graphs

- **Node Representation:** Each node in the graph corresponds to a sentence or paragraph in the text. The representation of text as nodes allows the model to process the document structurally and relationally.

- **Edge Construction:** Edges between nodes are established based on measures of similarity, which can be calculated through various methods, including cosine similarity of TF-IDF vectors, overlap of key terms, or semantic similarity metrics. These connections reflect the contextual and thematic relationships between text segments.

250

Centrality and Ranking

- **Centrality Measures:** Once the graph is constructed, centrality measures such as PageRank or betweenness centrality are applied to identify the most "central" nodes in the graph. These central nodes are presumed to hold the most informational value or to be most representative of the text's overall content.

- **Sentence Selection:** Sentences corresponding to nodes with the highest centrality scores are selected for inclusion in the summary. This selection is predicated on the assumption that sentences most connected to others are likely to contain key information about the text.

Applications of Graph-Based Models

Graph-based models are particularly effective in tasks requiring an understanding of the document's global structure and the interrelation of its parts, such as:

- **Multi-document Summarization:** These models excel in summarizing multiple documents by creating a unified graph that captures the similarities and differences across texts, helping to identify common themes or unique insights.

- **Content Overview:** Graph-based summarization can provide a coherent overview of lengthy documents or collections of documents by identifying the most central and informative sentences.

Strengths of Graph-Based Models

Contextual Awareness

Unlike frequency-based methods that might miss the broader context in which terms are used, graph-based models inherently consider the relationships between sentences, offering a more holistic view of the text's structure and thematic connections.

Flexibility

Graph-based summarization techniques are adaptable to various domains and languages since they rely on structural properties of the text rather than language-specific features. This universality makes them particularly versatile.

Scalability

These models can efficiently process large volumes of text, including multi-document collections, by leveraging scalable graph algorithms. This scalability is crucial for applications like news aggregation or literature review analysis.

By modeling text as a network of interconnected units, these models illuminate the most central and informative segments, enabling the creation of coherent and comprehensive summaries. As NLP technologies continue to evolve, the integration of graph-based models in extractive summarization tasks underscores the ongoing quest for more nuanced and context-aware methods of understanding and condensing written content.

Machine Learning Models:

Supervised learning models can be trained on annotated datasets to identify features that contribute to a sentence's importance, including positional cues, cue words, and syntactic structures.

Machine Learning Models for Extractive Summarization

Machine learning models for extractive text summarization are trained to evaluate and score sentences based on their likelihood of being included in a summary. This process typically involves two main steps: feature extraction and model training.

Feature Extraction

The first step in preparing data for machine learning-based summarization is to extract features from the text that can be indicative of a sentence's importance. Common features include:

- **Statistical Features:** Such as term frequency, sentence position, sentence length, and the presence of named entities or numerals.

- **Syntactic Features:** Including POS tag distributions, which can help the model understand the grammatical structure of sentences.

- **Semantic Features:** Such as the similarity of a sentence to the document's title or to other sentences, which can be measured using techniques like TF-IDF vectors or embeddings.

Model Training

Once features are extracted, various machine learning algorithms can be applied to train a model. The choice of algorithm can vary based on the task's complexity, the size of the dataset, and the desired accuracy.

- **Supervised Learning Models:** Algorithms like decision trees, support vector machines (SVM), and neural networks are commonly used. These models are trained on annotated datasets where sentences are labeled as either 'summary-worthy' or not.

- **Deep Learning Approaches:** More recently, deep learning models, especially those based on recurrent neural networks (RNNs) and transformers, have shown superior performance in extractive summarization by capturing the contextual relationships between sentences more effectively.

Advantages of Machine Learning Models

- **Adaptability:** Machine learning models can adapt to different genres or styles of text, as long as they are trained on representative data.

- **Scalability:** Once trained, these models can summarize new texts quickly and efficiently, making them suitable for applications that need to process large volumes of information.

- **Contextual Understanding:** Advanced models, particularly deep learning-based ones, excel at understanding the context and nuances of language, enabling them to identify relevant sentences more accurately.

Challenges and Considerations

- **Dependency on Annotated Data:** Supervised models require large annotated datasets for training, which can be resource-intensive to create.

- **Model Complexity:** Deep learning models, while effective, can be complex and computationally expensive, necessitating significant hardware and time investment.

- **Interpretability:** Machine learning models, especially deep learning ones, often act as "black boxes," making it difficult to understand the rationale behind their decisions. This can be a concern for applications where explainability is crucial.

By leveraging the advancements in machine learning and deep learning, these models offer powerful tools for identifying and extracting key information from documents, catering to the growing need for efficient information processing in the digital age. As the field of NLP progresses, the development and refinement of machine learning methodologies for extractive summarization will continue to be a key area of research, driven by the dual goals of improving summarization quality and meeting the scalability demands of real-world applications.

Advantages and Challenges

- **Advantages:** Extractive summarization maintains the original phrasing and factual accuracy since it directly uses sentences from the source text. It is also computationally less demanding than abstractive methods.

- **Challenges:** A key limitation is the potential lack of coherence in the generated summary, as selected sentences might not seamlessly connect. Additionally, extractive summaries may include redundant information if similar sentences are chosen.

Abstractive Text Summarization

Abstractive summarization goes beyond mere extraction, aiming to paraphrase and condense the original text. This approach generates new sentences that capture the essence of the source content, often resulting in summaries that are more coherent and succinct than extractive counterparts.

Methodologies

- **Sequence-to-Sequence (Seq2Seq) Models:** These models, often based on Recurrent Neural Networks (RNNs) or Long Short-Term Memory (LSTM) networks, map the input text to an internal representation, which is then used to generate a summary.

- **Attention Mechanisms:** The integration of attention mechanisms allows the model to focus on different parts of the source text while generating each word of the summary, improving relevance and coherence.

- **Transformers and Pre-trained Models:** Transformer architectures, particularly pre-trained models like BERT and GPT, have significantly advanced abstractive summarization. These models leverage vast amounts of data to learn complex language patterns, enabling them to generate summaries that closely mimic human paraphrasing.

Advantages and Challenges

- **Advantages:** Abstractive summaries can be more natural and concise, often providing better readability and a clearer overview of the source text's main points.

They allow for the inclusion of synthesis and interpretation, akin to human-generated summaries.

- **Challenges:** High computational complexity and the need for large, annotated datasets for training are significant hurdles. There's also a greater risk of factual inaccuracies or distortions since the generated text may inadvertently introduce or omit critical information.

Extractive and abstractive text summarization techniques, offer distinct approaches to condensing text, each with its own set of strengths and limitations. Extractive methods excel in preserving the original text's accuracy, while abstractive techniques provide summaries that are more fluid and succinct, akin to human summarization. The choice between these methods depends on the specific requirements of the application, including the desired summary length, coherence, and the feasibility of training complex models. As NLP technologies continue to evolve, the development and refinement of both extractive and abstractive summarization methods will remain central to the ongoing quest to automate the understanding and condensation of written content.

Summarization Using Graph-Based Algorithms:

Text summarization techniques are meticulously explored, with a notable focus on the use of graph-based algorithms and clustering. These approaches represent a sophisticated blend of computational linguistics and data science principles, tailored to distill essential information from vast texts or multiple documents. By leveraging the interconnectedness of textual elements and the natural grouping of similar content, these methodologies provide powerful tools for automated summary generation.

Graph-Based Algorithms in Text Summarization

Graph-based algorithms for text summarization construct a graph where nodes represent textual units (such as sentences or paragraphs), and edges denote the relationships (typically similarity or relevance) between these units. The essence of this approach lies in identifying the most central nodes in the graph, under the premise that these nodes contain the key information to be included in the summary.

Methodology

Construction of the Graph:

Text units are represented as nodes, and edges are established based on a similarity measure (e.g., cosine similarity of TF-IDF vectors). This setup models the text as a network, capturing the intricate relationships between different segments.

Constructing the Graph: A Step-by-Step Process

The construction of the graph for text summarization involves several key steps, each contributing to the transformation of unstructured text into a network of interrelated nodes (typically representing sentences or paragraphs) and edges (representing the relationships between these nodes).

Text Unit Identification

- **Node Representation:** The first step involves identifying the textual units that will be represented as nodes in the graph. In extractive summarization, these units are often individual sentences, but they can also be paragraphs or other text segments, depending on the granularity desired.

*   **Normalization:** Text units are preprocessed and normalized to facilitate accurate comparison and similarity measurement. This may include steps like lowercasing, stop word removal, stemming, or lemmatization.

Similarity Measurement

*   **Edge Establishment:** Edges between nodes are created based on a measure of similarity or relevance between the text units they represent. The choice of similarity measure is crucial, as it determines the structure and quality of the graph.

*   **Techniques for Similarity Measurement:** Common approaches include cosine similarity of TF-IDF vectors, Jaccard similarity for overlap of key terms, and more sophisticated methods leveraging word embeddings or semantic analysis to capture deeper relationships.

Graph Representation

*   **Weighted vs. Unweighted Edges:** The graph can be constructed with either weighted or unweighted edges. Weighted edges incorporate the degree of similarity between nodes directly into the graph structure, allowing for more nuanced analysis of node centrality and importance.

*   **Directed vs. Undirected Graphs:** While most summarization graphs are undirected, reflecting mutual similarity, directed graphs can be used in scenarios

where the directionality of relationships (e.g., temporal or causal sequences) is relevant.

Significance of Graph Construction in Text Summarization

The methodology of constructing the graph is foundational to the effectiveness of graph-based summarization approaches. The graph not only visualizes the text's structure but also encodes semantic and contextual relationships between its parts. This structured representation enables the application of graph theory and network analysis techniques to identify the most informative components of the text.

- **Centrality Analysis:** Various centrality measures, such as PageRank or betweenness centrality, can be applied to identify key nodes that are most central to the graph. These nodes, corresponding to the most significant text units, are prime candidates for inclusion in the summary.

- **Clustering within the Graph:** For methods incorporating clustering, the graph's structure facilitates the identification of densely connected subgraphs or communities. These clusters can represent different themes or topics within the text, guiding the selection of diverse and representative content for the summary.

By transforming unstructured text into a structured network of interconnected units, this methodology lays the groundwork for advanced analysis and selection processes that underpin effective summarization. The thoughtful representation of text as a graph not only captures its informational content but also the intricate relationships that give context and coherence to the narrative, enabling the generation of summaries that are both informative and reflective of the text's complexity.

Centrality Measurement:

Techniques like PageRank or other centrality metrics are employed to identify the most significant nodes. These central nodes are presumed to encapsulate the core themes or topics of the text.

Principles of Centrality Measurement

Centrality measurement in graph-based text summarization aims to identify nodes (textual units) that hold the most informational weight or are most representative of the document's content. Several centrality metrics can be applied, each offering a different perspective on what constitutes a 'central' node:

PageRank

- **Overview:** Originally designed for ranking web pages, PageRank is a widely used centrality measure in text summarization. It operates on the principle that nodes are important if they are linked to by other important nodes.

- **Application:** In text summarization, PageRank helps identify sentences that are most central to the information flow within the document, assuming that a sentence linked to by many other significant sentences is likely to be of high importance.

Betweenness Centrality

- **Overview:** Betweenness centrality measures the extent to which a node lies on the shortest paths between other nodes in the graph. It highlights nodes that serve as critical bridges within the network.

- **Application:** Sentences with high betweenness centrality are often crucial for maintaining the coherence of the summary, as they may connect diverse topics or ideas within the text.

Eigenvector Centrality

- **Overview:** Similar to PageRank, eigenvector centrality considers a node's importance to be proportional to the sum of the importances of the nodes it is connected to. It differs in its calculation, focusing on the eigenvectors of the adjacency matrix of the graph.

- **Application:** This metric is used to identify sentences that are not only significant but also connected to other significant sentences, ensuring the inclusion of content that is deeply embedded in the text's thematic structure.

Applications of Centrality Measurement in Text Summarization

Centrality measurement is pivotal for extractive summarization, guiding the selection of sentences that best represent the core information or narrative of the document. By applying these metrics, summarization systems can:

- **Generate Coherent Summaries:** Select sentences that contribute to a cohesive and comprehensive understanding of the document, maintaining logical flow and thematic integrity.

- **Ensure Content Diversity:** Identify key sentences across different parts of the document or from diverse topics, preventing the summary from being dominated by a single theme.

Advantages and Challenges

Advantages

- **Insight into Textual Structure:** Centrality measurement offers valuable insights into the structural and thematic organization of the text, beyond mere surface-level features.

- **Adaptability:** Various centrality metrics can be applied depending on the specific goals of the summarization task, whether focusing on thematic representation, narrative flow, or information density.

Challenges

- **Complexity of Computation:** For large documents or multi-document summarization tasks, the computation of centrality measures can become computationally intensive.

- **Selection of Appropriate Metric:** Choosing the most suitable centrality metric for a given text or summarization objective requires a deep understanding of both the text's nature and the implications of different centrality measures.

Through the strategic application of centrality metrics, summarization systems can discern the most informative and representative units of text, crafting summaries that are both concise and reflective of the original document's complexity. As the field of NLP advances, exploring and optimizing centrality measurement methodologies will continue to be crucial for enhancing the efficacy and efficiency of text summarization techniques, enabling more nuanced and insightful distillations of information.

Extraction of Summary:

Sentences corresponding to the highest-ranked nodes are extracted to form the summary. The selection process may also consider diversity to avoid redundancy and ensure a broad coverage of topics.

Techniques for Summary Extraction

Selecting Central Nodes

- **Rank-Based Selection:** Following centrality measurement, nodes (typically sentences) are ranked based on their centrality scores. The extraction process involves selecting the top-ranked nodes. The number of nodes selected may be predetermined or based on a proportion of the original text length.

- **Diversity Consideration:** To ensure that the summary covers a broad range of topics or themes present in the text, algorithms may incorporate diversity measures to select nodes that not only have high centrality scores but also represent different clusters or subtopics within the graph.

Handling Redundancy

- **Redundancy Elimination:** A common challenge in extractive summarization is avoiding redundancy, as central nodes may contain overlapping information. Techniques such as MMR (Maximal Marginal Relevance) can be employed to balance the relevance and novelty of selected sentences, ensuring that each contributes unique information to the summary.

- **Cluster-Based Extraction:** In methods that involve clustering, one approach is to extract one or more representative sentences from each identified cluster. This ensures that the summary encompasses a comprehensive overview of all major themes in the text.

Summary Construction

- **Preserving Logical Flow:** Extracted sentences are arranged to preserve the logical and narrative flow of the original text. This may involve ordering sentences based on their appearance in the source document or employing more sophisticated methods to reconstruct a coherent narrative.

- **Post-Extraction Refinement:** The draft summary may undergo additional refinement, including adjusting sentence transitions, ensuring coherence, and fine-tuning the length of the summary to meet specific requirements.

Challenges and Considerations

- **Balancing Brevity and Comprehensiveness:** One of the key challenges in summary extraction is balancing the need for brevity with the desire to provide a comprehensive overview of the text. Achieving this balance requires careful selection and prioritization of content.

- **Context Preservation:** Ensuring that the extracted summary maintains the context and significance of the original text is crucial. This involves not only selecting central nodes but also understanding the relationships and dependencies between them.

- **Scalability and Efficiency:** The extraction process must be scalable and efficient, capable of summarizing large volumes of text or multiple documents within a reasonable timeframe.

By leveraging the structural and thematic relationships within texts, these methodologies facilitate the generation of summaries that are not only concise but also richly informative and representative of the source material. As NLP continues to evolve, the refinement of summary extraction techniques will remain at the forefront of efforts to enhance our ability to distill and communicate the essential contents of vast and varied textual landscapes, underscoring the transformative potential of advanced NLP technologies in the realm of text summarization and generation.

Advantages

- **Flexibility:** Graph-based summarization is adaptable across different types of texts and domains, as it relies on the universal principle of relational significance among text units.

- **Context Preservation:** By considering the entire text network, graph-based methods maintain a high level of contextual integrity, ensuring that the extracted summary is representative of the original content.

- **Scalability:** This approach is effective for both single-document and multi-document summarization tasks, capable of handling large datasets efficiently.

Clustering for Text Summarization

Clustering involves grouping text units based on similarity, aiming to identify natural clusters that represent the main themes or topics in the text. Summaries are then generated by selecting representative sentences from each cluster, ensuring a comprehensive overview of the text's content.

Methodology

- **Feature Extraction:** Initially, features are extracted from the text to represent each unit in a multidimensional space, often using techniques like TF-IDF or word embeddings.

- **Clustering Algorithm Application:** Algorithms such as K-means, hierarchical clustering, or DBSCAN are applied to group similar text units into clusters. The choice of algorithm depends on the specific characteristics of the text and the desired granularity of the summary.

- **Representative Selection:** For each cluster, representative sentences are selected based on criteria such as centrality within the cluster or closeness to the cluster centroid.

Advantages

- **Comprehensiveness:** Clustering ensures that the summary covers a broad range of topics or themes present in the original text, providing a holistic overview.

- **Efficiency:** This approach can significantly reduce the volume of text to be processed in the later stages of summarization, particularly in multi-document summarization tasks.

- **Adaptability:** Clustering methods can adjust to the inherent structure and thematic diversity of the text, making them versatile across various summarization contexts.

As the field of NLP advances, the exploration and optimization of these techniques will continue to enhance our ability to synthesize and interpret the ever-growing expanse of digital text, paving the way for more intelligent and efficient information processing systems.

Neural Approaches to Text Summarization:

These models have revolutionized the field of natural language processing by enabling machines to transform input sequences into output sequences, a capability that is particularly well-suited to tasks like text summarization. This section delves into the neural underpinnings of Seq2Seq models, their application in text summarization, and the advancements they have brought to the domain.

Overview of Sequence-to-Sequence Models

Seq2Seq models are a type of neural network architecture designed to handle variable-length input and output sequences. Central to Seq2Seq models are two components: an encoder and a decoder. The encoder processes the input sequence (the text to be summarized) and condenses it into a fixed-length vector representation, capturing the essence of the input. The decoder then takes this representation and generates the output sequence (the summary), one token at a time.

Seq2Seq models are a type of neural network architecture designed to convert sequences from one domain into sequences in another domain, making them ideal for applications such as machine translation, chatbots, and notably, text summarization. At their core, Seq2Seq models consist of two main components: an encoder and a decoder.

Encoder

The encoder processes the input sequence (the text to be summarized) and converts it into a fixed-dimensional context vector. This vector aims to encapsulate the essential information from the input text, serving as a compressed representation of its content. The encoder typically employs a Recurrent Neural Network (RNN) or one of its more advanced variants, such as Long Short-Term Memory (LSTM) networks or Gated Recurrent Units (GRUs), to manage the variable-length input sequences effectively.

Decoder

The decoder takes the context vector produced by the encoder as its input and generates the output sequence (the summary) one token at a time. Like the encoder, the decoder often utilizes RNNs, LSTMs, or GRUs to generate the summary, aiming to capture the main points of the original text while maintaining coherence and fluency. The decoder operates in a step-by-step manner, with each step producing a token of the summary until the entire summary is generated.

The Role of Attention Mechanisms

A significant advancement in Seq2Seq models is the integration of attention mechanisms, which allow the decoder to focus on different parts of the input sequence while generating each token of the summary. This process mimics human cognitive attention by dynamically adjusting which parts of the input text are most relevant at each step of the generation process. Attention mechanisms enhance the model's ability to deal with long input sequences and improve the quality and relevance of the generated summaries.

Training Seq2Seq Models for Text Summarization

Training Seq2Seq models for summarization typically involves a large corpus of text-summary pairs. The model learns to predict the summary sequence given the input text sequence, optimizing parameters to minimize the difference between the generated summary and the reference summary. Advanced training techniques, such as teacher forcing and scheduled sampling, may be employed to accelerate convergence and improve model performance.

Advantages of Seq2Seq Models in Text Summarization

- **Flexibility:** Seq2Seq models can handle variable-length input and output sequences, accommodating a wide range of text lengths and summary styles.

- **Contextual Understanding:** Through the use of recurrent layers and attention mechanisms, Seq2Seq models achieve a deep understanding of the text context, enabling them to generate summaries that are both relevant and coherent.

- **Abstractive Capabilities:** Unlike extractive summarization methods, Seq2Seq models can paraphrase and rephrase the input text, producing abstractive summaries that can convey the essence of the original text in new ways.

By leveraging the power of encoder-decoder architectures and attention mechanisms, Seq2Seq models offer a dynamic and effective solution for condensing text into informative summaries. As NLP continues to evolve, the refinement and application of Seq2Seq models will undoubtedly play a crucial role in advancing the state-of-the-art in text summarization, enabling more sophisticated, accurate, and human-like summaries of textual data.

Encoder-Decoder Architecture

- **Encoder:** Typically an RNN, LSTM, or GRU, the encoder reads the input text and transforms it into a context vector. This vector aims to encapsulate the entire meaning of the input sequence.

- **Decoder:** Mirroring the architecture of the encoder, the decoder then takes the context vector and sequentially generates the summary, often employing attention mechanisms to focus on different parts of the input text during the generation process.

Neural Approaches in Text Summarization

The adaptation of Seq2Seq models for text summarization has led to the development of both abstractive and extractive methodologies within the neural framework.

Abstractive Summarization

Seq2Seq models excel in abstractive summarization, where the goal is to paraphrase and condense the original text. By learning to generate new sentences that capture the core information of the source text, Seq2Seq models can produce concise and coherent summaries that may not necessarily use the exact phrasing found in the input.

- **Attention Mechanisms:** The integration of attention mechanisms allows the model to dynamically focus on different parts of the input text while generating each word of the summary, enhancing the relevance and accuracy of the generated summary.

- **Copy Mechanisms:** Some Seq2Seq models incorporate copy mechanisms to directly include key phrases or terms from the source text in the summary, combining the strengths of extractive and abstractive summarization.

Extractive Summarization

While primarily known for their abstractive capabilities, Seq2Seq models can also be adapted for extractive summarization. This is typically achieved by training the model to predict which sentences in the input should be included in the summary, treating it as a classification problem.

Advancements and Challenges

Seq2Seq models have significantly advanced the field of text summarization, enabling more natural, coherent, and informative summaries. However, challenges remain, such as:

- **Handling Long Texts:** The fixed-length context vector can become a bottleneck for long texts, potentially leading to a loss of information.

- **Model Complexity:** Seq2Seq models, especially those with attention and copy mechanisms, can be complex and require substantial computational resources for training and inference.

- **Data Requirements:** High-quality, large-scale datasets are necessary to train Seq2Seq models effectively, which can be a limiting factor in resource-constrained scenarios.

Through the innovative use of encoder-decoder architectures, coupled with attention and copy mechanisms, Seq2Seq models offer a versatile framework for both abstractive and extractive summarization tasks. As NLP technologies continue to evolve, further refinement and innovation in Seq2Seq models will undoubtedly play a pivotal role in enhancing our ability to automatically summarize textual content, opening new vistas in the understanding and generation of human language.

Text Generation Techniques:

These techniques embody the advances in computational linguistics and artificial intelligence that enable machines to generate human-like text, contributing to a variety of applications such as content creation, chatbots, and automated storytelling. This section provides an in-depth exploration of these text generation techniques, highlighting their methodologies, applications, and the technological progress they represent.

Markov Chains for Text Generation

Markov chains, a statistical model, lay the groundwork for early text generation systems. They generate text by predicting the next word in a sequence based on the probability distribution of words following a given state or set of states in the text.

Methodology

- **State Representation:** In the context of text generation, a state typically represents one or more words. The model transitions between states based on observed probabilities in the training data, effectively capturing the stylistic and syntactic patterns of the source text.

- **Chain Construction:** A Markov chain is constructed from a corpus by analyzing the frequency and sequence of words. The transition probabilities from one word or group of words to the next are calculated, forming the basis for text generation.

Applications and Limitations

- **Applications:** Markov chains have been used for simple text generation tasks, including automated poetry or prose generation, where the complexity of the generated text is not paramount.

- **Limitations:** The primary limitation of Markov chains is their reliance on immediate preceding states without a broader context, leading to generated text that can lack coherence and logical progression over longer spans.

LSTM Networks for Text Generation

Long Short-Term Memory (LSTM) networks, a type of Recurrent Neural Network (RNN), represent a significant advancement in text generation, addressing the limitations of Markov chains by considering longer contexts and dependencies in the text.

Methodology

- **Sequential Processing:** LSTMs process text sequences one token at a time, maintaining a hidden state that captures information from previously seen tokens. This allows LSTMs to remember and utilize a much longer context for predictions.

- **Handling Long-Term Dependencies:** LSTMs are specifically designed to avoid the vanishing gradient problem common in traditional RNNs, making them adept at capturing long-term dependencies in text.

Applications and Advancements

- **Applications:** LSTMs have been employed in more complex text generation tasks, including machine translation, dialogue systems, and automated story generation, where coherence and context understanding are crucial.

- **Advancements:** The ability of LSTMs to generate contextually rich and coherent text over extended sequences marked a leap forward in artificial text generation capabilities.

GPT Models for Text Generation

The introduction of Generative Pre-trained Transformer (GPT) models has set new standards in text generation, leveraging deep learning and large-scale language modeling to produce text that can be indistinguishable from human-written content.

Methodology

- **Transformer Architecture:** GPT models utilize the transformer architecture, which relies on self-attention mechanisms to weigh the importance of different words in the input. This allows for parallel processing of sequences and a deeper understanding of context.

- **Pre-training and Fine-tuning:** GPT models are first pre-trained on vast corpora of text, learning a wide range of language patterns and structures. They can then be fine-tuned on specific tasks or styles to generate targeted text outputs.

Applications and Impact

- **Applications:** GPT models have been applied to a breadth of text generation tasks, including high-quality article writing, creative writing, and effective conversational agents, demonstrating unparalleled versatility and creativity.

- **Impact:** The advent of GPT models has significantly broadened the possibilities for text generation, challenging the boundaries between human and machine capabilities in linguistic creativity.

Each technique offers unique strengths, from the simplicity and ease of implementation of Markov chains to the deep contextual understanding and generative prowess of GPT models. As these technologies continue to evolve, the future of text generation promises even more sophisticated tools for creating compelling, diverse, and contextually rich text, further blurring the lines between human and machine-generated content.

Conclusion

The advancements in deep learning models, such as Bidirectional LSTMs, CRFs, and Transformers, have not only enhanced the accuracy and fluency of these tasks but also opened new avenues for innovation. As NLP continues to progress, the exploration and refinement of text summarization and generation techniques will undoubtedly continue to reshape our interaction with textual content, bridging the gap between human creativity and machine intelligence.

Chapter 7: Dialogue Systems and Chatbots

Dialogue systems and chatbots are presented as pivotal applications of NLP, embodying the intersection of computational linguistics, artificial intelligence, and human-computer interaction. These systems are designed to simulate conversational interactions with humans, providing responses that are coherent, contextually relevant, and, ideally, indistinguishable from those a human would provide.

Evolution of Dialogue Systems and Chatbots

The evolution of dialogue systems and chatbots traces back to simple rule-based systems that responded to user inputs with predefined scripts. Over time, advancements in machine learning and NLP have led to the development of more sophisticated systems capable of understanding natural language queries, maintaining context over a conversation, and generating responses that adapt to the user's intent and emotional state.

The Early Days: Rule-Based Systems

The origins of dialogue systems can be traced back to simple rule-based systems that operated on predefined patterns and responses. One of the earliest and most famous examples is ELIZA, developed in the mid-1960s by Joseph Weizenbaum. ELIZA simulated conversation by matching user inputs to a set of rules and responding with pre-scripted replies. Though limited in scope and understanding, ELIZA demonstrated the potential for machines to mimic human-like interactions, laying the groundwork for future developments in dialogue systems.

Advancements in AI and Machine Learning

The advent of more sophisticated AI and machine learning techniques marked a significant shift in the development of dialogue systems and chatbots. The introduction of statistical models and later, machine learning algorithms, allowed for more flexible and dynamic conversation capabilities. Systems could now learn from vast datasets of real conversations, improving their ability to understand natural language inputs and generate appropriate responses. This era saw the development of more advanced systems like PARRY, a more complex conversational agent developed in the early 1970s, which demonstrated improved conversational abilities and a deeper level of simulated understanding.

The Rise of Neural Networks and Deep Learning

The introduction of neural networks and deep learning technologies propelled dialogue systems and chatbots into a new era of possibilities. Recurrent Neural Networks (RNNs), particularly Long Short-Term Memory (LSTM) networks, enabled systems to remember and utilize context from earlier parts of a conversation, significantly enhancing the coherence and relevance of responses. The development of the Seq2Seq model architecture further advanced the field by allowing end-to-end training of dialogue systems, streamlining the process of converting natural language inputs into meaningful outputs.

Breakthroughs with Transformer Models

The introduction of transformer models, such as OpenAI's Generative Pre-trained Transformer (GPT) series and Google's BERT, marked a groundbreaking advancement in NLP. These models, pre-trained on extensive corpora of text, exhibited unprecedented understanding of language context, nuance, and semantics. Their ability to generate human-like text and engage in complex dialogues has significantly narrowed the gap between human and machine communication, enabling the development of chatbots and conversational agents with sophisticated conversational capabilities.

Current Landscape and Future Directions

Today, dialogue systems and chatbots are integrated into various aspects of daily life and industry, from customer service and e-commerce to personal assistants and beyond. The evolution from rule-based to AI-driven conversational agents has not only improved the functionality and usability of these systems but also opened up new avenues for human-computer interaction. Looking forward, advancements in AI, machine learning, and computational linguistics promise to further enhance the intelligence, adaptability, and personalization of dialogue systems, pushing the boundaries of what is possible in automated conversational technologies.

This progression underscores the synergistic relationship between advancements in technology and the expanding role of conversational agents in society. As we continue to explore and innovate in the realms of AI and NLP, the future of dialogue systems and chatbots holds exciting possibilities for even more seamless, intuitive, and enriching human-computer interactions.

Methodologies

Dialogue systems and chatbots are built upon several core NLP methodologies, each contributing to the system's ability to parse, understand, and respond to human language.

- **Natural Language Understanding (NLU):** At the heart of dialogue systems, NLU processes and interprets user inputs, extracting intent and relevant entities. This step is crucial for determining the appropriate response or action the system should take.

- **Dialogue Management:** This component maintains the state and context of the conversation, enabling the system to provide coherent and contextually appropriate responses. Dialogue management often involves decision-making processes to determine the next best response or question to further the dialogue.

- **Natural Language Generation (NLG):** NLG enables chatbots to construct responses in natural language. This can range from selecting appropriate predefined responses to dynamically generating replies based on the conversation's context, leveraging techniques like template-based generation, statistical models, and neural networks.

Key Challenges

Developing effective dialogue systems and chatbots involves navigating several challenges, including:

- **Understanding Context and Ambiguity:** One of the primary challenges is ensuring that the system accurately understands the context of the conversation and can handle ambiguous or incomplete user inputs.

- **Maintaining Coherence Over Long Interactions:** As conversations progress, maintaining coherence and remembering previous interactions become increasingly challenging but are essential for providing a seamless user experience.

- **Managing Varied User Intentions:** Users may interact with chatbots for myriad reasons, from seeking information to completing transactions or simply engaging in casual conversation. Adapting to these varied intentions requires sophisticated NLU and dialogue management strategies.

Applications

Dialogue systems and chatbots have found applications across numerous domains, demonstrating their versatility and the broad interest in automating conversational interactions.

- **Customer Service:** Many businesses employ chatbots to handle customer inquiries, providing instant responses to common questions and escalating more complex issues to human representatives.

- **E-commerce and Retail:** Chatbots assist users in finding products, making recommendations based on preferences, and facilitating transactions.

- **Healthcare:** Dialogue systems can provide health information, symptom checking, and mental health support, offering accessible resources to users.

- **Education:** Educational chatbots support learning by answering questions, providing explanations, and even tutoring students in various subjects.

Overview Of Dialogue Systems:

These systems, designed to simulate conversational interactions with humans through text or speech, have undergone tremendous evolution, powered by advances in computational linguistics, artificial intelligence (AI), and machine learning.

Significance of Dialogue Systems and Conversational Agents

Dialogue systems and conversational agents represent a significant leap in how humans interact with machines. By enabling natural language communication, these systems break down the barriers between human intelligence and artificial intelligence, making technology more accessible, intuitive, and effective. From customer service bots and personal assistants to therapeutic and educational tools, dialogue systems have diverse applications that touch various aspects of daily life and industry.

Core Components

Dialogue systems typically comprise several key components that work together to process input, understand context, generate responses, and maintain the flow of conversation:

Natural Language Understanding (NLU):

This component interprets the user's input, extracting intent and entities that represent the semantic meaning of the request.

Significance of NLU in Dialogue Systems

NLU stands at the intersection of linguistics and artificial intelligence, serving as the foundational block that enables dialogue systems to process and understand human language inputs effectively. Unlike simpler text processing that may only look for keywords or specific phrases, NLU delves into the complexities of language, interpreting user intent, discerning nuances, and extracting relevant entities from natural language inputs. This deep understanding is crucial for generating appropriate and context-aware responses, making NLU a cornerstone of any effective dialogue system or conversational agent.

Functionalities of NLU

NLU encompasses several key functionalities that together facilitate a comprehensive understanding of language:

- **Intent Recognition:** One of the primary tasks of NLU is to determine the user's intention behind a given utterance. Whether it's booking a flight, asking a question, or expressing a concern, identifying the intent is essential for the system to proceed with relevant actions or responses.

- **Entity Extraction:** Beyond understanding the user's intent, NLU also involves recognizing and extracting named entities (such as dates, locations, product names, and quantities) from the input text. These entities often provide the specific details necessary to fulfill the user's request.

- **Contextual and Semantic Analysis:** NLU systems employ linguistic models and algorithms to analyze the context and semantics of conversations. This includes understanding the relationships between words, the implications of certain phrases, and even the sentiment behind the user's input, enabling the system to interact in a more human-like manner.

Challenges in NLU

Despite advancements in NLP technologies, NLU continues to face several challenges that impact the effectiveness of dialogue systems and conversational agents:

- **Ambiguity and Polysemy:** Natural language is inherently ambiguous, with many words and phrases having multiple meanings depending on context. Effectively resolving these ambiguities is a significant challenge for NLU systems.

- **Idiomatic and Colloquial Language:** People often use idioms, slang, and colloquial expressions in conversation, which can be difficult for NLU systems to interpret accurately.

- **Domain-Specific Language:** Conversations within specific domains (e.g., medical, legal, technical) may involve specialized vocabulary and concepts that require domain-specific knowledge and understanding for accurate interpretation.

Natural Language Understanding is a pivotal component of dialogue systems and conversational agents. It enables these systems to go beyond mere keyword recognition, allowing for a deeper, more nuanced interaction with users. By accurately interpreting intent, extracting entities, and analyzing context and semantics, NLU lays the groundwork for meaningful and effective communication between humans and machines. As NLU technologies continue to evolve, they promise to further enhance the capabilities of dialogue systems, making them more intuitive, responsive, and capable of handling the complexities of human language.

Dialogue Management:

Often considered the system's brain, this component manages the conversation's state and flow, deciding on the system's response strategy based on the context and the objectives of the dialogue.

Functionality of Dialogue Management

Dialogue management encompasses several key functions essential for the operation of dialogue systems and conversational agents:

- **State Tracking:** It keeps track of the conversation state, including the history of user inputs, system responses, identified entities, and user intents. This tracking enables the system to maintain context over the course of an interaction.

- **Context Handling:** Beyond tracking the immediate conversation state, dialogue management also involves understanding and utilizing broader context, such as the user's profile, preferences, and the specific situation or environment in which the dialogue occurs.

- **Decision Making:** Based on the current state and context, dialogue management determines the next action the system should take. This could involve generating a response directly, executing a backend action (like querying a database or calling an API), or asking the user for clarification or additional information.

Methodologies in Dialogue Management

Dialogue management can be implemented through various methodologies, each with its own set of strategies for managing conversations:

- **Rule-Based Systems:** Early dialogue systems often relied on a set of predefined rules to manage dialogues. These systems use if-then-else logic to map specific inputs or conversation states to corresponding responses or actions. While straightforward to implement, rule-based systems can become complex and hard to maintain as the number of possible interactions grows.

- **Finite State Machines (FSMs):** FSMs model dialogues as a series of states and transitions, with each state representing a point in the conversation and transitions triggered by user inputs or system actions. FSMs provide a structured way to manage dialogues but can struggle with highly dynamic or open-ended conversations.

- **Frame-Based Models:** These models structure conversations around "frames" or templates that capture the information needed to complete a task or fulfill an intent. Dialogue management involves filling in the slots of a frame with information provided by the user, guiding the conversation towards achieving the specified goal.

- **Machine Learning and Data-Driven Approaches:** More advanced dialogue systems leverage machine learning models, including reinforcement learning, to learn dialogue strategies from data. These approaches can adapt to a wide range of interactions, learning optimal pathways through conversations based on feedback and performance metrics.

Challenges in Dialogue Management

- **Scalability:** As the scope of possible interactions expands, managing all potential paths through a conversation becomes increasingly challenging, especially for rule-based and FSM approaches.

- **Adaptability:** Ensuring that dialogue systems can adapt to unexpected inputs, changes in user intent, or shifts in context requires sophisticated dialogue management strategies.

- **Naturalness and Flexibility:** Maintaining a natural and flexible conversational flow, especially in open-domain dialogues, is a significant challenge, requiring systems to balance goal orientation with the ability to engage in more exploratory or unstructured interactions.

Dialogue management is a fundamental component of dialogue systems and conversational agents. It encompasses the systems and strategies that enable these technologies to engage in meaningful and coherent dialogues with users. By effectively managing the state, context, and decision-making processes within a conversation, dialogue management systems pave the way for more sophisticated, adaptable, and engaging conversational agents. As advancements in AI and machine learning continue to push the boundaries of what's possible, dialogue management remains a key area of research and development, critical to realizing the full potential of human-computer interaction through dialogue.

Natural Language Generation (NLG):

This component is responsible for formulating the system's responses into natural language, ensuring that the output is coherent, contextually appropriate, and human-like.

Importance of NLG in Dialogue Systems

NLG stands as the bridge between machine understanding and human interaction within dialogue systems. It's the mechanism through which these systems communicate insights, decisions, and actions back to the user in an intelligible and natural manner. Without NLG, the ability of chatbots and conversational agents to participate in human-like dialogue would be severely limited, reducing their effectiveness and user satisfaction.

Operational Mechanisms of NLG

NLG processes in dialogue systems typically involve several key steps, each contributing to the generation of accurate, relevant, and contextually appropriate responses:

- **Content Determination:** This initial step involves deciding on the information to be conveyed in the response. Based on the input from the user, the system's knowledge base, and the current context of the conversation, NLG systems identify the key messages or actions that need to be communicated.

- **Structuring:** Once the content is determined, the NLG system organizes it into a logical order. For complex responses that convey multiple pieces of information, this step ensures that the output follows a coherent and easily understandable sequence.

- **Lexicalization:** This step involves choosing the specific words or phrases to express the content. The NLG system selects appropriate vocabulary to convey the intended meaning, considering factors like politeness, formality, and clarity.

- **Aggregation:** To produce fluent and concise responses, NLG systems may combine related pieces of information into single sentences, reducing repetition and enhancing the readability of the output.

- **Refinement and Realization:** The final steps involve refining the generated text to ensure grammatical correctness, adjusting for tone and style, and converting the structured representation into a final natural language output.

Challenges in NLG

The development of effective NLG components in dialogue systems faces several challenges, reflecting the complexities of human language and communication:

- **Variability and Creativity:** Generating responses that are varied and creative, rather than formulaic or repetitive, is a significant challenge. Users expect conversational agents to produce responses that feel personalized and engaging.

- **Contextual and Emotional Sensitivity:** Crafting responses that are appropriate to the context of the conversation, including understanding and responding to the user's emotional state, requires advanced linguistic and social awareness.

- **Coherence and Cohesion:** Maintaining coherence and cohesion in longer responses or across multiple turns in a conversation demands sophisticated linguistic models that can track and refer back to previous dialogue segments.

Natural Language Generation is a foundational component of dialogue systems and conversational agents. By enabling these systems to produce human-like text, NLG facilitates effective and natural interactions between humans and machines. The continual advancement of NLG technologies, driven by research in NLP, AI, and computational linguistics, promises to enhance the capabilities of dialogue systems, making them more versatile, engaging, and capable of meeting the diverse needs of users across various applications.

Types of Dialogue Systems

Dialogue systems can be categorized based on their functionality, interaction mode, and underlying technology:

- **Rule-Based vs. AI-Driven:** Early dialogue systems relied on rule-based frameworks where responses were generated based on a set of predefined rules. Modern systems increasingly leverage AI, particularly machine learning and deep learning, to understand and generate human-like responses dynamically.

- **Goal-Oriented vs. Open-Domain:** Goal-oriented systems are designed to accomplish specific tasks, such as booking a hotel or ordering food. In contrast, open-domain systems aim for more general conversational capabilities, engaging users on a wide range of topics without a specific end-goal.

- **Text-Based vs. Voice-Activated:** While some dialogue systems interact with users through written text, others use speech recognition and synthesis to enable voice-based interactions, broadening their accessibility and use cases.

Challenges in Developing Dialogue Systems

Creating effective dialogue systems presents several challenges, reflecting the complexity of human language and communication:

- **Understanding Context and Ambiguity:** Accurately interpreting user intent, especially in the presence of ambiguous or incomplete input, remains a significant challenge.

- **Maintaining Coherence Over Long Conversations:** Ensuring that the system can remember and reference earlier parts of the conversation to maintain coherence and relevance in its responses.

- **Generating Natural and Varied Responses:** Avoiding repetitive or formulaic responses to keep the conversation engaging and natural for the user.

- **Handling Diverse and Evolving Language:** Adapting to the nuances of human language, including slang, idioms, and cultural references, as well as changes in language use over time.

Through the integration of NLU, dialogue management, and NLG, these systems strive to replicate the complexities of human conversation, offering users a seamless and engaging experience. As technology continues to advance, the future of dialogue systems promises even greater capabilities, further blurring the lines between human and machine communication and opening new possibilities for automated interactions across all sectors of society and industry.

Rule-Based and Retrieval-Based Chatbots:

The exploration of dialogue systems and chatbots delves into various methodologies that underpin their operation, with particular attention to rule-based and retrieval-based models. These types of chatbots represent foundational approaches in the field of conversational AI, each with distinct mechanisms, applications, and implications for user interaction. This comprehensive section outlines the principles, advantages, and limitations of rule-based and retrieval-based chatbots, providing insights into their role in the broader landscape of NLP-driven dialogue systems.

Rule-Based Chatbots

Rule-based chatbots operate on a set of predefined rules and heuristics that guide their responses to user inputs. These rules are explicitly programmed by developers and often involve pattern matching and keyword recognition to interpret the user's intent and generate appropriate responses.

Principles and Operation

Rule-based chatbots function by matching user inputs to a predefined set of rules or patterns. These rules dictate the chatbot's responses, making the interaction predictable and consistent. The complexity of these chatbots can vary significantly, from simple bots that recognize keywords to more sophisticated systems that parse and understand grammatical structures.

Pattern Matching:

At the heart of rule-based systems is pattern matching, where the chatbot searches the user's input for specific keywords or phrases identified in its rule set. Upon finding a match, the chatbot selects the corresponding response.

Decision Trees:

For more complex interactions, rule-based chatbots may employ decision trees that guide users through a series of questions, narrowing down the user's intent and delivering more targeted responses based on their answers.

Advantages

- **Consistency and Reliability:** Rule-based chatbots offer a high level of consistency, providing the same response to specific inputs every time. This reliability is crucial in domains where accuracy and predictability are paramount.

- **Ease of Implementation:** These chatbots are relatively straightforward to develop and deploy, making them accessible for businesses and developers without extensive AI expertise.

- **Control over Responses:** Developers have complete control over the chatbot's responses, ensuring that the bot always communicates within the bounds of what is deemed appropriate for the interaction.

Challenges

- **Limited Scalability:** The effectiveness of rule-based chatbots is directly tied to the comprehensiveness of their rule set. Expanding the bot's capabilities requires manually adding new rules, which can become impractical as the scope of possible interactions grows.

- **Lack of Flexibility:** These chatbots struggle with variations in user input that haven't been explicitly accounted for in their rules, leading to potential frustration for users whose queries don't match any predefined patterns.

- **Minimal Contextual Understanding:** Rule-based systems generally lack the ability to understand or remember context from earlier in the conversation, which can limit their effectiveness in more complex or nuanced dialogues.

Applications

Despite their limitations, rule-based chatbots are highly effective in scenarios where interactions are straightforward and can be anticipated in advance. Common applications include:

- **Customer Support:** Handling frequently asked questions or providing standardized information about products and services.

- **Form Filling and Data Collection:** Guiding users through forms or surveys by asking predefined questions.

- **Instructional Guides:** Assisting users with step-by-step instructions for tasks such as setup processes, troubleshooting, or using software features.

While their lack of flexibility and contextual understanding poses challenges for more complex interactions, their predictability, ease of implementation, and control over responses make them invaluable for specific applications. As dialogue systems continue to evolve, the integration of rule-based mechanisms with more advanced AI technologies may offer pathways to enhancing their capabilities, bridging the gap between reliability and adaptability in conversational agents.

Principles and Operation

Pattern Matching:

Rule-based systems analyze incoming messages for specific patterns or keywords to determine the appropriate response. This can involve simple "if-then" logic or more complex algorithms for parsing and understanding user inputs.

Pattern Matching in Rule-Based Chatbots

Pattern matching in rule-based chatbots involves identifying specific keywords, phrases, or patterns within user inputs and mapping them to predefined responses. This process is guided by a set of rules crafted by developers, which dictate the chatbot's response to various inputs.

Methodologies

- **Exact Match:** The simplest form of pattern matching, where the chatbot looks for an exact match between the user's input and its database of predefined patterns. While straightforward, this method lacks flexibility and can fail if the user's input deviates slightly from the expected pattern.

- **Regular Expressions:** A more advanced form of pattern matching, regular expressions allow for the definition of complex patterns that can match a wide range of inputs. This method provides greater flexibility, enabling the chatbot to recognize inputs that follow a certain structure or contain variations of a keyword or phrase.

- **Keyword Matching:** This method involves identifying specific keywords within the user's input that signal the intent or topic. The chatbot then selects a response based on the presence of these keywords, allowing for a degree of variability in user inputs.

Applications

Pattern matching serves as the backbone for many rule-based chatbot applications, from customer service bots that provide information based on queries to interactive guides that assist users through predefined processes. Its effectiveness in these applications hinges on the ability to accurately predict and categorize user inputs, ensuring that the chatbot can respond appropriately to a wide range of requests.

Pattern Matching in Retrieval-Based Chatbots

Retrieval-based chatbots also employ pattern matching, but instead of triggering predefined responses, they use it to search a database of potential responses and select the one that best matches the user's query based on similarity measures.

Methodologies

- **Semantic Matching:** Advanced retrieval-based systems go beyond simple keyword or phrase matching to include semantic analysis, understanding the meaning behind user inputs. This approach often involves natural language processing techniques and machine learning models to evaluate the semantic similarity between the user's input and available responses.

- **Contextual Matching:** These chatbots may also consider the context of the conversation when matching patterns, using information from previous exchanges to inform the response selection process. This method enhances the relevance and coherence of responses, particularly in ongoing dialogues.

Challenges

Despite its widespread use, pattern matching faces several challenges, including:

- **Handling Ambiguity and Variability:** Natural language is inherently ambiguous and variable. Effectively dealing with the multitude of ways users can express similar intents or queries remains a significant challenge for pattern matching algorithms.

- **Scalability:** As the scope of potential user inputs expands, maintaining an exhaustive set of patterns or keywords becomes increasingly difficult, challenging the scalability of rule-based systems.

Pattern matching stands as a critical operational principle in the development and functionality of both rule-based and retrieval-based chatbots. By enabling these systems to interpret and respond to user inputs, pattern matching facilitates the automation of conversational exchanges across various applications. Advancements in natural language processing and machine learning continue to enhance the sophistication of pattern matching techniques, driving improvements in chatbot responsiveness, flexibility, and user satisfaction.

Decision Trees:

Many rule-based chatbots utilize decision trees to guide conversations along predetermined paths, offering users options or prompts based on their previous responses.

Decision Trees in Chatbot Design

Decision trees are a method of representing a series of branching choices, leading to different outcomes or responses based on user inputs. In the realm of chatbots, decision trees are employed to structure the conversation, allowing the bot to ask follow-up questions, provide information, or take actions based on the user's replies.

Methodology

- **Branching Logic:** Decision trees are structured around nodes and branches, where each node represents a point of decision (often a question posed by the chatbot) and each branch represents a potential response or outcome. The path taken through the tree depends on the user's inputs, guiding the conversation towards relevant responses or actions.

- **Design and Implementation:** Building a decision tree for a chatbot involves mapping out all possible conversational paths and outcomes. This requires a deep understanding of the chatbot's domain and the types of interactions it will engage in. Developers use these insights to create a comprehensive tree that covers various user intents and scenarios.

Advantages

- **Structured Conversations:** Decision trees provide a clear structure for interactions, ensuring that chatbots can handle conversations logically and coherently. This is particularly beneficial for goal-oriented chatbots, where the objective is to guide users to specific information or outcomes.

- **Predictability and Control:** By defining the conversational paths and outcomes, decision trees offer developers greater control over the chatbot's behavior, ensuring that it responds appropriately to a wide range of user queries.

- **Scalability in Specific Domains:** For chatbots operating within well-defined domains or with a narrow focus, decision trees can be scaled effectively by expanding the tree to cover more scenarios or by refining branches to handle more nuanced interactions.

Challenges

- **Complexity with Scale:** As the scope of the chatbot's functionality grows, the decision tree can become exceedingly complex, making it difficult to manage and update. This complexity can also lead to increased chances of errors or oversights in the conversational flow.

- **Limited Flexibility:** Decision trees operate within the confines of their predefined paths, limiting the chatbot's ability to handle unexpected user inputs or diverge from the scripted conversation. This can result in a less natural interaction experience for users.

Application Scenarios

Decision trees are particularly well-suited to certain types of chatbot applications, including:

- **Customer Support:** For handling common queries, guiding users through troubleshooting steps, or navigating service options.

- **Surveys and Data Collection:** Systematically collecting information from users by guiding them through a series of questions and responses.

- **E-commerce:** Assisting users in finding products, making recommendations based on preferences, or navigating the purchase process.

Conclusion

Decision trees serve as an integral component in the principles and operation of rule-based and retrieval-based chatbots. By enabling structured and logical conversational flows, decision trees enhance the capability of chatbots to engage users effectively within specific domains or tasks. Despite the challenges associated with complexity and flexibility, the strategic application of decision trees in chatbot design continues to be a valuable approach for creating reliable and functional conversational agents. As the field of conversational AI evolves, the integration of decision trees with more advanced technologies may offer new pathways to overcoming these limitations, further enriching the chatbot-user interaction experience.

Advantages

- **Simplicity and Control:** Rule-based chatbots are relatively straightforward to develop and deploy, offering developers precise control over the bot's behavior and responses.

- **Reliability:** Because their responses are pre-defined, rule-based chatbots provide consistent and predictable interactions, ensuring accuracy in specific domains where their rules apply.

Limitations

- **Scalability:** The complexity and usefulness of rule-based chatbots are limited by the number and specificity of the rules they are programmed with, making them less scalable and flexible in handling diverse or unexpected user inputs.

- **Limited Understanding:** These chatbots lack the ability to understand context or nuances in language beyond their programmed rules, leading to potential frustrations in user interactions.

Retrieval-Based Chatbots

Retrieval-based chatbots generate responses by selecting from a predefined repository of responses. Unlike rule-based bots that follow rigidly defined pathways, retrieval-based models use algorithms to determine the most relevant response to the user's input based on similarity measures or contextual cues.

Principles and Operation

- **Response Ranking:** Upon receiving an input, the chatbot searches its response database to find the most appropriate replies. It ranks these potential responses based on relevance to the input, often employing machine learning models to enhance the accuracy of this matching process.

- **Contextual Awareness:** More advanced retrieval-based systems incorporate contextual information from the conversation history to improve response relevance and coherence.

Advantages

- **Flexibility:** Retrieval-based chatbots can offer more varied and nuanced responses than rule-based systems, as they can draw from a large, diverse set of pre-defined responses.

- **Improved User Experience:** By providing responses that are contextually appropriate and diverse, these chatbots can facilitate more engaging and satisfying interactions.

Limitations

- **Dependence on Response Database:** The effectiveness of retrieval-based chatbots is heavily dependent on the quality and breadth of their response database. They may struggle with topics outside of this database.

- **Lack of Personalization:** While more flexible than rule-based systems, retrieval-based chatbots may still fall short in delivering personalized responses tailored to the user's specific needs or preferences.

Rule-based and retrieval-based chatbots, serve as essential building blocks in the development of conversational agents. Each type offers distinct advantages and faces specific challenges, reflecting the trade-offs between simplicity and control on one hand, and flexibility and adaptability on the other. As the field of NLP and conversational AI continues to advance, the integration of these models with more sophisticated AI techniques promises to enhance the capabilities of chatbots, driving towards more natural, intelligent, and user-centric conversational experiences.

Generative Chatbots Using Sequence-To-Sequence:

The exploration of generative chatbots marks a significant advance in the field of dialogue systems and conversational AI. Generative chatbots represent the cutting edge of technology, leveraging sophisticated neural network architectures such as sequence-to-sequence (Seq2Seq) models and Transformers to produce responses that are not pre-defined but generated in real-time. This comprehensive portion delves into the mechanics, advantages, and challenges of employing Seq2Seq models and Transformers in the creation of generative chatbots, underscoring their transformative impact on how machines understand and generate human language.

Generative Chatbots: An Overview

Generative chatbots are designed to go beyond selecting responses from a set of predefined options. Instead, they dynamically generate replies based on the input they receive, allowing for a more natural and varied conversation. This capability stems from their use of advanced neural network models that can understand context, infer intent, and produce linguistically coherent outputs.

Sequence-to-Sequence (Seq2Seq) Models

304

Seq2Seq models are pivotal in the development of generative chatbots. These models consist of two main components: an encoder that processes the input text and a decoder that generates the output text.

Encoder:

The encoder reads the input sentence and transforms it into a high-dimensional vector (or a set of vectors), capturing the semantic and syntactic properties of the input.

Encoder in Seq2Seq Models

The encoder of a Seq2Seq model acts as the initial processing unit, taking the user's input sentence and converting it into a fixed-size vector or a set of vectors known as the context or state vectors. This transformation is critical, as it prepares the ground for generating a relevant and coherent response by the decoder.

Mechanisms of Operation

Input Processing: The encoder starts by breaking down the input text into tokens, typically words or subwords, which are then converted into numerical representations, often using word embeddings. These embeddings capture semantic and syntactic properties of the tokens, facilitating a more nuanced understanding of the input.

Recurrent Layers: Most encoders in Seq2Seq models leverage Recurrent Neural Networks (RNNs), Long Short-Term Memory (LSTM) networks, or Gated Recurrent Units (GRUs). These layers are adept at processing sequences of data, allowing the encoder to handle inputs of varying lengths and maintain information across different parts of the sentence.

Context Vector Generation: As the encoder processes the input sequence, it aggregates information from each token, culminating in the generation of the context vectors. These vectors serve as a compressed representation of the entire input, capturing its essential meaning and context.

Importance of the Encoder

Contextual Understanding: The encoder's ability to distill complex and varied input into a dense representation is crucial for the chatbot's understanding of user queries or statements. This understanding forms the basis for generating relevant responses.

Handling Variable Input Lengths: Given the diversity of human language, user inputs can vary significantly in length and complexity. The encoder's design allows Seq2Seq models to accommodate this variability, ensuring consistent performance across different conversational scenarios.

Challenges and Considerations

- **Information Bottleneck:** The process of condensing the entire input sequence into a fixed-size context vector(s) can create an information bottleneck, potentially leading to a loss of detail or nuance, especially in longer sentences or more complex dialogues.

- **Sequential Processing:** Traditional encoder designs process the input sequentially, which can introduce challenges in capturing long-distance dependencies within the text and may limit the speed of processing due to the inherently sequential nature of RNNs and their variants.

Evolution and Advances

- **Attention Mechanisms:** To mitigate the information bottleneck and enhance the encoder's effectiveness, attention mechanisms can be integrated, allowing the model to dynamically focus on different parts of the input sequence when generating the context vectors.

- **Transition to Transformers:** The introduction of Transformers has revolutionized the encoder's architecture by employing self-attention layers. These layers process the entire input sequence in parallel, improving efficiency and the model's ability to capture complex dependencies within the text.

The encoder component in sequence-to-sequence models plays an indispensable role in generative chatbots by transforming user inputs into rich contextual representations. This process lays the groundwork for generating coherent and contextually appropriate responses, making the encoder a cornerstone of effective dialogue systems. As NLP technology continues to evolve, innovations in encoder design and functionality are expected to further enhance the conversational capabilities of generative chatbots, pushing the boundaries of human-computer interaction.

Decoder:

The decoder then uses this vector to generate the output sentence, one word at a time, effectively translating the internal representation into a response.

The Role of the Decoder in Seq2Seq Models

The decoder in Seq2Seq models is tasked with generating the output sequence from the context vectors provided by the encoder. This process involves translating the dense, encoded representation of the input into a natural language response, step by step. The decoder's operation is central to the Seq2Seq model's ability to produce generative and dynamic responses in chatbots.

Mechanisms of Operation

Sequence Generation: Starting with the context vector(s) as the initial state, the decoder generates the output sequence one token at a time. At each step, it predicts the next token based on the current state and the previously generated tokens, effectively building the response incrementally.

Recurrent Layers: Similar to the encoder, the decoder often utilizes RNNs, LSTMs, or GRUs to maintain state across the generation process. This recurrent structure enables the decoder to consider both the overall context and the specific sequence of tokens already generated, ensuring coherence in the output.

Termination Condition: The decoding process continues until a termination condition is met, which is typically the generation of a special end-of-sequence token or reaching a maximum sequence length. This condition signals the completion of the response.

Importance of the Decoder

Contextual Relevance: The decoder ensures that the generated responses are not only grammatically correct but also contextually relevant to the input, drawing on the encoded information to address the user's intent and the conversational context.

Adaptability: By generating responses based on learned patterns and the specific context of each interaction, the decoder allows for a high degree of adaptability and personalization in chatbot responses, surpassing the capabilities of rule-based systems.

Challenges and Considerations

- **Complexity in Learning:** Training the decoder to generate coherent, contextually appropriate responses can be challenging, particularly for open-domain conversations that require a broad understanding of language and context.

- **Managing Long Sequences:** As the length of the desired output increases, maintaining coherence and relevance throughout the response becomes more difficult, posing a challenge for the decoder's recurrent architecture.

Evolution and Advances

- **Attention Mechanisms:** The integration of attention mechanisms allows the decoder to focus on different parts of the encoded input as it generates each token, improving the relevance and coherence of responses by dynamically adapting to the input's content.

- **Advancement with Transformers:** The advent of Transformer models has significantly enhanced the decoder's capabilities. Transformers use self-attention to process the entire sequence simultaneously, improving efficiency and the model's ability to capture complex dependencies. In a Transformer-based Seq2Seq model, the decoder can attend to all positions of the input sequence at once, leading to more nuanced and contextually aware generation.

The decoder component in sequence-to-sequence models is essential for the functioning of generative chatbots. It translates the context encapsulated by the encoder into natural language responses, enabling chatbots to engage in fluid, dynamic conversations. Through advancements in neural network architectures and techniques like attention mechanisms and Transformers, the decoder's ability to produce coherent, relevant, and engaging responses continues to evolve, pushing the boundaries of what is possible in automated dialogue systems and enhancing the interactivity and human-like quality of conversational agents.

Attention Mechanisms:

Many Seq2Seq implementations incorporate attention mechanisms, which allow the model to weigh different parts of the input as it generates each word in the output, enhancing the relevance and coherence of the responses.

The Role of Attention Mechanisms in Seq2Seq Models

Attention mechanisms augment Seq2Seq models by dynamically selecting which parts of the input sequence to focus on during each step of the decoding process. Instead of relying solely on a fixed context vector to generate the entire output sequence, attention allows the model to access the entire input sequence at each step, effectively "remembering" more detailed information and how it relates to the task at hand.

Functionality

Dynamic Contextual Focus: Attention mechanisms compute a set of weights over the input tokens, indicating the relative importance of each token when generating the current output token. This process is repeated for each token in the output sequence, allowing the model to adapt its focus based on what it has already generated.

Weighted Sum: The attention weights are used to create a weighted sum of the encoder's output vectors, producing a context vector that is specific to the current step in the decoding process. This step-by-step context vector provides nuanced guidance for the generation of each output token.

Advantages of Attention Mechanisms

- **Improved Handling of Long Sequences:** By mitigating the information bottleneck associated with encoding the entire input into a single context vector, attention mechanisms enhance the model's ability to deal with long input sequences without loss of performance.

- **Enhanced Contextual Understanding:** Attention provides a mechanism for the model to "refer back" to the input sequence, enabling more accurate and contextually relevant responses, especially in complex conversational scenarios.

- **Increased Model Interpretability:** The attention weights offer insights into how the model is processing the input sequence to generate the output, allowing developers to understand and diagnose the model's behavior more effectively.

Applications in Generative Chatbots

The incorporation of attention mechanisms in Seq2Seq models has significantly advanced the capabilities of generative chatbots, enabling them to engage in more coherent and contextually rich conversations. Applications include:

- **Customer Support Bots:** Attention-enhanced Seq2Seq models can provide precise, informative responses to customer queries, even when handling complex, multi-step interactions that require referring to earlier parts of the conversation.

- **Language Translation Bots:** In multilingual chatbot interfaces, attention mechanisms improve the quality of machine translation by focusing on relevant parts of the input text, ensuring that the generated responses are both accurate and contextually appropriate.

Evolution and Integration with Transformers

The introduction of the Transformer architecture, which relies entirely on self-attention mechanisms, represents a further evolution of the attention concept. Transformers discard the sequential processing inherent in RNNs and LSTMs, instead processing the entire input sequence in parallel. This approach not only enhances the efficiency and effectiveness of attention but also scales up the capacity of models to handle the complexities of natural language, pushing the boundaries of what's possible in generative chatbots and conversational AI.

Attention mechanisms in sequence-to-sequence models have revolutionized the development of generative chatbots. By enabling models to focus dynamically on different parts of the input sequence during the response generation process, attention mechanisms facilitate the creation of more nuanced, relevant, and engaging conversational agents. As the field of NLP continues to evolve, the integration of attention mechanisms and their expansion through architectures like Transformers will undoubtedly continue to play a central role in shaping the future of dialogue systems and conversational AI.

Transformers

Transformers represent a significant evolution in the design of neural networks for NLP, including the development of generative chatbots. Unlike Seq2Seq models, Transformers do not process input sequentially; instead, they use self-attention mechanisms to consider all parts of the input simultaneously, leading to substantial improvements in efficiency and effectiveness.

Self-Attention:

This feature allows Transformers to dynamically focus on different parts of the input sentence as they generate each word in the response, facilitating a deeper understanding of context and relationships within the text.

Transformers: Revolutionizing NLP

Transformers, introduced in the seminal paper "Attention is All You Need" by Vaswani et al., represent a paradigm shift in natural language processing. Unlike their predecessors, which processed inputs sequentially, Transformers analyze entire sequences of data simultaneously, thanks to the self-attention mechanism. This allows for more efficient training and improved handling of long-range dependencies in text, making Transformers especially suited for generative chatbot applications.

Self-Attention: The Core of Transformers

Self-attention is a mechanism that allows each position in the input sequence to attend to all positions in the previous layer of the model simultaneously. This is achieved by computing a set of attention scores that determine how much focus should be placed on other parts of the input sequence when producing the output for a given position.

Mechanism and Operation

Attention Scores: For each token in the input sequence, the model calculates a score reflecting the relevance of every other token to the current one. These scores determine how much each token will contribute to the representation of the token being processed.

Weighted Sum: The attention scores are used to create a weighted sum of the input tokens, producing an output vector that contains aggregated information from across the entire sequence. This process is replicated for each token, generating a comprehensive context-aware representation.

Layer Stacking: Transformers consist of multiple layers of self-attention mechanisms stacked on top of each other, allowing the model to refine and deepen its understanding of the input sequence at each layer.

Advantages of Self-Attention in Dialogue Systems

- **Efficiency:** By processing all parts of the sequence simultaneously, Transformers are significantly more efficient than RNNs or LSTMs, especially for longer sequences.

- **Contextual Understanding:** Self-attention provides a nuanced understanding of the context and relationships within the text, capturing subtle dependencies and nuances that enhance the quality of generated responses.

- **Scalability:** The parallel processing capabilities of Transformers enable them to scale to very large datasets and models, facilitating the training of powerful generative chatbots on extensive corpora of conversational data.

Implications for Generative Chatbots

The adoption of Transformers and self-attention mechanisms in generative chatbots has led to notable advancements in conversational AI:

- **Improved Coherence and Relevance:** Chatbots powered by Transformers can generate responses that are more coherent, contextually relevant, and aligned with the flow of conversation, significantly improving user engagement and satisfaction.

- **Enhanced Language Modeling:** The ability of Transformers to capture complex linguistic patterns and structures has raised the bar for language modeling, enabling chatbots to handle a wide array of conversational topics and styles with greater fluency.

- **Versatility:** Transformer-based chatbots exhibit remarkable versatility, excelling in both specific, goal-oriented tasks and open-ended, conversational interactions.

Transformers, with their self-attention mechanism have revolutionized the development of generative chatbots. By offering a more efficient, contextually aware, and scalable approach to processing natural language, Transformers empower chatbots to engage in more meaningful, human-like conversations. As conversational AI continues to evolve, the Transformer architecture stands as a cornerstone of innovation, driving forward the capabilities of dialogue systems and setting new standards for natural language understanding and generation.

Pre-training and Fine-tuning:

Transformers are often pre-trained on vast corpora of text, learning general language patterns and structures. They can then be fine-tuned on specific conversational datasets, enabling them to excel in particular domains or conversational styles.

The Essence of Pre-training and Fine-tuning

Pre-training and fine-tuning constitute a two-phase approach to model development in NLP. Pre-training involves training a model on a large corpus of data, allowing it to learn a broad understanding of language patterns, structures, and contexts. Fine-tuning, on the other hand, adapts this pre-trained model to specific tasks or domains by further training it on a smaller, task-specific dataset.

Pre-training

- **Objective:** The goal of pre-training is to equip the model with a generalized language understanding. This is achieved by exposing the model to vast amounts of text data, enabling it to learn from the linguistic diversity and complexity inherent in natural language.

- **Techniques:** For sequence-to-sequence models and Transformers, pre-training often involves tasks like masked language modeling (predicting missing words in a sentence) or next sentence prediction, which help the model grasp syntax, semantics, and discourse.

Fine-tuning

- **Task-Specific Adaptation:** During fine-tuning, the pre-trained model is further trained on a dataset specific to the desired conversational domain or task. This process tailors the model's generalized understanding of language to the nuances and specific requirements of the chatbot's intended function.

- **Efficiency:** Fine-tuning requires significantly less data and computational resources than training a model from scratch, as the model has already acquired a foundational language understanding during pre-training.

Significance in Generative Chatbots

The pre-training and fine-tuning paradigm has profound implications for the development of generative chatbots:

- **Enhanced Performance:** By leveraging the comprehensive language understanding acquired during pre-training, chatbots can generate more coherent, contextually appropriate, and diverse responses.

- **Domain Specificity:** Fine-tuning allows developers to customize generative chatbots for particular domains or conversational scenarios, improving the relevance and accuracy of the chatbot's interactions within those contexts.

- **Resource Efficiency:** This approach significantly reduces the amount of labeled data and computational power needed to create effective chatbots, making advanced conversational AI more accessible.

Challenges and Considerations

While pre-training and fine-tuning offer considerable advantages, they also present challenges:

- **Data Quality and Bias:** The quality and representativeness of the pre-training and fine-tuning datasets are crucial. Biases or inaccuracies in the data can lead to suboptimal or even problematic behavior in chatbots.

- **Transfer Learning Limitations:** While pre-trained models offer a strong starting point, the effectiveness of fine-tuning can vary depending on the similarity between the pre-training tasks and the specific objectives of the chatbot.

Pre-training and fine-tuning represent a paradigm shift in how dialogue systems and generative chatbots are developed. By combining the broad language understanding acquired through pre-training with the nuanced, task-specific adaptations made during fine-tuning, this methodology enables the creation of chatbots that are both linguistically proficient and tailored to specific conversational needs. As the field of NLP continues to evolve, the strategic application of pre-training and fine-tuning will undoubtedly remain central to the advancement of conversational AI, driving forward the capabilities and applications of generative chatbots.

Advantages of Generative Chatbots

- **Flexibility and Novelty:** Generative chatbots can produce a wide variety of responses, including novel sentences that have never been explicitly programmed or observed during training, offering a more engaging conversational experience.

- **Contextual Awareness:** Thanks to models like Transformers, these chatbots excel in maintaining context over the course of an interaction, allowing for more coherent and meaningful conversations.

- **Personalization:** The ability to generate responses dynamically enables chatbots to tailor their language, tone, and content to the individual user, enhancing personalization and user satisfaction.

Challenges

- **Computational Resources:** Training and deploying state-of-the-art models like Transformers require significant computational power and data, which can be a barrier for some applications.

- **Maintaining Coherence:** While generative models can produce a wide range of responses, ensuring that these responses remain relevant and coherent, especially over long conversations, remains a challenge.

- **Safety and Control:** Generative chatbots may inadvertently produce inappropriate or undesirable responses, necessitating mechanisms to filter and control output.

Generative chatbots, powered by sequence-to-sequence models and Transformers represent a leap forward in the quest for machines that can engage in human-like dialogue. These models' ability to understand input, maintain context, and generate coherent, contextually appropriate responses has significantly expanded the potential applications for chatbots, making them more versatile, engaging, and effective tools for a wide range of conversational tasks. As NLP continues to evolve, generative chatbots are poised to play an increasingly central role in shaping the future of human-computer interaction.

Evaluation Metrics for Dialogue Systems:

The evaluation of dialogue systems and chatbots is presented as a critical aspect of their development and refinement. Given the complexity of human language and the diverse contexts in which conversational agents operate, determining the effectiveness of these systems requires a nuanced approach. Various metrics have been developed to assess different dimensions of performance, including the quality of responses, user satisfaction, and the system's ability to achieve specific tasks.

BLEU Score (Bilingual Evaluation Understudy)

Description: Originally developed for machine translation, the BLEU score measures how closely a system's generated text matches reference texts. In the context of chatbots, it can assess the similarity between a chatbot's response and a set of human-generated responses.

Application: While BLEU offers an objective measure of textual similarity, its applicability to dialogue systems is limited by its focus on surface-level matches, potentially overlooking the nuances of conversational context and appropriateness.

ROUGE Score (Recall-Oriented Understudy for Gisting Evaluation)

Description: The ROUGE score evaluates the quality of a summary by comparing it to one or more reference summaries. It includes several measures, such as ROUGE-N, which compares n-grams of the system's output with those of the reference texts.

Application: Similar to BLEU, ROUGE can be used to evaluate the similarity of chatbot responses to expected responses, with considerations for its limitations in capturing conversational dynamics.

Perplexity

Description: Perplexity is a measure of how well a probability model predicts a sample. In dialogue systems, it assesses the language model's ability to anticipate the next word in a sequence, offering insights into its linguistic proficiency.

Application: While useful for evaluating the model's understanding of language structure, perplexity does not directly measure the quality or relevance of chatbot responses in a conversational context.

F1 Score and Precision-Recall

Description: These metrics evaluate the chatbot's ability to retrieve or generate relevant information. Precision measures the proportion of relevant responses generated, while recall assesses the system's ability to generate all relevant responses. The F1 score provides a harmonic mean of precision and recall.

Application: Particularly relevant for information retrieval chatbots, these metrics balance the trade-off between providing accurate information and covering the breadth of possible relevant responses.

User Satisfaction

Description: User satisfaction surveys and ratings offer direct feedback on the users' perceived quality of interactions with the chatbot. These subjective measures can include aspects like helpfulness, ease of use, and overall satisfaction.

Application: User satisfaction is arguably the most comprehensive metric, capturing the end-to-end experience of interacting with the chatbot. However, it is influenced by a wide range of factors beyond the system's linguistic capabilities.

Task Success Rate

Description: For goal-oriented dialogue systems, the task success rate measures the chatbot's effectiveness in achieving the intended outcome of the conversation, such as completing a booking or accurately answering a query.

Application: This metric is critical for evaluating the functional performance of chatbots designed for specific tasks, providing a clear measure of effectiveness in real-world applications.

Dialogue Length and Turn-Taking

Description: These metrics assess the efficiency of conversations, measuring the number of turns or the length of dialogue required to achieve a resolution or maintain user engagement.

Application: Ideal dialogue length varies by context but can indicate the system's efficiency in guiding the conversation and maintaining user interest.

Evaluating dialogue systems and chatbots involves a multifaceted approach that considers linguistic accuracy, relevance, user experience, and task-specific effectiveness. The choice of evaluation metrics should align with the chatbot's objectives, ensuring a comprehensive assessment of its performance. As the field of conversational AI advances, the development of more sophisticated metrics and evaluation methods will be crucial for driving improvements, enhancing user satisfaction, and achieving more natural and productive human-computer interactions.

Conclusion

Dialogue systems and chatbots, represent a fascinating application of NLP technology, with the potential to transform how humans interact with machines. Through the integration of NLU, dialogue management, and NLG, these systems strive to provide meaningful, engaging, and helpful conversational experiences. As NLP and AI technologies continue to advance, the capabilities of dialogue systems and chatbots will undoubtedly expand, further enhancing their applicability and impact across a wide range of industries and domains.

Chapter 8: Language Translation

The domain of language translation, specifically machine translation (MT), is explored as a cornerstone application of NLP that has seen remarkable advancements over the years. Machine translation involves the automatic conversion of text or speech from one language to another by computers, striving to achieve human-like accuracy and fluency. This section provides a detailed overview of the evolution, methodologies, challenges, and the current state of machine translation, underscoring its significance in bridging language barriers and facilitating global communication.

Evolution of Machine Translation

The journey of machine translation begins with rule-based systems, which relied on linguistic rules and dictionaries to translate text. These systems, while pioneering, were limited by the complexity and variability of human languages. The advent of statistical machine translation (SMT) marked a significant advancement, using statistical models to infer the probability of translation equivalents. The field has further evolved with the introduction of neural machine translation (NMT), leveraging deep learning techniques to improve translation quality significantly.

Early Beginnings and Rule-Based Machine Translation (RBMT)

The journey of machine translation began in the 1950s, sparked by the dream of overcoming language barriers through technology. Early systems were based on rule-based machine translation (RBMT), which relied heavily on linguistic rules and bilingual dictionaries manually crafted by linguists. RBMT systems operated by analyzing the source text according to the rules of the source language, translating the constituent elements, and then synthesizing the target text based on the target language's rules.

Strengths: RBMT excelled in translating simple sentences and maintaining grammatical consistency.

Limitations: The rigid rule-based approach struggled with linguistic nuances, idiomatic expressions, and the vast diversity of language use, making it difficult to scale across languages and domains.

Statistical Machine Translation (SMT)

The 1990s witnessed the rise of statistical machine translation (SMT), which marked a significant departure from RBMT. SMT models were built on the principle that translation patterns could be learned from large corpora of bilingual text. By analyzing these corpora, SMT systems could infer the probability of certain words or phrases being accurate translations of each other.

Methodology: SMT relied on statistical algorithms to align segments of text between the source and target languages, using these alignments to generate translations based on probability models.

Impact: SMT represented a leap forward in MT, offering greater flexibility and scalability than RBMT. It enabled translations that were more adaptable to context and varied language use, though challenges remained in handling complex sentences and maintaining coherence across longer texts.

Neural Machine Translation (NMT)

The advent of neural machine translation (NMT) in the mid-2010s ushered in the current era of MT. NMT leverages deep neural networks, particularly sequence-to-sequence (Seq2Seq) models, to translate text. Unlike its predecessors, NMT considers the entire input sentence as a whole, enabling it to produce more fluent and accurate translations.

- **Breakthroughs:** The introduction of attention mechanisms within NMT models allowed for even finer control over the translation process, addressing the issue of long-range dependencies by focusing on relevant parts of the input for each segment of the output.

- **Advantages:** NMT systems have significantly outperformed SMT in terms of translation quality, particularly for languages with sufficient training data. They offer improved handling of nuances, context, and the overall fluency of translations.

The Era of Transformers and Beyond

Transformers, a type of model introduced by Vaswani et al. in 2017, have further revolutionized NMT. Characterized by their self-attention mechanisms, Transformers process entire sentences simultaneously, making them more efficient and effective than previous models.

- **Innovation:** The Transformer architecture has led to the development of models like BERT and GPT, which, when applied to MT, achieve unprecedented translation quality across a wide range of languages.

- **Future Directions:** Ongoing research focuses on improving NMT for low-resource languages, reducing biases in translations, and enhancing the interpretability and trustworthiness of MT systems.

The evolution of machine translation, as chronicled in mirrors the broader advances in computational linguistics and artificial intelligence. From rule-based systems to the neural network-driven approaches of today, each stage has contributed to breaking down language barriers, facilitating global communication, and enriching cross-cultural understanding. As MT continues to evolve, it stands as a testament to the ingenuity and collaborative spirit of the research community, driving towards a future where language no longer divides us.

Methodologies in Machine Translation

Rule-Based Machine Translation (RBMT)

Description: RBMT systems translate based on an extensive set of linguistic rules and bilingual dictionaries for each language pair. These rules dictate how words, phrases, and grammatical structures should be converted from the source to the target language.

Limitations: The main drawback is the need for exhaustive, manually crafted rules and dictionaries, which makes scaling across languages and domains challenging.

Statistical Machine Translation (SMT)

Description: SMT models translation as a statistical problem, using large corpora of aligned texts (parallel corpora) in both the source and target languages to learn translation probabilities.

Advancements: Techniques like phrase-based SMT improved translation quality by considering the context around individual words or phrases, leading to more coherent translations.

Neural Machine Translation (NMT)

Description: NMT employs deep neural networks, particularly sequence-to-sequence (Seq2Seq) models with attention mechanisms, to learn to translate texts in an end-to-end manner. NMT systems have significantly outperformed their predecessors in terms of translation quality and fluency.

Impact: The use of recurrent neural networks (RNNs), convolutional neural networks (CNNs), and more recently, Transformer models, has enabled NMT to capture complex linguistic patterns and dependencies, producing translations that are often indistinguishable from human translations.

Challenges in Machine Translation

Handling Ambiguity and Context: One of the primary challenges in MT is dealing with lexical and structural ambiguities inherent in human languages. Context plays a crucial role in determining the meaning of words and phrases, requiring sophisticated models to accurately capture and interpret it.

Maintaining Fluency and Coherence: Ensuring that translated texts are not only accurate but also fluent and coherent over long passages remains a significant challenge, especially for languages with diverse grammatical structures and idiomatic expressions.

Domain-Specific Terminology: Specialized domains, such as legal, medical, or technical fields, often require precise translations of terminology, which can be difficult to achieve without extensive domain-specific training data.

Current State and Future Directions

The current state of machine translation is characterized by the dominance of NMT, particularly Transformer-based models, which have set new standards for accuracy, fluency, and speed. The integration of advanced techniques like transfer learning, domain adaptation, and multilingual models offers promising pathways to further improvements. Additionally, the exploration of unsupervised and semi-supervised learning methods aims to reduce the reliance on large parallel corpora, making high-quality translation accessible for a broader range of languages and domains.

Introduction To Machine Translation:

The introduction to machine translation (MT) and language translation tasks sets the stage for understanding one of the most ambitious and impactful applications of natural language processing. Machine translation seeks to bridge the gaps between languages, enabling the automatic conversion of text or spoken language from one language (source) to another (target) while preserving meaning, nuance, and context. This foundational section explores the objectives, significance, and complexities of MT, providing a gateway to the subsequent in-depth exploration of its evolution, methodologies, and challenges.

Objectives of Machine Translation

The primary objective of machine translation is to produce accurate and coherent translations without human intervention. MT aims to achieve several key goals:

Accessibility:

By breaking down language barriers, MT makes information, knowledge, and communication accessible to a broader audience, fostering global connectivity.

Breaking Down Linguistic Barriers

One of the primary objectives of machine translation is to eliminate the barriers posed by language differences. In an increasingly globalized world, the need for swift, accurate translation has never been more critical. MT systems strive to provide instant translation services that enable individuals and organizations to access and share information across linguistic boundaries, fostering global communication and understanding.

Facilitating Cross-Cultural Communication

MT plays a crucial role in facilitating cross-cultural communication by allowing people to interact and collaborate with others from different linguistic backgrounds. This accessibility is vital in various contexts, including international diplomacy, global business operations, and multicultural communities, where clear and effective communication across languages can bridge cultural divides.

Democratizing Access to Information

Accessibility through machine translation extends to the democratization of information. By providing translations of web content, academic papers, legal documents, and more, MT systems ensure that knowledge is not confined to those who speak certain languages. This democratization is particularly important in education and research, where access to the latest findings and literature should not be limited by language.

Supporting Language Learning and Preservation

Machine translation also supports language learning and preservation. For learners, MT tools offer immediate translations that can aid comprehension and language acquisition. For lesser-spoken languages, MT contributes to preservation efforts by providing translation capabilities that increase the language's visibility and usability online, potentially encouraging its use and study.

Enhancing User Experience in Technology

In the digital age, MT enhances user experience by enabling multilingual interfaces and content in software applications, websites, and digital platforms. This inclusivity ensures that technology products can reach a wider audience, catering to users in their native languages and thus broadening the technology's impact and appeal.

Challenges in Achieving Accessibility

Despite these objectives, achieving accessibility through machine translation is not without challenges. Issues such as translation accuracy, handling of idiomatic expressions, and cultural nuances pose ongoing hurdles. Additionally, the disparity in resource availability between languages—where some languages have vast amounts of data to train models on, while others have very little—can lead to uneven translation quality and coverage.

The objective of enhancing accessibility through machine translation underscores the transformative potential of this technology. By breaking down linguistic barriers, facilitating cross-cultural communication, democratizing access to information, and supporting language learning and preservation, MT plays a crucial role in fostering a more inclusive, interconnected global community. As the field of NLP continues to advance, the pursuit of more accurate, nuanced, and equitable machine translation remains a key endeavor, promising to further expand the horizons of accessibility and understanding across languages.

Efficiency:

MT offers a rapid translation solution compared to manual translation processes, crucial for time-sensitive or voluminous translation tasks.

Defining Efficiency in Machine Translation

Efficiency in machine translation encompasses both the speed of translation and the ability to process large volumes of content within limited time frames. It involves the development of systems that can instantly translate text, making information accessible across language barriers without the delay inherent in manual translation processes.

Speed of Translation

Instantaneous Results: One of the most significant advantages of MT is its ability to provide immediate translations, which is particularly crucial for dynamic environments like live communication, customer support, and real-time information dissemination.

Scalability

Handling Large Volumes: MT systems are designed to handle vast amounts of data efficiently, enabling the translation of large corpora, websites, and documentation that would be impractical or exceedingly time-consuming for human translators.

Benefits of Efficient Machine Translation

Global Communication: By facilitating quick and scalable translations, MT contributes to breaking down language barriers, enhancing global communication, and fostering cross-cultural understanding.

Economic Advantages: Efficiency in MT can significantly reduce the cost associated with translating vast amounts of information, making it an economically viable solution for businesses and organizations seeking to internationalize their content.

Accessibility of Information: The speed and scalability of MT allow for a broader dissemination of knowledge and information, making content accessible to non-native speakers almost immediately after its original publication.

Challenges in Achieving Efficiency

While the pursuit of efficiency is a key objective, achieving it poses several challenges:

- **Quality vs. Speed:** Ensuring high-quality translations while maintaining speed is a significant challenge. The complexity of natural language and the nuances of meaning can sometimes necessitate trade-offs between speed and the accuracy or fluency of translations.

- **Resource Intensity:** Advanced MT models, particularly those based on deep learning, require substantial computational resources for training and inference, which can impact the speed and scalability of translations, especially for languages with limited computational support.

- **Language and Domain Variability:** The efficiency of MT systems can vary across languages and specific domains. Languages with limited resources or highly specialized terminology may pose challenges to the speed and scalability of translations.

Technological Advancements Addressing Efficiency

Advancements in NLP and computational hardware continue to address these challenges:

- **Optimization of Neural Networks:** Ongoing research aims to optimize neural MT models, improving their speed without compromising translation quality.

- **Hardware Improvements:** Advances in computational hardware, including GPUs and specialized chips for AI tasks, enhance the efficiency of MT systems, enabling faster processing and translation of large datasets.

- **Hybrid Approaches:** Combining the strengths of different MT approaches, such as using rule-based pre-processing steps or incorporating statistical methods, can improve the efficiency of neural MT systems, particularly for challenging languages and domains.

Efficiency stands as a cornerstone objective of machine translation. By aiming to produce instantaneous, scalable translations, MT technologies strive to unlock a world where language is no longer a barrier to information, opportunity, and understanding. As MT continues to evolve, the balance between speed, quality, and resource efficiency will remain a central focus, driving innovation and expanding the frontiers of accessible, global communication.

Scalability:

Automated translation systems can handle vast amounts of data and support multiple languages, addressing the increasing demand for multilingual content across digital platforms.

The Importance of Scalability in Machine Translation

Scalability is essential for machine translation to meet the diverse and expanding needs of global communication. As businesses, organizations, and individuals increasingly operate in a multilingual world, the demand for translation services spans a vast array of languages, dialects, and specialized domains. Scalability ensures that MT systems can handle these varied demands efficiently, providing high-quality translations across different scales of operation.

Handling Diverse and Large-Scale Data

- **Volume:** Scalable MT systems can process large volumes of text swiftly, crucial for translating websites, documents, and data sets that grow exponentially.

- **Variety:** Effective MT must accommodate a wide range of languages and dialects, including less commonly spoken languages, ensuring inclusivity and broader access to information.

Benefits of Scalable Machine Translation

- **Global Reach:** Scalability enables businesses and content creators to reach a global audience by translating content into multiple languages without significant delays or prohibitive costs.

- **Real-time Communication:** In settings requiring instant translation, such as customer support or international conferences, scalable MT systems provide immediate language translation services, facilitating seamless cross-lingual interactions.

- **Accessibility:** By efficiently translating educational materials, legal documents, and other critical information, scalable MT systems play a vital role in making knowledge and services accessible to non-native speakers.

Challenges to Achieving Scalability

Scalability in machine translation faces several challenges, from technological constraints to the intricacies of human language:

- **Computational Resources:** The intensive computational demands of training and running advanced neural MT models can limit scalability, especially for real-time applications and languages with complex grammatical structures.

- **Language Coverage:** Ensuring comprehensive language coverage, particularly for low-resource languages with limited training data, poses a significant challenge to scalability.

- **Quality Maintenance:** As the scope of MT expands, maintaining consistent translation quality across languages and domains becomes increasingly challenging, requiring continual refinement of models and algorithms.

Advances Enhancing Scalability

Technological innovations and research in NLP are continually addressing the scalability challenges in MT:

- **Efficient Model Architectures:** Development of more efficient neural network architectures, such as Transformer models, has significantly improved the speed and efficiency of MT systems, enhancing their scalability.

- **Multilingual Models:** The advent of multilingual MT models capable of translating multiple languages with a single system has streamlined the translation process, reducing the need for separate models for each language pair and thereby improving scalability.

- **Dynamic Resource Allocation:** Advances in cloud computing and AI hardware enable dynamic allocation of computational resources, allowing MT systems to scale up for large tasks or scale down for smaller, more routine translations.

Scalability stands as a critical objective of machine translation. It embodies the capability of MT systems to adapt and efficiently manage the growing and diversifying demands of global communication. Through ongoing advancements in NLP technologies and computational infrastructure, scalability in machine translation continues to evolve, promising to enhance the accessibility of information, foster global connectivity, and bridge language divides more effectively than ever before.

Significance of Language Translation Tasks

Language translation tasks are pivotal in various domains, impacting everything from international business and diplomacy to education and entertainment. These tasks involve not just the literal translation of words but also the adaptation of cultural references, idiomatic expressions, and specialized terminology to ensure that the translated content is culturally and contextually appropriate.

Cultural Sensitivity:

Effective translation requires an understanding of cultural nuances, ensuring that translations are not only linguistically accurate but also culturally respectful and relevant.

Cultural Sensitivity in Language Translation

Cultural sensitivity in language translation refers to the ability of MT systems to account for and adapt to the cultural contexts and nuances inherent in different languages. This involves more than mere word-for-word translation; it requires an understanding of idioms, cultural references, societal norms, and the subtle connotations that words and phrases may carry in different cultures.

Importance of Cultural Sensitivity

- **Accurate Contextual Translation:** Culturally sensitive translation ensures that the meaning and intent behind the source text are preserved in the target language, accounting for cultural differences that could affect interpretation.

- **Prevention of Miscommunication:** By recognizing and appropriately translating cultural nuances, MT systems can avoid potential misunderstandings or offenses that might arise from culturally insensitive translations.

- **Enhanced User Experience:** Translations that reflect an understanding of cultural context resonate more deeply with users, fostering greater engagement and trust in the translated content.

Challenges to Achieving Cultural Sensitivity

Incorporating cultural sensitivity into machine translation presents several challenges, largely due to the complexity of human cultures and the subtleties of linguistic expression:

- **Variability Across Cultures:** The vast diversity of cultural practices, beliefs, and norms across different societies makes it challenging to create MT systems that can universally account for these variations.

- **Idiomatic and Non-Literal Language:** Idioms, proverbs, and culturally specific references often do not have direct equivalents in other languages, requiring translators to find creative, contextually appropriate solutions.

- **Evolving Language and Culture:** Language and culture are not static; they evolve over time. Keeping MT systems updated with current cultural contexts and linguistic usage is an ongoing challenge.

Technological and Methodological Approaches

Advancements in NLP and computational linguistics have led to innovative approaches to enhance cultural sensitivity in MT:

- **Context-Aware Translation Models:** Development of neural machine translation models that can consider broader context and cultural cues in their translations, improving the ability to handle idiomatic and culturally nuanced language.

- **Incorporation of Cultural Knowledge Bases:** Integrating extensive cultural knowledge bases into MT systems can aid in identifying and appropriately translating culturally specific references or norms.

- **Human-in-the-Loop Systems:** Combining automated translation with human review and correction processes can ensure that translations meet cultural sensitivity standards, particularly for high-stakes or nuanced texts.

The significance of cultural sensitivity in language translation tasks highlights a crucial dimension of machine translation that transcends technical accuracy to embrace the human aspects of language use. Achieving cultural sensitivity in MT is pivotal for creating translations that are not only linguistically correct but also culturally resonant and respectful. As MT technologies continue to advance, the integration of cultural understanding into translation processes remains a key objective, reflecting the evolving nature of language as a tool for both communication and cultural expression.

Domain-specific Challenges:

Specialized fields such as legal, medical, and technical domains present additional challenges due to their precise terminology and the critical importance of accuracy.

Domain-specific Challenges in Language Translation

Domain-specific challenges in language translation stem from the need to accurately and appropriately translate content that contains specialized terminology, concepts, and stylistic conventions unique to a particular field. These challenges highlight the intricacy of language and its deep interconnection with professional knowledge and context.

Complexity of Specialized Terminology

- **Terminology Accuracy:** Precision in translating domain-specific terms is crucial, as even minor errors can lead to significant misunderstandings. This requires MT systems to have an extensive understanding of the specialized lexicon.

- **Contextual Variability:** Many terms and concepts have different meanings or implications depending on their context within the domain, complicating the translation process.

Stylistic and Conventional Norms

- **Adherence to Style Guides:** Certain domains follow strict stylistic and formatting guidelines that translations must comply with to be considered accurate and professional.

- **Consistency:** Maintaining consistency in terminology and style across multiple documents or within large projects is essential for clarity and coherence.

Implications of Domain-specific Challenges

The presence of domain-specific challenges in machine translation has profound implications for the accuracy, reliability, and trustworthiness of translated content.

- **Risk of Misinformation:** Inaccurate translations can lead to the dissemination of misinformation, with potentially grave consequences in fields like medicine and law.

- **Impact on Professional Practice:** Errors or inconsistencies in translation can affect professional practice, decision-making, and compliance with regulations.

Strategies for Addressing Domain-specific Challenges

Tackling domain-specific challenges in MT requires targeted strategies that leverage both technological advancements and human expertise.

- **Customized Machine Translation Models:** Developing MT models tailored to specific domains can improve accuracy. This involves training models on large corpora of domain-specific texts to learn the relevant terminology and stylistic conventions.

- **Terminology Management:** Implementing terminology management systems within MT workflows helps ensure consistency and accuracy in the use of specialized terms. This can involve the use of glossaries or controlled vocabularies.

- **Human Expertise:** Integrating human expertise through post-editing processes or human-in-the-loop systems allows for the refinement of machine-translated content, ensuring that translations meet domain-specific standards.

- **Continuous Learning and Adaptation:** MT systems must be designed to continually learn and adapt to new developments and changes within specific domains, incorporating the latest terminology and conventions.

The domain-specific challenges in language translation underscore the complexity of translating specialized content accurately and effectively. Addressing these challenges requires a multifaceted approach that combines advanced MT technologies with deep domain knowledge and human expertise. As MT continues to evolve, the development of more sophisticated, domain-adapted models and the strategic integration of professional knowledge will be key to overcoming these challenges, enhancing the quality and reliability of domain-specific translations, and further bridging the gaps in global communication.

Complexities of Machine Translation

Machine translation is fraught with complexities that stem from the inherent properties of language and the diversity of linguistic expressions:

Ambiguity and Polysemy: Words and phrases often carry multiple meanings, and the correct interpretation depends heavily on context, making disambiguation a significant challenge for MT systems.

Syntactic and Grammatical Differences: Variations in grammar, sentence structure, and word order between languages pose challenges in maintaining the natural flow and coherence of translated text.

Idiomatic Expressions and Cultural References: Translating idioms or culture-specific references requires not just a direct linguistic translation but often a reimagining of the expression to convey the intended meaning in the target language.

Approaches to Machine Translation

MT approaches have evolved significantly over time, reflecting advancements in computational linguistics and artificial intelligence:

Rule-Based Machine Translation (RBMT): Early MT efforts relied on linguistic rules and dictionaries for each language pair, offering structured but inflexible translations.

Statistical Machine Translation (SMT): SMT introduced statistical models that learn translation probabilities from bilingual corpora, improving flexibility and scalability. **Neural Machine Translation (NMT):** The advent of NMT, particularly with sequence-to-sequence models and attention mechanisms, has dramatically enhanced the quality and fluidity of translations by leveraging deep learning techniques.

The introduction to machine translation and language translation tasks highlights the ambitious goal of automating linguistic translation and the challenges that arise from the complex nature of human languages. As MT continues to evolve, driven by advances in NLP and AI, its potential to transform global communication and information exchange grows, making it a cornerstone of modern linguistic technology. The pursuit of more accurate, natural, and accessible translations remains a dynamic field of research and development, reflecting the ongoing quest to build bridges between the world's languages and cultures.

Statistical Machine Translation (SMT):

The exploration of statistical machine translation (SMT) represents a pivotal chapter in the evolution of machine translation technologies. SMT marked a significant departure from the rule-based systems that dominated the early years of machine translation, introducing a data-driven approach that leverages statistical models to translate text from one language to another. This comprehensive section delves into the nuances of phrase-based SMT and the transition to neural approaches, detailing their methodologies, strengths, and the transformative impact they have had on the field of machine translation.

Statistical Machine Translation: An Overview

Statistical machine translation relies on the analysis of bilingual text corpora to learn how words and phrases in one language correspond to those in another. By building statistical models from these alignments, SMT systems can predict the most likely translation of a given sentence based on the probabilities derived from the training data.

Foundations of Statistical Machine Translation

Statistical Machine Translation is grounded in the idea that the translation process can be modeled statistically. The core premise is that the best translation of a given text is one that maximizes the probability of producing a target language text from a source language text, based on the evidence found in bilingual corpora.

Data-Driven Approach: Unlike its rule-based predecessors, SMT relies on analyzing large volumes of bilingual text to learn translation patterns. This corpus-based approach allows for more flexibility and adaptability in translation.

Language and Translation Models: SMT systems typically consist of a language model, which ensures the fluency of the generated text in the target language, and a translation model, which determines the likelihood of certain words or phrases being translations of each other.

Evolution to Phrase-Based Models

Phrase-based SMT represents an evolution from earlier word-based approaches, addressing some of the limitations associated with translating single words in isolation. Phrase-based models consider chunks of words, or "phrases," as the basic units of translation, allowing for more contextually appropriate translations by capturing idiomatic expressions and local context.

Phrase Extraction and Alignment: This involves identifying and aligning phrases in bilingual corpora, from which the system learns probable translations. The alignment process is crucial for determining which phrases in the source text correspond to phrases in the target text.

Decoding and Scoring: The decoding process in phrase-based SMT searches for the most probable translation based on a combination of the language model and translation model scores. This includes evaluating different phrase orderings and selecting the output that best represents the source text meaning while adhering to the syntactic and stylistic conventions of the target language.

Transition Towards Neural Approaches

The advent of Neural Machine Translation (NMT) has shifted the paradigm once again, offering a more sophisticated approach to capturing the nuances of language. NMT utilizes deep learning and neural network architectures, such as sequence-to-sequence models with attention mechanisms, to provide end-to-end translation capabilities.

From Statistical to Neural: While SMT models translations based on statistical probabilities derived from bilingual corpora, NMT approaches translation as a continuous space problem. This allows for a deeper understanding of linguistic features and context, significantly improving translation quality.

Impact of Neural Networks: The introduction of neural networks in MT has enabled systems to learn complex mappings between languages directly, considering entire sentences or larger text units. This holistic approach has led to translations that are not only more accurate but also more fluent and coherent.

The exploration of statistical machine translation underscores its significance as a foundational technology that paved the way for modern advancements in machine translation. From its statistical beginnings to the development of phrase-based models, and ultimately the transition to neural approaches, SMT has been instrumental in advancing the pursuit of automated, high-quality language translation. As the field continues to evolve, the lessons learned from SMT and its phrase-based methodologies remain integral to the ongoing refinement and innovation in machine translation technologies, driving forward the capabilities and understanding of computational linguistics.

Phrase-Based SMT

Phrase-based SMT represented an advancement over earlier word-based models by translating sequences of words—or phrases—rather than individual words in isolation. This approach acknowledges that words often carry meaning in groups and that their translation can depend significantly on the context provided by adjacent words.

Methodology:

Phrase-based SMT systems align phrases in bilingual corpora and use these alignments to generate a translation model. During translation, the source text is segmented into phrases, which are then translated and re-ordered according to a statistical model.

Phrase-based SMT operates on the principle that translating sequences of words—or "phrases"—together rather than individually leads to more accurate and contextually appropriate translations. This approach acknowledges the importance of local context and the way words interact within phrases to convey meaning.

Core Components of Phrase-Based SMT

- **Phrase Extraction and Alignment:** The first step involves extracting potential phrase pairs from a parallel corpus, which is a collection of texts and their translations. Alignment algorithms identify which phrases in the source language correspond to phrases in the target language, based on statistical likelihood derived from the corpus.

- **Translation Model:** This model computes probabilities for phrase translations, determining how likely it is for a source language phrase to be translated into a particular target language phrase. These probabilities are learned from the frequency and patterns of phrase alignments in the training data.

- **Language Model:** Integral to ensuring the fluency of the output, the language model predicts the likelihood of a phrase occurring in the target language. It helps in selecting the most probable sequence of phrases that not only translates the source text accurately but also maintains coherence and grammatical integrity in the target language.

- **Reordering Model:** Phrase-based SMT must account for differences in sentence structure between languages. The reordering model manages the position and order of translated phrases, addressing syntactic variations to produce sentences that are structurally appropriate in the target language.

- **Decoding:** The decoder is the component that searches for the best translation by considering the combined scores from the translation model, language model, and reordering model. It navigates through the vast space of possible translations to select the output that maximizes overall translation quality according to the models' probabilities.

Advantages of Phrase-Based SMT

- **Contextual Awareness:** By translating phrases as units, phrase-based SMT captures local contextual nuances more effectively than word-based approaches, leading to translations that are more syntactically and semantically aligned with the target language.

- **Handling of Idiomatic Expressions:** This methodology is better equipped to translate idiomatic expressions and collocations, as it is more likely to encounter these phrases as units in the training data.

- **Flexibility and Adaptability:** Phrase-based models offer flexibility in adapting to different languages and domains, as the quality of translation largely depends on the breadth and depth of the parallel corpus used for training.

Challenges and Limitations

- **Complexity and Resource Intensity:** The effectiveness of phrase-based SMT depends on extensive bilingual corpora and significant computational resources for training and decoding, which can be limiting factors, especially for less-resourced languages.

- **Long-Distance Dependencies:** While phrase-based SMT handles local context well, it struggles with long-distance dependencies and maintaining coherence over longer text spans, limitations that would later be addressed by neural models.

The methodology of phrase-based statistical machine translation represents a critical leap forward in machine translation technology. By focusing on phrases as the fundamental units of translation, phrase-based SMT introduced a more nuanced understanding of language and context into the machine translation process. This approach laid the groundwork for the subsequent development of neural machine translation models, which build upon and extend the capabilities of phrase-based SMT to deliver even more sophisticated and contextually aware translations, pushing the boundaries of what is possible in automated language translation.

Neural Machine Translation (NMT)

The advent of neural machine translation represented a paradigm shift in SMT, introducing models that utilize deep neural networks to learn to translate texts. NMT models, particularly those based on the sequence-to-sequence (Seq2Seq) architecture, process and generate entire sentences, considering the full context of the input.

Architecture: NMT systems typically employ an encoder-decoder framework, where the encoder processes the input sentence to generate a context-rich representation, and the decoder generates the translation based on this representation. Attention mechanisms further enhance NMT by allowing the model to focus on different parts of the input sentence during translation, addressing the limitations of phrase-based systems in handling long-range dependencies.

Impact: NMT has dramatically improved the quality of machine translations, offering unprecedented fluency and accuracy. Neural models excel in understanding the nuanced meanings of sentences and generating coherent, contextually appropriate translations.

Challenges: Despite their strengths, NMT systems require substantial computational resources for training and operation. They also necessitate large amounts of bilingual training data, which can be a limitation for languages with fewer resources.

Statistical machine translation, from phrase-based to neural approaches has significantly advanced the capabilities of machine translation. While phrase-based SMT laid the groundwork by introducing a more context-aware translation process, the transition to neural machine translation has unlocked new levels of fluency and accuracy, making translations more natural and accessible than ever before. As NMT continues to evolve, it promises to further refine and expand the possibilities of machine translation, making it an indispensable tool in the global exchange of information and ideas.

Neural Machine Translation (NMT):

A detailed exploration of phrase-based statistical machine translation (SMT) illuminates this crucial advancement in the realm of machine translation. Phrase-based SMT marked a significant evolution from earlier word-based models by adopting phrases as the basic units of translation, thereby capturing linguistic nuances more effectively.

Phrase-Based SMT Methodology

Phrase-based SMT operates on the principle that translating sequences of words - or "phrases" - together rather than individually leads to more accurate and contextually appropriate translations. This approach acknowledges the importance of local context and the way words interact within phrases to convey meaning.

Core Components of Phrase-Based SMT

Phrase Extraction and Alignment:

The first step involves extracting potential phrase pairs from a parallel corpus, which is a collection of texts and their translations. Alignment algorithms identify which phrases in the source language correspond to phrases in the target language, based on statistical likelihood derived from the corpus.

Phrase Extraction and Alignment: An Overview

Phrase extraction and alignment are foundational to the operation of phrase-based SMT systems. These processes involve identifying statistically significant sequences of words (phrases) in the source language and determining their most likely translations in the target language, based on analysis of bilingual text corpora.

Principles of Phrase Extraction

- **Identification of Candidate Phrases:** The first step involves analyzing aligned sentences in a parallel corpus to identify all possible sequences of words (phrases) that could constitute meaningful units for translation.

- **Statistical Significance:** Not all identified phrases are equally likely to be useful for translation. Statistical measures are applied to determine the significance of each phrase pair based on their frequency of co-occurrence and alignment patterns in the parallel corpus.

Alignment Process

- **Word Alignment:** Initially, individual words in the source and target sentences are aligned using statistical models. This alignment serves as the basis for identifying potential phrase pairs.

- **Phrase Pair Extraction:** Based on word alignments, algorithms extract pairs of phrases (source-target pairs) that represent potential translations of each other. The extraction process considers various combinations and lengths of sequences to maximize coverage and translation accuracy.

- **Consistency Check:** Extracted phrase pairs undergo a consistency check to ensure that they align properly without conflicting with the word-level alignments. Only consistent phrase pairs are retained for the translation model.

Methodologies for Phrase Extraction and Alignment

The methodologies for phrase extraction and alignment have evolved to incorporate sophisticated statistical models and heuristics designed to optimize translation quality:

Heuristic-Based Extraction: Early methods relied on heuristics to guide the extraction of phrase pairs, setting constraints on phrase lengths and alignments to manage computational complexity.

Statistical Optimization: Advanced approaches use statistical optimization techniques to refine the selection of phrase pairs, enhancing the precision and recall of extracted translations by evaluating their likelihood in a probabilistic framework.

Implications for Phrase-Based SMT

The process of phrase extraction and alignment directly impacts the effectiveness of phrase-based SMT systems:

- **Translation Quality:** Accurate phrase extraction and alignment lead to translations that better capture the syntactic and semantic nuances of the source text, resulting in more fluent and coherent output.

- **Coverage and Flexibility:** By extracting a wide range of phrase pairs, phrase-based SMT systems gain the flexibility to handle varied linguistic structures and idiomatic expressions, enhancing their applicability across different languages and domains.

Phrase extraction and alignment serve as pivotal components in the architecture of phrase-based statistical machine translation. These processes enable machine translation systems to capture and utilize the complex interplay of words within phrases, significantly advancing the field's ability to produce accurate and contextually appropriate translations. As machine translation technologies continue to evolve, the methodologies underpinning phrase extraction and alignment remain fundamental to the quest for improved linguistic understanding and translation performance.

Translation Model:

This model computes probabilities for phrase translations, determining how likely it is for a source language phrase to be translated into a particular target language phrase. These probabilities are learned from the frequency and patterns of phrase alignments in the training data.

Translation Model in Phrase-Based SMT: An Overview

The translation model in phrase-based SMT systems is responsible for assigning probabilities to potential translations based on how likely a source language phrase is to be translated into a target language phrase. It forms the backbone of the translation process, guiding the selection of phrases that make up the final translated output.

Operation of the Translation Model

Probability Estimation: The translation model estimates the probabilities of phrase pairs (source-target pairs) extracted during the phrase extraction and alignment process. These probabilities are calculated based on the frequency of occurrence of each pair within the aligned bilingual corpus, reflecting how often a particular source phrase is translated as a given target phrase.

Contextual Dependency: While primarily focused on direct phrase pair probabilities, advanced models may also consider additional contextual factors, such as the position of phrases within a sentence or the presence of neighboring words, to refine the probability estimates.

Significance of the Translation Model

The translation model is crucial for several reasons:

- **Accuracy of Translation:** By prioritizing phrase pairs with higher probabilities, the translation model ensures that the most likely translations are selected, enhancing the accuracy and naturalness of the output.

- **Handling Ambiguity:** The model plays a key role in resolving translation ambiguities, as multiple target phrases might be valid translations for a single source phrase. Probability scores help in selecting the most contextually appropriate option.

- **Efficiency:** Efficient computation of translation probabilities allows for rapid translation decisions, making phrase-based SMT systems practical for real-time applications.

Challenges in Developing Translation Models

Developing effective translation models within phrase-based SMT systems presents several challenges:

- **Data Sparsity:** For less common phrases or those with few occurrences in the training data, accurately estimating translation probabilities can be difficult, potentially leading to less reliable translations.

- **Phrase Pair Explosion:** The vast number of possible phrase pairs extracted from large corpora can lead to computational challenges, requiring sophisticated models and optimization techniques to manage the explosion of potential translations.

- **Domain Adaptation:** The model's performance can vary significantly across different domains or genres, as specialized terminology or stylistic differences may not be adequately represented in the training data.

Advances and Innovations

To address these challenges, several advances have been made in the development of translation models for phrase-based SMT:

- **Smoothing Techniques:** To mitigate data sparsity issues, smoothing techniques are employed, allowing the model to assign non-zero probabilities to unseen phrase pairs based on similar or related data.

- **Feature-Rich Models:** Modern translation models incorporate a broader range of linguistic and contextual features, including syntactic and semantic information, to improve translation quality.

- **Domain-Specific Training:** Tailoring the training process to specific domains or incorporating domain-adaptive techniques helps enhance the model's performance on specialized texts.

Through the statistical estimation of phrase pair probabilities, the translation model guides the selection of the most appropriate translations, underpinning the system's ability to generate fluent and accurate output. Ongoing advancements in model development and training methodologies continue to refine the capabilities of phrase-based SMT, pushing the boundaries of machine translation accuracy and efficiency.

Language Model:

Integral to ensuring the fluency of the output, the language model predicts the likelihood of a phrase occurring in the target language. It helps in selecting the most probable sequence of phrases that not only translates the source text accurately but also maintains coherence and grammatical integrity in the target language.

Function of the Language Model in Phrase-Based SMT

The language model in phrase-based SMT systems plays a pivotal role in generating translations that are not only accurate but also naturally fluent. It evaluates the likelihood of a sequence of words appearing together in the target language, essentially guiding the translation process towards outputs that resemble native language usage.

Generating Fluent Translations

- **Probability Evaluation:** The language model assigns probabilities to sequences of words (phrases or sentences) based on their occurrence and co-occurrence frequencies within a large corpus of the target language. This statistical measure helps in selecting the most likely word sequences during the translation process.

- **Handling Ambiguity:** In situations where the translation model suggests multiple possible translations for a source phrase, the language model helps in choosing the option that best fits within the context of the surrounding text in the target language, thereby maintaining coherence and fluency.

Importance of the Language Model

- **Enhanced Readability:** By ensuring that translations conform to the syntactic and stylistic norms of the target language, the language model significantly improves the readability and naturalness of the translated text.

- **Contextual Appropriateness:** The language model aids in contextually appropriate word choice, which is crucial for maintaining the meaning and tone of the original text while adhering to the linguistic preferences of the target language audience.

Methodologies in Developing Language Models

The development of effective language models for phrase-based SMT involves several methodological considerations, leveraging vast corpora of the target language to learn patterns of language use.

- **N-gram Models:** Traditional language models often rely on n-grams, sequences of 'n' words, to predict the likelihood of a word sequence. While simple, n-gram models can be powerful tools for ensuring fluency, especially when trained on extensive and varied language corpora.

- **Smoothing Techniques:** Given the impossibility of covering all potential word sequences in any corpus, smoothing techniques are employed to assign non-zero probabilities to unseen n-grams, ensuring the model can handle novel phrases gracefully.

- **Neural Language Models:** More recent advancements have seen the incorporation of neural networks into language modeling, offering improved predictions by capturing deeper linguistic patterns and contexts beyond what n-gram models can achieve. These models use distributed representations of words to better generalize over the language.

The language model within phrase-based statistical machine translation is instrumental in producing translations that not only convey the source text's meaning accurately but also respect the linguistic characteristics of the target language. By prioritizing fluency and grammatical correctness, language models address the crucial aspect of readability, making translated texts more accessible and engaging for readers. As SMT continues to evolve, especially with the integration of neural approaches, the sophistication and effectiveness of language models are set to further enhance the quality and naturalness of machine-generated translations.

Reordering Model:

Phrase-based SMT must account for differences in sentence structure between languages. The reordering model manages the position and order of translated phrases, addressing syntactic variations to produce sentences that are structurally appropriate in the target language.

The Role of the Reordering Model in Phrase-Based SMT

The reordering model is integral to phrase-based SMT systems, designed to manage the syntactic and grammatical differences in sentence structure across languages. It ensures that the translated phrases are arranged in an order that conforms to the grammatical rules and stylistic conventions of the target language, contributing to the fluency and coherence of the output.

Addressing Word Order Differences

- **Cross-Linguistic Variability:** Languages exhibit significant variability in their preferred word order. For example, a Subject-Verb-Object (SVO) structure in one language might correspond to a Subject-Object-Verb (SOV) structure in another. The reordering model navigates these differences, adjusting the position of translated phrases accordingly.

- **Local and Global Reordering:** Reordering can be local (affecting words and phrases within a sentence) or global (affecting the structure of entire sentences or paragraphs). The reordering model accounts for both, ensuring logical and natural progression in the translated text.

Significance of the Reordering Model

- **Enhancing Translation Quality:** By accurately reordering translated phrases, the model significantly enhances the readability and naturalness of translations, making them more comprehensible and engaging for readers in the target language.

- **Improving Contextual Accuracy:** Proper reordering is essential for maintaining the intended meaning of the original text, as incorrect word order can lead to misinterpretations or loss of critical information.

Methodologies Employed in Reordering Models

Developing effective reordering models involves sophisticated algorithms and linguistic insights to predict the optimal arrangement of phrases in the target language.

- **Distance-Based Reordering:** Early reordering models often relied on distance-based metrics, penalizing excessive movement of phrases from their original positions. While simple, this approach could be overly rigid, failing to accommodate the natural fluidity of language.

- **Syntactic and Semantic Models:** More advanced reordering strategies incorporate syntactic and semantic analyses to guide the repositioning of phrases. These models leverage linguistic rules and patterns identified in the target language, offering more nuanced and context-aware reordering.

- **Machine Learning Approaches:** Recent advancements have seen the application of machine learning techniques to learn reordering patterns from large corpora of bilingual text. These data-driven models can adaptively predict the most likely word order based on the context and content of the translation.

Challenges and Evolution

- **Complexity and Ambiguity:** Accurately predicting the optimal order of phrases involves navigating the inherent complexity and ambiguity of language, posing significant challenges to reordering models.

- **Integration with Neural Models:** The transition towards neural machine translation (NMT) has reshaped the approach to reordering. NMT models, particularly those employing attention mechanisms and Transformer architectures, inherently address reordering challenges by considering the entire input sequence holistically, reducing the need for separate reordering models.

The reordering model within the phrase-based statistical machine translation framework plays a crucial role in bridging the syntactic and structural divides between languages. By ensuring that translated phrases are presented in an order that reflects the linguistic norms of the target language, reordering models significantly contribute to the fluency, coherence, and overall quality of translations. As machine translation continues to evolve, particularly with the integration of neural approaches, the principles underlying effective reordering remain central to the quest for more accurate, natural, and accessible cross-lingual communication.

Decoding:

The decoder is the component that searches for the best translation by considering the combined scores from the translation model, language model, and reordering model. It navigates through the vast space of possible translations to select the output that maximizes overall translation quality according to the models' probabilities.

Function of Decoding in Phrase-Based SMT

Decoding in phrase-based SMT is the process by which the system constructs the final translated text from the source language input. This involves navigating through the complex lattice of possible phrase combinations and sequences, informed by the translation model, language model, and reordering model, to identify the most likely target language output that conveys the intended meaning of the source text.

Key Tasks of the Decoder

- **Phrase Selection:** The decoder selects phrases from the set identified by the phrase extraction and alignment process, considering their statistical likelihood and compatibility with the rest of the selected phrases.

- **Phrase Sequencing:** Beyond selecting phrases, the decoder must sequence them in a manner that is grammatically and stylistically appropriate for the target language, taking into account the guidance provided by the reordering model.

- **Optimization:** The decoder optimizes this selection and sequencing process to maximize the overall translation quality, typically defined in terms of the combined scores from the translation, language, and reordering models.

Methodologies Employed in Decoding

The decoding process in phrase-based SMT employs various algorithms and strategies to efficiently search through the space of possible translations and identify the optimal output.

- **Beam Search:** A widely used decoding strategy, beam search limits the breadth of the search space at each step, considering only a fixed number of the most promising options. This approach balances the trade-off between search completeness and computational feasibility.

- **N-best Lists:** Decoders often generate lists of the N best translation options according to their scores, allowing for subsequent rescoring or refinement based on additional models or post-processing steps.

- **Dynamic Programming:** Some decoding algorithms utilize dynamic programming techniques to efficiently manage the combinatorial explosion of possible phrase sequences, storing and reusing partial results to avoid redundant computations.

Challenges in Decoding

The decoding process faces several significant challenges that phrase-based SMT systems must address to produce high-quality translations.

- **Search Space Complexity:** The sheer volume of possible phrase combinations and orderings can make the search space prohibitively large, requiring sophisticated strategies to explore effectively.

- **Quality vs. Speed Trade-off:** Achieving the highest possible translation quality often requires exhaustive search strategies that may not be computationally practical. Decoding algorithms must navigate this trade-off, seeking to optimize translation quality within acceptable computational constraints.

- **Integration of Models:** Effectively combining the outputs of the translation, language, and reordering models during the decoding process is complex, as each contributes differently to the overall translation quality.

Decoding is a critical component of phrase-based statistical machine translation. It represents the culmination of the translation process, where the intricate interplay of phrase selection, ordering, and optimization unfolds to produce the final translated text. The effectiveness of the decoding process directly influences the quality, coherence, and fluency of translations, highlighting its importance in the development and operation of SMT systems. As the field of machine translation continues to evolve, particularly with the increasing prominence of neural approaches, the principles and challenges of decoding remain central to the pursuit of more accurate and natural language translation.

Advantages of Phrase-Based SMT

- **Contextual Awareness:** By translating phrases as units, phrase-based SMT captures local contextual nuances more effectively than word-based approaches, leading to translations that are more syntactically and semantically aligned with the target language.

- **Handling of Idiomatic Expressions:** This methodology is better equipped to translate idiomatic expressions and collocations, as it is more likely to encounter these phrases as units in the training data.

- **Flexibility and Adaptability:** Phrase-based models offer flexibility in adapting to different languages and domains, as the quality of translation largely depends on the breadth and depth of the parallel corpus used for training.

Challenges and Limitations

- **Complexity and Resource Intensity:** The effectiveness of phrase-based SMT depends on extensive bilingual corpora and significant computational resources for training and decoding, which can be limiting factors, especially for less-resourced languages.

- **Long-Distance Dependencies:** While phrase-based SMT handles local context well, it struggles with long-distance dependencies and maintaining coherence over longer text spans, limitations that would later be addressed by neural models.

The methodology of phrase-based statistical machine translation represents a critical leap forward in machine translation technology. By focusing on phrases as the fundamental units of translation, phrase-based SMT introduced a more nuanced understanding of language and context into the machine translation process. This approach laid the groundwork for the subsequent development of neural machine translation models, which build upon and extend the capabilities of phrase-based SMT to deliver even more sophisticated and contextually aware translations, pushing the boundaries of what is possible in automated language translation.

Evaluation Metrics for Machine Translation:

The evaluation of machine translation (MT) systems is meticulously examined through the lens of key metrics such as BLEU, METEOR, and Translation Edit Rate (TER). These metrics offer distinct approaches to quantifying the performance of MT systems, providing insights into their accuracy, fluency, and overall effectiveness in translating text from one language to another.

BLEU (Bilingual Evaluation Understudy)

The BLEU score is one of the most widely used metrics for evaluating the quality of machine-translated text against a set of reference translations. BLEU measures the similarity between the machine-generated text and the human translations, focusing on the precision of n-grams (contiguous sequences of n words) in the translated text.

BLEU: Methodology

The BLEU score measures the quality of machine-generated translations by comparing them with one or more human reference translations. The core of BLEU's methodology lies in calculating the precision of n-grams (contiguous sequences of 'n' words) in the machine-translated text relative to the reference texts.

- **N-gram Precision:** BLEU evaluates the overlap of n-grams between the machine-translated text and the reference translations. It calculates precision scores for various n-gram lengths (typically up to 4-grams), reflecting both lexical and structural accuracy.

- **Brevity Penalty:** To penalize overly short translations, which might artificially inflate precision scores, BLEU incorporates a brevity penalty. This ensures that the translated text's length is suitably comparable to that of the reference translations, encouraging translations that are not only accurate but also adequately verbose.

Strengths of BLEU

- **Standardization:** BLEU provides a standardized and objective measure for evaluating translation quality across different systems and languages, facilitating comparative analyses and benchmarking.

- **Reproducibility:** Due to its straightforward computational methodology, BLEU scores are easy to reproduce, enabling consistent evaluation across studies and applications.

- **Scalability:** BLEU can efficiently handle large datasets, making it suitable for evaluating extensive corpora of machine-translated text against reference translations.

Limitations of BLEU

- **Surface Matching:** BLEU primarily focuses on the surface overlap of n-grams, which can overlook deeper aspects of translation quality, such as semantic accuracy, grammatical correctness, and fluency.

- **Context Ignorance:** BLEU does not account for the context within which words and phrases are used, potentially missing nuances in meaning that depend on broader textual or situational contexts.

- **Reference Dependence:** The quality of the reference translations significantly impacts BLEU scores. A lack of high-quality, diverse reference texts can lead to misleading evaluations, especially for languages or domains with limited resources.

Impact on Machine Translation

Despite its limitations, BLEU has had a profound impact on the development and refinement of MT systems. It has served as a critical benchmark in the evolution from statistical to neural machine translation, providing a quantifiable measure of progress in the field. Moreover, BLEU's widespread adoption has spurred the development of complementary and more sophisticated evaluation metrics, pushing the boundaries of automated translation quality assessment.

The BLEU metric remains a fundamental tool in the arsenal of machine translation evaluation, embodying a balance between simplicity and effectiveness. While the pursuit of more comprehensive and nuanced evaluation metrics continues, BLEU's legacy as a pioneer in the objective assessment of machine translation quality endures, underscoring the ongoing challenge of quantifying the intricacies of human language translation through computational means.

METEOR (Metric for Evaluation of Translation with Explicit Ordering)

METEOR is designed to address some of the limitations of BLEU by incorporating synonymy and stemming, aiming for a more nuanced evaluation of translation quality that better aligns with human judgments.

METEOR: Methodology

METEOR distinguishes itself from BLEU by employing a more sophisticated approach to translation evaluation, aiming to align more closely with human perceptions of translation quality.

- **Flexible Matching:** METEOR uses a combination of exact, stem, synonym, and paraphrase matches to compare the machine-translated text against reference translations. This flexibility allows for a more comprehensive assessment of meaning preservation across translations.

- **Alignment-Based Scoring:** The metric employs an alignment algorithm that pairs words and phrases in the machine translation with those in the reference text, minimizing crossing alignments to reflect the natural order of words.

- **Harmonic Mean of Precision and Recall:** Unlike BLEU, which primarily focuses on precision, METEOR calculates both precision (the accuracy of the machine-translated words against the reference) and recall (the proportion of reference words captured in the machine translation). The final METEOR score is the harmonic mean of these two measures, adjusted by a penalty for word order differences to account for fluency.

Strengths of METEOR

- **Improved Correlation with Human Judgment:** By considering synonyms, stemming, and paraphrases, METEOR aligns more closely with human evaluations of translation quality, especially in terms of semantic accuracy.

- **Penalty for Word Order Differences:** The inclusion of a penalty for improper word order helps ensure that translations not only convey the correct meaning but also adhere to the syntactic norms of the target language, contributing to fluency and readability.

- **Language Adaptability:** METEOR is designed to be extensible for different languages, with parameters that can be adjusted to accommodate linguistic characteristics specific to each language.

Limitations of METEOR

- **Computational Complexity:** The sophisticated analyses involved in METEOR, particularly its alignment algorithm and synonym matching, make it more computationally intensive than BLEU, potentially limiting its scalability for large datasets.

- **Dependency on External Resources:** METEOR's effectiveness, particularly for synonym and paraphrase matching, relies on the availability of comprehensive linguistic resources, which may not exist for all languages or might be of varying quality.

Impact on Machine Translation Evaluation

METEOR has significantly contributed to the advancement of MT evaluation by providing a metric that better captures the nuances of translation quality. Its development has spurred further research into evaluation metrics that balance computational efficiency with the depth of linguistic analysis, leading to a broader understanding of what constitutes a successful translation.

METEOR represents an important step forward in the evaluation of machine translation, offering a more nuanced and linguistically informed approach compared to its predecessors. By emphasizing semantic and syntactic congruity alongside traditional precision and recall metrics, METEOR provides a more holistic assessment of translation quality, pushing the boundaries of automated evaluation closer to the complexities of human judgment and understanding in translation tasks.

TER (Translation Edit Rate)

TER is an edit-distance-based metric that measures the number of edits required to change a machine-translated text into one of the reference translations. It focuses on the effort needed to correct the MT output to match human translations.

TER: Methodology

TER quantifies the quality of a machine translation by calculating the minimum number of edit operations needed to match a reference translation. These operations include insertions, deletions, substitutions, and shifts (moves) of words or phrases.

- **Calculation of Edit Distance:** TER computes the edit distance between the machine-generated text and the reference text, considering the least number of edits needed for convergence.

- **Normalization:** The total count of edits is then normalized by the number of words in the reference translation, providing a rate that reflects the proportion of the text that requires modification.

Advantages of TER

- **Post-Editing Insight:** TER offers a direct measure of the effort required to post-edit machine translations, aligning with practical considerations in translation workflows.

- **Complementarity to Other Metrics:** While BLEU and METEOR focus on precision and semantic alignment, TER provides an additional dimension of evaluation related to the editability and practical usability of translations.

- **Applicability Across Languages and Domains:** TER's edit-based approach makes it broadly applicable across different languages and domains, as it measures the universal process of editing text.

Limitations of TER

- **Potential for Ambiguity:** The focus on edit operations does not always account for the nuances of translation quality, such as stylistic preferences or the acceptability of alternate translations that might not align word-for-word with the reference but are still valid.

- **Sensitivity to Reference Quality:** Like other MT evaluation metrics, the effectiveness of TER is influenced by the quality and representativeness of the reference translations. High variability in reference quality can lead to inconsistent TER scores.

- **Shift Operations Complexity:** While the inclusion of shifts (or moves) as an edit operation allows TER to account for word order differences, it also adds complexity to the calculation, potentially affecting the metric's sensitivity and specificity.

Role in Machine Translation Evaluation

TER has carved out a unique niche in the landscape of MT evaluation metrics by highlighting the practical aspects of translation quality, such as the ease of post-editing. This focus is particularly relevant for translation service providers and clients who need to assess the cost-effectiveness and efficiency of integrating MT into their workflows.

- **Feedback for System Improvement:** TER scores can inform developers about the aspects of their MT systems that most frequently require post-editing, guiding targeted improvements.

- **Benchmarking Tool:** In combination with other metrics, TER serves as a valuable benchmarking tool, enabling a comprehensive evaluation of MT systems from both linguistic and operational perspectives.

The Translation Edit Rate (TER) metric plays an indispensable role in the evaluation of machine translation quality by focusing on the editability and practical efficiency of translations. By measuring the effort required to refine machine-generated text to meet professional standards, TER complements metrics like BLEU and METEOR, enriching the toolkit available for assessing and improving MT systems. Through its unique emphasis on post-editing effort, TER underscores the importance of not just achieving linguistic accuracy but also facilitating efficient translation workflows, thereby contributing to the advancement of machine translation technologies and their application in real-world settings.

The evaluation metrics BLEU, METEOR, and TER play critical roles in assessing and guiding the development of machine translation systems. Each metric offers unique insights into different aspects of translation quality, from n-gram overlap to semantic equivalence and post-editing effort. Together, they provide a comprehensive toolkit for researchers and practitioners to measure the performance of MT systems, identify areas for improvement, and drive the field towards more accurate, fluent, and human-like translations.

Conclusion

Machine translation represents a dynamic and rapidly evolving field within NLP. The progression from rule-based to neural-based approaches has dramatically enhanced the ability of machines to translate languages, reducing barriers to global communication and information exchange. As research continues to push the boundaries of what's possible in machine translation, we can anticipate even more sophisticated systems that better understand and preserve the nuances of human language across cultural and linguistic divides.

Chapter 9: Advanced NLP Techniques

A comprehensive exploration of advanced NLP techniques is presented, showcasing the latest methodologies and technologies that have propelled the field into new frontiers of language understanding and generation. These advanced techniques leverage deep learning, machine learning, and linguistic theory to tackle complex NLP tasks, offering insights into semantics, syntax, and the nuanced dynamics of human language.

Contextual Embeddings

Contextual embeddings represent a significant advancement over traditional word embeddings by capturing the context in which a word appears within a sentence. This approach allows for the same word to have different representations based on its surrounding words, thereby addressing polysemy and improving the model's understanding of word meaning in different contexts.

Principles of Contextual Embeddings

Contextual embeddings are advanced representations of words that dynamically change based on the words' context in a sentence. Unlike traditional word embeddings, which assign a single static vector to each word regardless of its usage, contextual embeddings adjust this representation to capture the semantic and syntactic nuances influenced by surrounding words.

- **Dynamic Word Representations:** Each instance of a word is represented by a unique vector that reflects its specific meaning in the given context, enabling the model to distinguish between different senses of the same word.

- **Deep Contextualization:** These embeddings are typically generated using deep learning models that analyze entire sentences or larger text units, ensuring that the word representations are informed by a broad understanding of the surrounding context.

Significance of Contextual Embeddings

Contextual embeddings represent a significant leap forward in NLP by addressing the limitations of static embeddings and enabling a more nuanced understanding of language.

- **Polysemy and Homonymy:** By providing context-sensitive representations, these embeddings effectively handle words with multiple meanings, enhancing the accuracy of NLP tasks like word sense disambiguation.

- **Improved Model Performance:** The introduction of contextual embeddings has led to remarkable improvements across a wide range of NLP tasks, including but not limited to, named entity recognition, sentiment analysis, and question answering.

Methodologies for Generating Contextual Embeddings

The generation of contextual embeddings relies on sophisticated deep learning architectures that are trained on large corpora of text. Two notable models that have pioneered the use of contextual embeddings are ELMo (Embeddings from Language Models) and BERT (Bidirectional Encoder Representations from Transformers).

- **ELMo:** ELMo utilizes a bidirectional LSTM (Long Short-Term Memory) network trained as a language model to generate deep contextualized word representations. The embeddings are derived from the internal states of the LSTM, capturing both left and right context.

- **BERT:** BERT leverages the Transformer architecture to pre-train deep bidirectional representations by jointly conditioning on both left and right context in all layers. As a result, the generated embeddings are deeply bidirectional, leading to even more profound contextualization.

Applications of Contextual Embeddings

The versatility and efficacy of contextual embeddings have led to their widespread adoption in various NLP applications, significantly enhancing performance and enabling new capabilities.

- **Machine Translation:** Incorporating contextual embeddings has resulted in translations that better capture the subtleties of source texts, improving both fluency and accuracy.

- **Text Classification and Sentiment Analysis:** Models equipped with contextual embeddings offer more precise classification and sentiment detection by understanding the context-dependent meanings of words.

- **Information Extraction and Question Answering:** These tasks benefit from the enhanced ability of models to understand and interpret the semantic relationships in text, leading to more accurate extraction of information and more relevant answers to questions.

Contextual embeddings have fundamentally transformed the landscape of NLP, offering models a dynamic and nuanced understanding of language. By considering the context in which words appear, these embeddings have bridged a significant gap in computational linguistics, paving the way for more sophisticated and human-like language processing capabilities. The ongoing development and application of contextual embeddings continue to drive the advancement of NLP, opening up new possibilities for research and practical applications alike.

Technologies:

Models like BERT (Bidirectional Encoder Representations from Transformers) and ELMo (Embeddings from Language Models) are pioneering examples of contextual embeddings, offering deep contextualized word representations that have dramatically improved performance across a range of NLP tasks.

Transformer Architectures

The introduction of Transformer architectures has been a pivotal advancement in NLP technology. Designed to overcome the limitations of previous sequence modeling and transduction systems, Transformers utilize self-attention mechanisms to weigh the importance of different words within a sentence or document.

- **Self-Attention Mechanism:** Unlike traditional models that process words in sequence, the Transformer can attend to all parts of the input data simultaneously, allowing it to capture complex dependencies and contextual nuances more effectively.

- **BERT and GPT:** Transformer-based models like BERT (Bidirectional Encoder Representations from Transformers) and GPT (Generative Pretrained Transformer) have set new standards in NLP for a range of tasks, from text classification and machine translation to question answering and text generation.

Deep Learning Frameworks

The surge in NLP capabilities is largely attributable to advances in deep learning frameworks that provide the tools and libraries necessary for designing, training, and deploying neural networks.

- **TensorFlow and PyTorch:** Frameworks like TensorFlow and PyTorch have become cornerstones in the development of NLP applications, offering extensive support for deep learning models, automatic differentiation, and GPU acceleration. These frameworks facilitate the rapid prototyping and scaling of NLP models, accelerating research and application development.

- **Hugging Face's Transformers:** This library offers a collection of pre-trained models based on Transformer architectures, simplifying the process of leveraging state-of-the-art NLP models for a wide range of languages and tasks.

Specialized Hardware for AI Computation

The computational demands of training large-scale NLP models have driven the development and adoption of specialized hardware optimized for deep learning tasks.

- **GPUs and TPUs:** Graphics Processing Units (GPUs) and Tensor Processing Units (TPUs) have emerged as critical hardware components for training deep learning models, including those used in NLP. These specialized processors can handle the massive parallel computations required for model training significantly faster than traditional CPUs.

- **Cloud-based AI Services:** Cloud platforms offer access to these specialized hardware resources, along with managed machine learning services, making it easier for researchers and practitioners to train and deploy advanced NLP models without the need for substantial on-premises infrastructure.

The technologies driving advanced NLP techniques have catalyzed a paradigm shift in how machines process and understand human language. From Transformer architectures that provide deep contextual understanding to the deep learning frameworks and specialized hardware that power these computational models, the landscape of NLP is evolving rapidly. As these technologies continue to advance, they promise to unlock even more sophisticated capabilities in language understanding, generation, and interaction, pushing the boundaries of what is possible in the field of natural language processing.

Transfer Learning in NLP

Transfer learning has revolutionized NLP by enabling models trained on large datasets to be fine-tuned for specific tasks with relatively small amounts of data. This technique has significantly reduced the barrier to entry for building competitive NLP models, democratizing access to state-of-the-art results.

Principles of Transfer Learning in NLP

Transfer learning in NLP is predicated on the observation that language exhibits hierarchical structures and patterns that are common across different tasks and domains. By pre-training models on large corpora of text data, these models learn a rich representation of language that can be fine-tuned to specific NLP tasks with relatively minimal additional training.

- **Pre-training:** Involves training a model on a large, general-language dataset to learn a wide range of linguistic features and relationships. This phase aims to develop a comprehensive understanding of language that is not specific to any particular task.

- **Fine-tuning:** The pre-trained model is then adapted to a specific NLP task by continuing the training process on a smaller, task-specific dataset. Fine-tuning adjusts the model's parameters to optimize performance for the target task, leveraging the general-language knowledge acquired during pre-training.

Methodologies and Technologies

The advent of deep learning architectures, particularly Transformer models, has been central to the successful implementation of transfer learning in NLP.

- **BERT (Bidirectional Encoder Representations from Transformers):** BERT represents a breakthrough in transfer learning for NLP, employing a deep Transformer network that is pre-trained on unsupervised language tasks, such as masked language modeling and next-sentence prediction, before being fine-tuned on a wide array of downstream tasks.

- **GPT (Generative Pretrained Transformer):** GPT and its successors (e.g., GPT-2, GPT-3) utilize a similar approach, focusing on generative pre-training followed by task-specific fine-tuning. GPT models are distinguished by their ability to generate coherent and contextually rich text sequences, making them highly effective across tasks that involve text generation.

Impact of Transfer Learning in NLP

Transfer learning has democratized access to advanced NLP capabilities, enabling researchers and practitioners with limited resources to leverage pre-trained models for high-quality language processing tasks.

- **Performance Gains:** Transfer learning has led to unprecedented improvements in a variety of NLP tasks, including but not limited to text classification, question answering, sentiment analysis, and machine translation. These gains are especially pronounced in scenarios where task-specific training data is scarce.

- **Efficiency and Scalability:** By reducing the need for extensive task-specific data and computational power, transfer learning makes it feasible to develop and deploy NLP models more efficiently and at a larger scale.

- **Adaptability and Generalization:** Models pre-trained on diverse language corpora exhibit a remarkable ability to generalize across tasks and domains, often with minimal fine-tuning. This adaptability underscores the potential of transfer learning to address a broad spectrum of NLP challenges.

Transfer learning represents a cornerstone of modern NLP, enabling models to leverage generalized language understanding for specific tasks. The methodology has not only propelled the field to new heights of performance and efficiency but also opened avenues for innovation and application across domains. The continued evolution of transfer learning techniques and technologies promises to further enhance the capabilities of NLP systems, making sophisticated language processing more accessible and impactful across a myriad of applications.

Application: Transfer learning is central to models like BERT, GPT (Generative Pretrained Transformer), and ULMFiT (Universal Language Model Fine-tuning), which are pre-trained on general tasks and then adapted to specific NLP tasks such as text classification, question answering, and more.

Sequence-to-Sequence Models

Sequence-to-sequence (Seq2Seq) models have transformed tasks that involve generating sequences, such as machine translation, text summarization, and conversational modeling. These models consist of an encoder that processes the input sequence and a decoder that generates the output sequence, facilitating complex transformations of text.

Overview of Sequence-to-Sequence Models

Seq2Seq models are a class of deep neural network architectures designed to convert sequences from one domain (e.g., sentences in a source language) to sequences in another domain (e.g., sentences in a target language) while preserving the semantic meaning of the input. These models are characterized by their encoder-decoder structure:

- **Encoder:** The encoder processes the input sequence, capturing its informational content in a fixed-size context vector, which serves as a compressed representation of the input sequence's meaning.

- **Decoder:** The decoder then uses this context vector to generate the output sequence step-by-step, ensuring that the output faithfully reflects the content and intent of the input sequence.

Significance of Seq2Seq Models

Seq2Seq models have significantly impacted NLP by providing a flexible framework for handling a wide range of sequence transformation tasks. Their ability to model complex, variable-length input and output sequences has opened up new avenues for research and application in language processing:

- **Machine Translation:** Seq2Seq models have substantially improved the quality of machine-generated translations by enabling more accurate and contextually appropriate translations.

- **Text Summarization:** These models have been applied to generate concise and relevant summaries of long texts, balancing the retention of critical information with brevity.

- **Conversational Agents:** Seq2Seq architectures underpin the development of sophisticated chatbots and conversational interfaces that can engage in more natural and coherent dialogues with users.

Methodological Advances

The evolution of Seq2Seq models has been marked by several methodological advances that have enhanced their performance and applicability:

- **Attention Mechanisms:** The integration of attention mechanisms allows the decoder to focus on different parts of the input sequence while generating each element of the output sequence, addressing the limitations of fixed-size context vectors by providing a dynamic, content-based approach to accessing the encoded information.

- **Bidirectional Encoders:** Utilizing bidirectional layers in the encoder allows the model to capture context from both directions (forward and backward) of the input sequence, enriching the context vector with a more comprehensive understanding of the input sequence.

- **Transformer Models:** The introduction of Transformer models, which rely entirely on self-attention mechanisms without recurrent layers, has further advanced the Seq2Seq framework, leading to significant improvements in translation quality, training efficiency, and the ability to handle longer sequences.

Challenges and Future Directions

While Seq2Seq models have brought about significant advancements, they continue to face challenges, particularly in handling extremely long sequences and maintaining coherence over lengthy outputs. Future directions in the development of Seq2Seq models involve enhancing their capacity to model complex dependencies and exploring more efficient training methodologies to improve scalability and performance.

Sequence-to-sequence models, represent a transformative approach in NLP, enabling machines to perform sophisticated sequence transformation tasks with increasing accuracy and fluency. The continuous evolution of Seq2Seq architectures, coupled with innovations like attention mechanisms and Transformer models, underscores the dynamic nature of research in NLP. As these models become more refined, they promise to unlock even greater capabilities in language understanding and generation, further bridging the gap between human and machine communication.

Innovation:

The integration of attention mechanisms within Seq2Seq models has further enhanced their ability to focus on relevant parts of the input sequence when generating each word of the output, improving both accuracy and fluency in tasks like translation.

The Innovation of Seq2Seq Models

Seq2Seq models represent a significant departure from traditional models by adopting an encoder-decoder framework that processes variable-length input sequences to produce variable-length output sequences, all while maintaining the semantic integrity of the data.

Encoder-Decoder Architecture

- **Encoder:** The encoder part of a Seq2Seq model reads and processes the entire input sequence. For each input token, it generates a vector representation, capturing the information and context of the sequence up to that point. The final set of vectors encapsulates the complete input sequence in a condensed form.

- **Decoder:** Starting from the encoded context, the decoder generates the output sequence one token at a time. It uses the context information along with what it has generated so far to predict the next token in the sequence. This stepwise generation allows it to handle sequences of arbitrary lengths.

Breakthroughs Enabled by Seq2Seq Models

Seq2Seq models have facilitated several breakthroughs in NLP, thanks to their flexible architecture and capacity to model complex language phenomena.

- **Attention Mechanism:** Perhaps the most significant innovation within Seq2Seq models is the introduction of attention mechanisms. Attention allows the model to dynamically focus on different parts of the input sequence as needed when generating each token of the output. This solves the problem of information bottleneck in long sequences and improves the model's ability to retain and use context.

- **Handling Long Dependencies:** With the integration of attention, Seq2Seq models can better manage long-range dependencies within the text, capturing relationships between elements that are far apart in the sequence. This capability is crucial for understanding and generating coherent and contextually accurate text.

- **Transformer Architecture:** Building on the concept of attention, the Transformer model further innovates by relying entirely on self-attention mechanisms, dispensing with recurrence and convolution. This leads to significant improvements in training efficiency and model performance, particularly for tasks involving long sequences.

Applications Revolutionized by Seq2Seq Models

The innovations introduced by Seq2Seq models have revolutionized a wide array of NLP applications, demonstrating their versatility and effectiveness.

- **Machine Translation:** Seq2Seq models have dramatically improved the quality of machine translation, enabling more accurate and fluent translations that consider the broader context of sentences.

- **Text Summarization:** In automatic text summarization, Seq2Seq models can condense long documents into concise summaries, maintaining the core message and relevant details.

- **Dialog Systems:** For chatbots and conversational AI, Seq2Seq models facilitate the generation of natural, context-aware responses, enhancing the user experience in automated dialogues.

The innovation of sequence-to-sequence models marks a pivotal evolution in NLP. By introducing a flexible framework capable of understanding and generating complex language structures, Seq2Seq models have unlocked new possibilities across various NLP tasks. The advent of attention mechanisms and the Transformer architecture represent key milestones in this journey, offering both theoretical insights and practical solutions to longstanding challenges in language processing. As NLP continues to advance, the foundational concepts and innovations of Seq2Seq models will undoubtedly continue to inspire and inform future developments in the field.

Attention Mechanisms

Attention mechanisms have become a cornerstone of advanced NLP models, allowing them to dynamically weight the importance of different parts of the input data. This technique has been instrumental in addressing the limitations of traditional Seq2Seq models, particularly in handling long input sequences.

Principles of Attention Mechanisms

Attention mechanisms are inspired by the human ability to focus on specific parts of a visual scene or pieces of information while ignoring others. In the context of NLP, they allow models to weigh the importance of different input tokens differently when generating each token in the output sequence.

- **Contextual Relevance:** The core idea behind attention is to assign different levels of importance to different parts of the input sequence, based on their relevance to the task at hand. This is achieved by calculating attention scores or weights that indicate how much focus the model should put on each input token for each step of the output.

- **Dynamic Weighting:** Unlike static models that treat all parts of the input equally, attention mechanisms provide a dynamic, content-based approach to handling input data. The model recalculates attention weights for each output token, allowing it to adaptively select the most relevant information from the input.

Impact of Attention Mechanisms

The introduction of attention mechanisms has led to substantial improvements in model performance, particularly for tasks involving long sequences or complex dependencies.

- **Improved Handling of Long Sequences:** By enabling models to focus on relevant parts of the input, attention mechanisms overcome the limitations of fixed-size context vectors in traditional Seq2Seq models, significantly enhancing the ability to capture long-range dependencies and nuances in the data.

- **Increased Model Interpretability:** Attention weights provide insights into the model's decision-making process, showing which parts of the input were deemed most important for generating a specific output. This has implications for model interpretability and debugging.

Applications of Attention Mechanisms

Attention mechanisms have found broad applications across various NLP tasks, revolutionizing how models understand and generate language.

- **Machine Translation:** In machine translation, attention mechanisms have led to more accurate and contextually appropriate translations by allowing the model to consider the entire input sequence when generating each word in the translation.

- **Text Summarization:** For automatic text summarization, attention helps models to identify and focus on the key pieces of information in the source text, enabling the generation of concise and informative summaries.

- **Question Answering and Reading Comprehension:**
  Attention mechanisms enhance models' ability to
  extract relevant information from long texts to answer
  questions, by focusing on the segments of the text most
  likely to contain the answer.

- **Speech Recognition and Generation:** In speech
  processing, attention mechanisms improve the
  performance of models by focusing on relevant parts of
  the audio signal when transcribing speech to text or
  generating speech from textual input.

Evolution and Future Directions

The success of attention mechanisms has spurred
further innovation in NLP, leading to the development of
Transformer models, which rely entirely on attention
without recurrence. This has opened new avenues for
research and application, pushing the boundaries of what's
possible in language understanding and generation.

Attention mechanisms represent a significant
advancement in NLP techniques, offering a more nuanced
and flexible approach to processing sequence data. By
enabling models to adaptively focus on the most relevant
parts of the input, attention mechanisms have enhanced the
performance and interpretability of NLP models,
contributing to groundbreaking improvements across a
wide array of tasks. The continued exploration and
refinement of attention-based models promise to drive
further progress in the field, expanding the capabilities and
applications of natural language processing.

Breakthroughs:

The Transformer architecture, which relies solely on attention mechanisms without recurrent layers, has set new standards for efficiency and effectiveness in NLP, underpinning models like BERT and GPT.

Transformer Models

The introduction of Transformer models represents a paradigm shift in NLP. Unlike previous sequence-based models that processed data in order, Transformers use self-attention mechanisms to weigh the significance of all parts of the input data simultaneously. This breakthrough:

- **Efficiency and Scalability:** Allows for more parallelization during training, drastically reducing computation time and enabling models to handle longer sequences of data more effectively.

- **Enhanced Language Understanding:** Offers a deeper understanding of context and relationships within text, significantly improving performance on tasks like machine translation, text summarization, and sentiment analysis.

Contextual Embeddings

Contextual embeddings, such as those generated by BERT (Bidirectional Encoder Representations from Transformers) and ELMo (Embeddings from Language Models), have revolutionized how machines understand words in context. These embeddings dynamically adjust based on the surrounding text, enabling:

- **Polysemy Resolution:** More accurate interpretations of words with multiple meanings, improving the nuances captured in tasks like word sense disambiguation and named entity recognition.

- **Rich Language Models:** The development of pre-trained models that can be fine-tuned for a wide range of tasks, significantly lowering the barrier to entry for advanced NLP applications.

Unsupervised Learning in NLP

The advancements in unsupervised learning techniques have been pivotal in leveraging the vast amounts of unlabelled text data available. Techniques such as autoencoders, GANs (Generative Adversarial Networks), and self-supervised learning approaches have enabled:

- **Language Model Pre-training:** Creation of powerful language models that understand the structure and nuances of language before being fine-tuned on specific NLP tasks, enhancing model performance across the board.

- **Data Augmentation:** Generation of synthetic text data for training, mitigating the challenges associated with scarce or imbalanced datasets.

Advancements in Language Understanding and Generation

Recent breakthroughs have dramatically improved machines' abilities to understand and generate human-like text, leading to more sophisticated applications:

- **Machine Translation:** Models like Google's BERT and OpenAI's GPT (Generative Pretrained Transformer) series have set new benchmarks in the quality of machine translation, making it indistinguishable from human translations in some contexts.

- **Conversational AI:** Advances in understanding context and generating coherent responses have led to more natural and effective chatbots and virtual assistants, transforming customer service, entertainment, and personal productivity.

- **Text Summarization and Generation:** Enhanced models now produce summaries that retain the original text's essential points with remarkable accuracy and can generate creative, contextually relevant content in various styles.

The breakthroughs in advanced NLP techniques signify a monumental leap forward in how computational systems understand, interpret, and generate human language. These advancements not only refine the execution of specific NLP tasks but also deepen the theoretical understanding of language processing. As the field continues to evolve, these breakthroughs lay the groundwork for future innovations, promising even greater capabilities and applications that will further bridge the gap between human linguistic complexity and computational understanding.

Applications of Advanced NLP Techniques

The advancements in NLP techniques have broad and transformative applications across various domains:

- **Machine Translation:** Enhanced by Seq2Seq models and attention mechanisms, offering more fluent and accurate translations.

- **Sentiment Analysis:** Improved through contextual embeddings and transfer learning, providing more nuanced understanding of sentiment and opinion.

- **Conversational AI:** Advanced by all the aforementioned techniques, leading to more natural and context-aware chatbots and virtual assistants.

- **Information Extraction:** Benefited from the deep contextual understanding afforded by these techniques, enabling more precise extraction of structured information from unstructured text.

Advanced Topic Modeling Techniques:

The exploration of advanced topic modeling techniques unveils the intricacies and applications of two pivotal methods: Latent Dirichlet Allocation (LDA) and Latent Semantic Analysis (LSA). These techniques are fundamental in extracting meaningful patterns and topics from large collections of text, aiding in the understanding and organization of unstructured data.

Latent Dirichlet Allocation (LDA)

LDA is a generative probabilistic model that assumes each document in a corpus contains a mixture of topics, and each topic is characterized by a distribution over words. LDA aims to reverse engineer this process, uncovering the latent topics that pervade the documents.

Mechanics of LDA

- **Topic Distribution:** LDA models each document as a mixture of various topics. It starts with random assignments and iteratively refines the topic distributions within documents and word distributions within topics based on the co-occurrence of words and their distribution across documents.

- **Dirichlet Priors:** The model incorporates Dirichlet priors for topic distributions within documents and word distributions within topics, encoding assumptions about the sparsity of these distributions and allowing for more robust topic inference.

Applications and Advantages

- **Content Summarization:** LDA provides a high-level overview of the main themes present in large text corpora, facilitating content summarization and exploration.

- **Document Classification and Organization:** By identifying the dominant topics within documents, LDA can enhance document classification, search, and recommendation systems.

- **Insights into Unstructured Data:** LDA is widely used in social media analysis, customer feedback analysis, and other areas where insights into large volumes of text are valuable.

Latent Semantic Analysis (LSA)

LSA, also known as Latent Semantic Indexing (LSI) when applied to search and retrieval tasks, is a technique that applies singular value decomposition (SVD) to a term-document matrix, uncovering the latent semantic structure of words and documents.

Mechanics of LSA

- **Term-Document Matrix:** LSA constructs a matrix representing the occurrences of terms in documents. Each cell in the matrix contains the frequency or a weighted frequency (like TF-IDF) of a term in a document.

- **Singular Value Decomposition:** By applying SVD to this matrix, LSA reduces its dimensionality, capturing the most significant relationships between terms and documents while filtering out noise and redundancy.

Applications and Advantages

- **Improving Information Retrieval:** LSA enhances search engines and information retrieval systems by allowing them to find documents related by meaning, not just by exact keyword matches.

- **Understanding Document Similarities:** The dimensional reduction in LSA helps in visualizing document similarities, aiding in document clustering and organization.

- **Semantic Analysis:** LSA's ability to capture the underlying semantic relationships between words makes it useful for synonym detection and concept categorization.

Challenges and Considerations

Both LDA and LSA face challenges in topic modeling, including determining the optimal number of topics, handling polysemy and synonymy, and scaling efficiently with large datasets. While LDA provides a more detailed probabilistic model that can capture topic distributions within documents, it can be computationally intensive. LSA, on the other hand, offers a simpler linear algebra-based approach but may lose some interpretability in its lower-dimensional semantic space.

The advanced topic modeling techniques of Latent Dirichlet Allocation and Latent Semantic Analysis represent powerful tools in the NLP toolkit for uncovering the hidden thematic structure of text. By enabling the automated discovery of topics and facilitating a deeper understanding of large text corpora, LDA and LSA have broadened the horizons of text analysis, content management, and information retrieval. As NLP continues to evolve, these techniques remain at the forefront, driving innovation and application across diverse domains.

Syntax And Dependency Parsing:

The exploration of advanced NLP techniques delves into the critical area of syntax and dependency parsing for grammatical analysis. These techniques are instrumental in dissecting the grammatical structure of sentences, providing a foundation for numerous NLP applications by revealing the hierarchical organization of words and the relationships between them. This comprehensive section discusses the principles of syntax and dependency parsing, methodologies, challenges, and their profound impact on enhancing machine understanding of human language.

Syntax and Dependency Parsing: An Overview

Syntax parsing, often referred to as syntactic analysis or parsing, involves analyzing sentences to determine their grammatical structure according to the rules of a given language. Dependency parsing, a subset of syntax parsing, focuses on identifying the dependencies between words in a sentence, mapping out how words relate to each other to convey meaning.

- **Syntactic Structure:** Understanding the syntactic structure helps in identifying the roles played by each word or phrase in a sentence, such as subjects, verbs, objects, and other grammatical elements.

- **Dependency Relations:** Dependency parsing aims to construct a dependency tree or graph that represents the linguistic dependencies among words, such as who is doing what to whom, specifying relationships like "nsubj" (nominal subject) and "dobj" (direct object).

Methodologies in Syntax and Dependency Parsing

Advancements in NLP have led to the development of several effective methodologies for syntax and dependency parsing, each with its unique approach to tackling the complexity of human language.

- **Constituency Parsing:** This approach involves breaking down a sentence into its constituent parts, often represented by a parse tree. Techniques like Context-Free Grammars (CFGs) and parsing algorithms such as the Cocke-Younger-Kasami (CYK) algorithm have been foundational in this space.

- **Transition-Based Parsing:** A popular approach for dependency parsing that incrementally constructs a parse tree by making a series of decisions based on the current state and input. This method is efficient and can be easily integrated with machine learning models.

- **Graph-Based Parsing:** This method treats parsing as a graph problem, where the goal is to find the optimal tree that spans all the words in a sentence, based on a scoring function for different possible trees.

Challenges in Syntax and Dependency Parsing

Despite significant advancements, syntax and dependency parsing continue to face challenges, including:

- **Ambiguity:** Natural language is inherently ambiguous. Disambiguating sentences with multiple valid parses or interpreting complex or nested structures accurately remains challenging.

- **Cross-Linguistic Variability:** Languages vary greatly in their syntactic structures. Developing parsing techniques that can be generalized across languages or adapted to language-specific features requires extensive linguistic knowledge and resources.

- **Integration with Semantic Analysis:** Moving beyond structural understanding to capture the semantic relationships and nuances conveyed by syntax in context is an ongoing area of research.

Impact on NLP Applications

Syntax and dependency parsing are foundational to numerous NLP applications, enabling more sophisticated and accurate processing of text:

- **Machine Translation:** Understanding the grammatical structure of sentences improves translation accuracy, especially for languages with significantly different syntax.

- **Information Extraction:** Parsing helps identify entities and their relations within sentences, facilitating the extraction of structured information from unstructured text.

- **Question Answering and Natural Language Understanding (NLU):** Parsing is crucial for interpreting the structure of queries and sentences to determine their intent and extract relevant information, enhancing the performance of QA systems and NLU tasks.

Syntax and dependency parsing represent essential components of advanced NLP techniques. By enabling a deep understanding of grammatical structures and relationships within text, these parsing methodologies enhance the ability of machines to process and interpret human language accurately. As NLP technologies continue to evolve, the innovations and applications of syntax and dependency parsing will undoubtedly play a pivotal role in bridging the gap between human linguistic complexity and computational analysis, driving forward the capabilities of NLP systems across a wide array of tasks and domains.

Coreference Resolution:

Coreference resolution is highlighted as a pivotal advanced NLP technique, crucial for understanding the referential relationships within texts. Coreference resolution seeks to identify when different expressions in a text refer to the same entity in the world, an essential task for achieving deep text comprehension, enhancing natural language understanding, and improving the performance of various NLP applications. This comprehensive portion explores the significance, methodologies, challenges, and applications of coreference resolution in the broader context of natural language processing.

Significance of Coreference Resolution

Coreference resolution addresses the challenge of deciphering which words or phrases (referred to as "mentions") in a text refer to the same entity. This task is fundamental for:

- **Text Coherence:** Understanding how different parts of a text are interconnected, contributing to a cohesive understanding of the narrative or argument.

- **Information Extraction:** Extracting and aggregating information about entities from multiple references across a text.

- **Enhanced Language Understanding:** Providing a more comprehensive representation of the text's meaning by resolving ambiguities related to entity references.

Methodologies in Coreference Resolution

Coreference resolution techniques have evolved from rule-based systems to sophisticated machine learning models, with recent approaches leveraging deep learning for improved accuracy.

- **Rule-Based Systems:** Early methods relied on manually crafted linguistic rules to identify coreferent mentions based on grammatical patterns, pronoun usage, and semantic compatibility. These systems, while interpretable, often lacked scalability and flexibility.

- **Machine Learning Approaches:** Supervised learning models trained on annotated corpora represented a significant advancement, using features extracted from the text to classify pairs or clusters of mentions as coreferent or not. These models required extensive feature engineering and domain-specific knowledge.

- **Deep Learning Models:** Recent advancements leverage neural networks to automatically learn representations of mentions and their contexts, obviating the need for manual feature engineering. Approaches like end-to-end neural coreference resolution models use representations from pre-trained language models (e.g., BERT) to better capture the complexities of coreference in text.

Challenges in Coreference Resolution

Despite advancements, coreference resolution remains a challenging task due to:

- **Ambiguity and Variety of Expressions:** Entities can be referenced in numerous ways, including pronouns, names, or descriptive phrases, increasing the difficulty of accurately linking mentions.

- **Contextual and World Knowledge:** Resolving coreferences often requires understanding beyond the immediate text, including common-sense knowledge or specific domain insights, posing challenges for purely data-driven models.

- **Long-Distance Relationships:** Identifying coreferent mentions that are far apart in a text requires models to effectively manage long-range dependencies, a task that is inherently difficult for many NLP models.

Applications of Coreference Resolution

Coreference resolution enhances the capabilities of numerous NLP applications, including:

- **Document Summarization:** By identifying and consolidating information related to the same entities, coreference resolution aids in generating concise summaries that accurately reflect the document's content.

- **Question Answering:** Understanding referential relationships is crucial for answering questions that involve references to entities mentioned elsewhere in a text.

- **Sentiment Analysis:** Analyzing sentiments expressed about entities requires accurately identifying all mentions of those entities, regardless of how they are referenced.

Coreference resolution is a sophisticated technique that significantly advances the state of NLP by enabling a deeper understanding of textual relationships and entity representations. Through the development of advanced methodologies and the application of deep learning, the field continues to make strides in accurately resolving referential relationships, thereby enhancing machine comprehension of natural language and improving the performance of downstream NLP tasks. The ongoing research and development in coreference resolution promise further enhancements in natural language understanding, pushing the boundaries of what automated systems can achieve.

Ethical Considerations In NLP:

In "Natural Language Processing (NLP): The Complete Guide," a crucial section is dedicated to the ethical considerations in NLP, highlighting the importance of addressing bias, fairness, and privacy in the development and application of advanced NLP technologies. As NLP systems increasingly influence various aspects of daily life, from content recommendation to decision-making processes, it becomes imperative to scrutinize these systems for ethical implications that could affect individuals and societies.

Ethical Considerations in NLP

The ethical landscape of NLP is complex, encompassing a range of issues that necessitate careful consideration and responsible action from researchers, developers, and practitioners.

Bias in NLP Systems

- **Source and Amplification of Bias:** NLP systems can inherit and even amplify biases present in their training data. These biases can manifest in various forms, including gender, racial, and socioeconomic biases, leading to unfair or discriminatory outcomes.

- **Implications:** The perpetuation of bias in NLP applications, such as sentiment analysis, language translation, and job application screening, can have serious implications for equality and fairness. For instance, biased sentiment analysis tools might systematically favor or disfavor certain groups.

Fairness in NLP

- **Equitable Treatment:** Fairness in NLP entails ensuring that NLP systems treat all individuals and groups equitably, without discrimination. This involves careful consideration of how systems are designed, trained, and deployed.

- **Operationalizing Fairness:** Achieving fairness requires identifying and operationalizing relevant fairness criteria for each application, which can include demographic parity, equality of opportunity, or other fairness metrics tailored to specific contexts.

Privacy in NLP

- **Data Sensitivity:** Many NLP applications process sensitive personal information, raising concerns about individual privacy. Ensuring that NLP systems respect privacy involves safeguarding the data used for training and inference.

- **Anonymization and Consent:** Techniques such as data anonymization and obtaining explicit consent for data usage are essential for maintaining privacy. Additionally, advances in privacy-preserving technologies like federated learning and differential privacy are being explored within NLP contexts.

Strategies for Addressing Ethical Challenges

Mitigating the ethical challenges in NLP involves a multifaceted approach, integrating technical, regulatory, and societal efforts.

- **Diverse and Representative Data:** Ensuring that training data is diverse and representative can help reduce biases in NLP systems. This involves actively seeking out and including data from underrepresented groups and perspectives.

- **Ethical Guidelines and Audits:** Developing and adhering to ethical guidelines for NLP research and development, along with conducting regular audits of NLP systems for bias, fairness, and privacy concerns, are critical for ethical accountability.

- **Transparency and Explainability:** Enhancing the transparency and explainability of NLP systems can aid in identifying and addressing ethical issues. This includes making model decisions understandable to users and stakeholders.

- **Community Engagement:** Engaging with diverse communities affected by NLP applications ensures that a broad spectrum of perspectives is considered in addressing ethical challenges, fostering more inclusive and equitable NLP solutions.

The ethical considerations of bias, fairness, and privacy are paramount in the advancement of NLP technologies. Addressing these ethical challenges is not only a technical necessity but also a moral imperative to ensure that NLP systems contribute positively to society. By adopting responsible practices and striving for ethical excellence, the field of NLP can navigate the complexities of modern technology, ensuring that advancements benefit all members of society equitably while safeguarding individual rights and dignity.

Conclusion

The advanced NLP techniques represent the cutting edge of research and application in the field. From contextual embeddings and transfer learning to Seq2Seq models and attention mechanisms, these techniques offer a deep and nuanced understanding of language, driving innovations that impact both theoretical linguistics and practical applications. As NLP continues to evolve, these advanced techniques will undoubtedly play a central role in shaping the future of how machines understand and interact with human language, unlocking new possibilities and applications that further bridge the gap between human cognition and artificial intelligence.

Chapter 10: Practical Applications

A dedicated exploration of practical applications and case studies vividly illustrates the transformative impact of NLP technologies across various sectors. Through detailed narratives and analyses, this section demonstrates how NLP has been leveraged to solve real-world problems, enhance decision-making processes, and streamline operations. This comprehensive overview delves into a diverse array of applications, including sentiment analysis in social media monitoring, machine translation in global communication, chatbots in customer service, and more, showcasing the versatility and potential of NLP to revolutionize industries.

Sentiment Analysis for Social Media Monitoring

One notable application of NLP is sentiment analysis, particularly in monitoring and analyzing social media content. Businesses and organizations utilize sentiment analysis to gauge public opinion, brand reputation, and customer satisfaction. A case study involving a major retail brand could illustrate how sentiment analysis helped the company identify emerging trends and issues from customer feedback on social media, leading to strategic adjustments in their marketing and product development efforts.

- **Outcome:** Improved customer engagement and targeted marketing strategies, resulting in increased customer satisfaction and brand loyalty.

Machine Translation in Global Communication

Machine translation stands out as a pivotal application of NLP, facilitating seamless cross-lingual communication in a globalized world. A case study on an international organization using machine translation to bridge language barriers among its multinational teams could highlight its effectiveness in enhancing collaboration and productivity.

- **Outcome:** Streamlined communication processes, reduced linguistic barriers, and fostered a more inclusive and collaborative international work environment.

Chatbots in Customer Service

Chatbots, powered by NLP, have redefined customer service by providing timely, personalized, and efficient assistance. A detailed case study of a financial institution that deployed chatbots for handling customer inquiries and transactions can showcase the technology's capability to improve service delivery and operational efficiency.

- **Outcome:** Enhanced customer satisfaction through 24/7 support, reduced response times, and decreased operational costs by automating routine inquiries.

Information Extraction for Legal Document Analysis

NLP techniques in information extraction have proven invaluable in processing and analyzing complex legal documents. A case study on a legal firm using NLP to extract relevant information from legal texts for case preparation and research could exemplify how the technology streamlines legal workflows and improves the accuracy of legal analyses.

- **Outcome:** Increased efficiency in legal research and document analysis, leading to more informed decision-making and strategic legal planning.

Predictive Text and Assistive Technologies

NLP has also made significant strides in developing predictive text systems and assistive technologies that enhance accessibility for individuals with disabilities. A case study on the development of an assistive communication app that employs predictive text algorithms to aid individuals with speech impairments could demonstrate the social impact of NLP.

- **Outcome:** Empowered users with improved communication abilities, fostering greater independence and participation in social and professional activities.

Conclusion

NLP technologies have permeated various facets of modern life, offering solutions to complex challenges, optimizing workflows, and creating new opportunities for innovation and growth. The tangible benefits observed across diverse sectors underscore the potential of NLP to continue driving technological advancements and societal progress. As the field of NLP evolves, its applications are bound to expand, further demonstrating the versatility and transformative power of natural language processing in addressing real-world needs.

Real-World Applications Of NLP:

The section dedicated to practical applications and case studies showcases the transformative impact of NLP across diverse domains, from healthcare and finance to social media. By highlighting real-world applications, this comprehensive exploration underscores not only the versatility of NLP technologies but also their potential to drive significant advancements and solve complex challenges in various sectors. This section delves into specific applications of NLP in these fields, illustrating how NLP technologies are being leveraged to enhance efficiency, decision-making, and user engagement.

Healthcare

The integration of NLP in healthcare has revolutionized patient care, research, and administration by enabling the extraction of valuable insights from unstructured medical data.

- **Clinical Decision Support:** NLP tools analyze patient records, clinical notes, and research articles to provide healthcare professionals with actionable insights, aiding in diagnosis, treatment planning, and patient monitoring.

- **Sentiment Analysis in Patient Feedback:** NLP is used to gauge patient satisfaction and concerns by analyzing feedback from surveys, social media, and online forums, helping healthcare providers improve service quality.

- **Drug Discovery and Research:** By swiftly reviewing and synthesizing vast amounts of scientific literature, NLP accelerates the research process, supporting the identification of new drug candidates and treatment approaches.

Finance

In the financial sector, NLP has become indispensable for analyzing market sentiment, automating customer service, and enhancing regulatory compliance.

- **Sentiment Analysis for Market Prediction:** NLP analyzes news articles, social media, and financial reports to gauge market sentiment, assisting traders and analysts in making informed investment decisions.

- **Automated Customer Support:** Chatbots and virtual assistants powered by NLP handle inquiries and transactions, improving customer experience while reducing operational costs for banks and financial institutions.

- **Regulatory Compliance Monitoring:** NLP tools scrutinize communication and documents to ensure adherence to financial regulations, helping firms mitigate risks and avoid penalties.

Social Media

The pervasive influence of social media has made it a rich source of data for NLP applications, offering insights into public opinion, consumer behavior, and social trends.

- **Social Media Monitoring:** Companies use NLP to monitor brand mentions and customer feedback across platforms, enabling real-time responses and strategic insights into brand perception.

- **Content Recommendation:** NLP algorithms analyze user interactions and content preferences to personalize recommendations, enhancing engagement and user experience on social media platforms.

- **Trend Analysis:** By aggregating and analyzing posts, comments, and hashtags, NLP tools identify emerging trends and public sentiment on social issues, guiding content creation and marketing strategies.

Cross-Domain Case Studies

- **Healthcare Case Study:** A leading hospital implemented an NLP system to extract and structure information from electronic health records (EHRs), significantly reducing manual data entry and enabling more accurate patient risk assessment and treatment personalization.

- **Finance Case Study:** A global financial services firm deployed NLP for real-time analysis of financial news and reports, integrating these insights into its trading algorithms to capitalize on market movements influenced by news events.

- **Social Media Case Study:** A social media analytics company utilized NLP to develop a tool for sentiment analysis and trend detection, providing brands with detailed insights into consumer attitudes and behaviors, shaping marketing and product development strategies.

Case Studies Demonstrating the Use Of NLP:

The segment on practical applications and case studies vividly illustrates how NLP techniques have been applied to solve specific, real-world problems across various domains. This section provides an in-depth look into several case studies, each highlighting the unique challenges faced by organizations and how the strategic application of NLP technologies offered solutions that enhanced operations, improved customer experiences, and drove innovation. These case studies span a range of industries including healthcare, customer service, and environmental monitoring, showcasing the versatility and impact of NLP.

Case Study 1: Enhancing Patient Care Through Clinical Text Analysis in Healthcare

Problem: A healthcare provider sought to improve patient outcomes by more effectively identifying patients at risk for chronic diseases earlier in their care journey. Traditional methods relied heavily on structured data, missing valuable insights hidden within unstructured clinical notes.

Solution: By implementing an NLP system designed to analyze and extract information from unstructured clinical text, the healthcare provider was able to identify early indicators of chronic diseases such as diabetes and heart disease. The NLP system used a combination of medical ontologies and machine learning algorithms to interpret the free text, recognize medical entities, and understand their relationships and implications.

Outcome: The application of NLP enabled the healthcare provider to significantly enhance early diagnosis rates, tailor treatment plans more accurately, and improve overall patient care and outcomes. This approach also facilitated a more comprehensive analysis of patient records, contributing to research and the development of new treatment protocols.

Case Study 2: Automating Customer Support for a Major Retailer

Problem: A global retailer faced challenges managing the volume of customer inquiries received through its online platforms, leading to long response times and decreased customer satisfaction.

Solution: The retailer implemented an NLP-powered chatbot capable of understanding and responding to customer inquiries in natural language. The chatbot was trained on a vast dataset of customer service interactions, enabling it to handle a wide range of queries from order tracking to product recommendations and returns policies.

Outcome: The chatbot significantly reduced response times, handled up to 70% of routine inquiries autonomously, and improved customer satisfaction scores. It also freed human customer service representatives to focus on more complex issues, enhancing overall service quality.

Case Study 3: Monitoring Environmental Compliance Through Social Media Analysis

Problem: An environmental agency sought to improve its monitoring of industrial compliance with environmental regulations by detecting early signs of violations reported by the public.

Solution: Leveraging NLP techniques, the agency developed a system to monitor social media platforms for mentions of specific industrial activities and potential environmental concerns. The system used sentiment analysis and entity recognition to identify relevant posts and assess public sentiment, flagging potential issues for further investigation.

Outcome: This proactive approach enabled the environmental agency to swiftly address and investigate reports of environmental violations, often before formal complaints were filed. The system not only improved regulatory compliance but also demonstrated the agency's commitment to environmental protection to the public.

These case studies underscore the transformative potential of NLP technologies in addressing complex challenges across diverse sectors. By harnessing the power of language analysis and understanding, organizations are able to uncover insights from vast amounts of unstructured data, automate and improve services, and engage with stakeholders in more meaningful ways. As NLP continues to evolve, its applications are set to expand further, driving innovation and solving problems in novel and impactful ways.

Best Practices for Building NLP Applications:

From data preparation and model selection to ethical considerations and system deployment, these best practices are pivotal for leveraging the full potential of NLP technologies.

Data Preparation and Management

- **High-Quality Datasets:** The foundation of any successful NLP application is high-quality data. Collect diverse, representative datasets that cover the nuances and variations of natural language specific to your application domain.

- **Data Cleaning and Preprocessing:** Perform thorough data cleaning and preprocessing to remove noise and standardize text data. This includes tokenization, normalization, removal of stop words, and handling of missing or ambiguous data.

- **Ethical Data Collection:** Ensure that data collection methods are ethical, respecting privacy laws and consent. Consider the impact of data biases on model performance and fairness.

Model Selection and Training

- **Model Complexity:** Choose the right model complexity for your task. While deep learning models offer state-of-the-art performance, simpler models can be more interpretable, easier to deploy, and require less computational resources.

- **Transfer Learning:** Leverage pre-trained models and fine-tune them on your specific dataset. This approach can significantly reduce training time and improve model performance, especially when data is scarce.

- **Regularization and Generalization:** Implement regularization techniques to prevent overfitting and ensure that your model generalizes well to unseen data.

Evaluation and Iteration

- **Comprehensive Evaluation Metrics:** Use a comprehensive set of evaluation metrics that reflect the specific goals of your application. Consider accuracy, precision, recall, F1 score, and domain-specific metrics to fully understand model performance.

- **Cross-validation:** Employ cross-validation techniques to assess how the model performs across different subsets of your data, ensuring reliability and robustness.

- **Iterative Development:** NLP model development is an iterative process. Continuously refine your model based on performance feedback and retrain it as new data becomes available.

Deployment and Scalability

- **Deployment Strategy:** Develop a clear strategy for deploying and integrating your NLP model into existing systems. Consider factors such as latency, throughput, and hardware requirements.

- **Scalability:** Ensure that your NLP system is scalable, capable of handling increases in data volume and user demand without significant degradation in performance.

- **Monitoring and Maintenance:** Once deployed, continuously monitor the system's performance and update it as necessary to address emerging challenges or changes in the application context.

Ethical Considerations and Fairness

- **Bias Detection and Mitigation:** Actively seek to identify and mitigate biases in your data and model. Implement fairness-aware modeling techniques to ensure equitable outcomes across different groups.

- **Transparency and Explainability:** Strive for transparency and explainability in your NLP systems. Users should understand how decisions are made, particularly in applications with significant social impact.

- **Privacy and Security:** Adhere to best practices for data privacy and security. Protect sensitive information and comply with relevant regulations and standards.

Building NLP applications and systems involves a multidisciplinary approach that combines technical expertise with ethical considerations and domain knowledge. Following these best practices helps practitioners navigate the complexities of NLP development, from data preparation to deployment and beyond. By emphasizing quality, fairness, and scalability, developers can create NLP solutions that are not only effective but also responsible and sustainable, driving positive impact across a multitude of domains.

Future Directions and Emerging Trends In NLP:

A critical exploration of future directions and emerging trends in NLP offers a glimpse into the evolving landscape of this dynamic field. As NLP continues to intersect with various disciplines and technologies, it stands at the forefront of innovations that promise to redefine how we interact with machines, process information, and understand natural language. This comprehensive portion delves into key trends that are shaping the future of NLP, including advancements in machine learning, the integration of multimodal data, the pursuit of ethical AI, and the expansion of NLP applications across industries.

Advancements in Machine Learning Techniques

- **Self-supervised Learning:** A significant trend is the shift towards self-supervised learning models that can learn from unlabeled data, reducing reliance on large annotated datasets and democratizing access to NLP technologies.

- **Neural Architecture Search (NAS):** NAS and automated machine learning (AutoML) are streamlining the design of neural network architectures, enabling the discovery of optimal models for specific NLP tasks with minimal human intervention.

Integration of Multimodal Data

- **Multimodal NLP:** The integration of text with other data types, such as images, video, and audio, is expanding the capabilities of NLP systems. Multimodal NLP enables more comprehensive understanding and generation of content, opening new avenues for applications in content creation, augmented reality, and assistive technologies.

- **Cross-lingual and Cross-modal Transfer Learning:** Leveraging knowledge across languages and modalities enhances the generalizability of models, facilitating the development of more versatile and robust NLP systems.

Pursuit of Ethical AI and Fairness

- **Bias Detection and Mitigation:** As awareness of bias in AI systems grows, there is an increasing focus on developing methodologies for detecting and mitigating biases in NLP models, ensuring fair and unbiased outcomes.

- **Explainable AI (XAI):** The demand for transparency and explainability in AI decisions is driving research in explainable NLP, aiming to make models more interpretable to humans and build trust in AI systems.

Expansion of NLP Applications

- **Healthcare:** NLP is revolutionizing healthcare by enhancing patient care through advanced analytics, automating administrative tasks, and enabling real-time monitoring of public health through social media analysis.

- **Environmental Monitoring:** Leveraging NLP for environmental monitoring and sustainability efforts, such as analyzing social media and satellite data to track climate change impacts and biodiversity loss.

- **Augmented Creativity:** NLP is being used to augment human creativity in fields such as literature, music, and art, offering tools that assist in the creative process and generate novel content.

Emerging Interfaces and Technologies

- **Voice and Conversational Interfaces:** The proliferation of voice-activated assistants and conversational AI is making natural language interaction with technology increasingly seamless, reshaping consumer expectations and experiences.

- **Quantum NLP:** Although in its nascent stages, the exploration of quantum computing for NLP tasks holds the potential for exponential improvements in processing speed and model complexity, promising breakthroughs in language understanding.

The future directions and emerging trends in NLP underscore the field's vibrant and rapidly evolving nature. From cutting-edge machine learning techniques and multimodal data integration to the critical pursuit of ethical AI and the expansion of NLP applications, these trends are setting the stage for a future where NLP technologies play an integral role in various aspects of society. As NLP continues to advance, it promises not only to enhance our interaction with technology but also to offer profound insights into the complexities of human language and communication.

Conclusion

As explored in "Natural Language Processing (NLP): The Complete Guide," the practical applications and case studies of NLP across healthcare, finance, and social media domains reveal the profound impact of NLP technologies in addressing real-world challenges and enhancing decision-making processes. By leveraging the vast amounts of unstructured data prevalent in these sectors, NLP not only facilitates a deeper understanding of complex patterns and trends but also drives innovation and efficiency. As NLP continues to evolve, its integration into various domains is poised to unlock further advancements, transforming industries and reshaping the way organizations operate and interact with their stakeholders.